How to Fight City Hall...

The IRS, Banks, Corporations, Your Local Airport & Other Nuisances

Joel D. Joseph, J.D.

Contemporary Books, Inc.
Chicago

Library of Congress Cataloging in Publication Data

Joseph, Joel D.
   How to fight city hall—the IRS, banks
corporations, your local airport, and other
nuisances.

   1. Government liability—United States—Popular works.
2. Corporation law—United States—Popular works.
3. Liability (Law)—United States—Popular works.
4. Actions and defenses—United States—Popular
works.   I. Title.
KF1321.Z9J67   1983   342.73'088   83-15052
ISBN 0-8092-5548-0   347.30288

To my father, Harold Joseph, and to my wife, Arlene Singer, both
of whom are fighters who refuse to give in where matters of principle
are concerned.

Published by Contemporary Books, Inc.
180 North Michigan Avenue, Chicago, Illinois 60601
Manufactured in the United States of America
Library of Congress Catalog Card Number: 83-15052
International Standard Book Number: 0-8092-5548-0

Published simultaneously in Canada by Beaverbooks, Ltd.
195 Allstate Parkway, Valleywood Business Park
Markham, Ontario L3R 4T8 Canada

Contents

Forms

How to Fight City Hall...

The IRS, Banks, Corporations, Your Local Airport & Other Nuisances

1

You Can Fight City Hall . . . and Win!

Suing the government or another large bureaucracy can be frustrating. But it can also be very challenging. An individual, or a small group of people, has certain advantages over a bureaucracy. You must take advantage of its weaknesses and your strengths.

The first major strength of a government agency or a large corporation is that it will survive forever. We mere mortals eventually die. The government knows this and takes advantage of it. For example, an Indians' claims case was delayed by the Justice (Injustice?) Department for more than one hundred years! The Justice Department lawyers filed every conceivable delaying motion and made numerous requests for extensions. However, the United States Supreme Court finally ruled in the Indians' favor, and the descendants from the original case prevailed. Now those Indians want the land itself back, not monetary compensation as their forefathers originally sought. Indian claims like these are throwing the land title insurance companies into havoc. Two things can be learned from this example. First, if you persevere, you or your heirs can prevail against the almighty government. Second, a long battle usually complicates matters and may work against the government and the taxpayers who support it.

The second major strength of the bureaucracy is that it stays in one place. Americans, on the other

hand, move about constantly. This advantage works in conjunction with the first one. Together they provide the reason behind the slogan, "You can't fight city hall."

But you *can* fight city hall . . . and win. Many people have done so. And some of the battles have been won quickly. They have been won quickly by fierce attacks at governmental weaknesses.

The most important weakness is publicity. Governments and corporations despise adverse publicity. The Love Canal battle was won, more than anything else, by publicity. In Washington, D. C., a small group of civic-minded homeowners settled a case with the regional subway authority; but only after the newspapers and television stations widely broadcast the story. The Washington Metropolitan Area Transit Authority (WMATA) was dumping wastes, and a gasoline storage tank was leaking into a small creek, the Little Falls Branch. The Little Falls Branch runs through several small towns on the outskirts of Washington, D. C., including Somerset, Friendship Heights, and Chevy Chase, Maryland.

At first, homeowners smelled gasoline fumes coming from the creek. They joined together with other homeowners in the area and found allies among local businesses who were affected by the pollution. An attorney, formerly with the U.S. Environmental Protection Agency, advised the group that because the pollution was of "waters of the United States," the Federal Water Pollution Control Act could be invoked.

Under the federal water pollution act, as under many laws, official notice of intent to sue must be given at least 60 days before suit can be brought. This group sent the notice and informed the press; the pressure and publicity which resulted caused the governmental agency (WMATA) to settle the case.

This case will be discussed at greater length in Chapter 17, How to Make a Federal Case Out of Water Pollution.

How does one go about getting publicity? There are three basic methods. The traditional method is to hold a press conference. A press release is also very common. Another method is wearing out shoe leather, or your index finger, by visiting and calling press contacts. Details on these techniques are included in Chapter 3, The Care and Feeding of the Press.

There is, indeed, strength in numbers. You should not have to fight city hall by yourself. If you have a problem, most likely you are not alone. Some others might not consider your problem to be their problem. But you will have comrades and allies. The problem, then, is how to organize. Chapter 4, How to Form a Non-Profit Organization, will be concerned with these matters.

The major advantage of the individual over the bureaucracy is flexibility. You are like the guerrilla warrior fighting against the regimented army. You can hit and run. You react much more quickly. One of my law professors called it "guerrilla law." You can have a press conference one day, be on talk shows the next, and file suit the same week. Not so· with government. At least three levels of bureaucracy in the government have to approve everything that is done. And then it has to be revised again and again. The same is true for large corporations.

Use your strengths to attack their weaknesses, and you can beat city hall. You must have patience and carefully plan your attack. But victory shall be yours if you think hard enough, work hard enough, and persevere.

2

How to Write a Complaint Letter

The first step in many dispute resolutions is to write a complaint letter. Before writing the letter, it is usually preferable to call first to find out the name of the proper official to write to. A letter addressed to a person by name will usually prompt a better response than one to a department or to the company in general.

DEADLINES

Put a specific deadline in your letter. For example, state, "If I do not hear from you by January 15th, I will refer the matter to my attorney for legal action." A specific deadline will insure that you get a response.

COORDINATE WITH PRESS RELEASE

You may want to release the text of your letter to the press. For example, say that you have learned that your city was giving away prime real estate at low prices to developers. You could write various city officials, demanding an explanation. Your key letter would be addressed to the head of the program involved. Quotes from the letter, along with a copy, could be sent to the local press in the form of a press release. See Chapter 3, the Care and Feeding of the Press.

REFERENCE IN THE LETTER

At the top of the letter a reference will direct the letter to the proper file. The abbreviation "re" is used, and it means "with regard to:" For example, if Mr. Smith went to a Good Foods Grocery Store, bought a jar of Tasty-Brand cherries, and found one with a pit inside, his reference could be one of the following:

1. *Re: Smith v. Good Foods;*
2. *Re: Smith v. Tasty-Brand;* or
3. *Re: Defective Tasty-Brand Cherries.*

CARBON COPIES

At the bottom left side of many letters you will notice the letters "cc." This means that a copy of the letter was sent to the persons listed next to the "cc." You will often get a better response to letters if the addressee of the letter knows that someone is watching. If you have a consumer problem, a carbon copy to a consumer protection group or agency is useful. If the product in question is a food or drug, send a carbon to your state food and drug office and the Federal Food and Drug Administration. If you feel that a legislative inquiry concerning the matter would be possible, send a copy to state or federal legislators who may have an interest in a particular area. Another device is the blind carbon copy or "bcc." This means that a copy of the letter has been sent to another party, but the addressee is not informed about it. This device can be useful when you provide a carbon copy to a committee that may investigate a problem but wants to keep a low profile.

Concerning the pit-in-the-cherry controversy, the following letter may get results:

KEEP A COPY

The first rule of law is keep a copy of everything you do. This will create a lot of paperwork, but organize it before it gets out of hand. Buy a cardboard expanding file to start with, and file your letters with their response in alphabetical order. If you need an attorney later, you will have your case well documented.

FORM 2-1

Sample Complaint Letter

December 30, 1980

Russell Jones
Consumer Relations Office
Tasty-Brand, Inc.
1111 Tasty Lane
Hanover, Nebraska 78901

RE: SMITH V. TASTY-BRAND

Dear Mr. Jones,

I bought a jar of Tasty-Brand cherries on December 15, 1980, at my local Good Foods store. My daughter, Phyllis, was eating the cherries, when she bit down and I heard a crunching noise. She broke a filling and was in a great deal of pain because there was a pit in the cherry. And your bottle states that these are "pitless" cherries!

My dentist examined Phyllis immediately and repaired the broken dental work. He charged me $50.00. I have enclosed a copy of the dentist's statement and report.

If you would reimburse me for the dental charges, I would be pleased. Send me a check for $50.00 by January 15, 1981, and I will consider the matter closed. If I do not hear from you by that date, I will refer the matter to my attorney, who will sue for considerably more than $50.00.

Sincerely yours,

Robert Smith

cc: Franklin Ross, Action TV News
    Barney O'Malley, Chairman,
        New York Food and Drug Office
    Harvey Rogers, Food and Drug
        Administration

(See Form 21-1 for another sample complaint letter).

3

The Care and Feeding of the Press

Not all of the articles in the *Washington Post* get there by investigative reporting. Some of the articles walk in the door. The press needs stories. Reporters like people to do their work for them. They, like all writers, are basically lazy, and would just as soon rewrite your press release as write the article from scratch. Some small newspapers will use your press release verbatim.

Before we get to the form for a press release, you should develop a press list. This list can be used for mailing releases, and it can be used for giving notice of press conferences. Make a list of all of the TV and radio stations, magazines, and newspapers that you want to give you publicity. Look in the Yellow Pages for ideas. Your library will have a book called the *Ayer Directory of Publications*, which includes most newspapers and periodicals. Look through the publications at the library and make a list of names and addresses. Note the names of the writers who have written articles on the subject matter with which you are concerned. You should address individuals by name. Large newspapers get hundreds of mailings every day, and yours could get lost. It doesn't hurt to send two or three releases to the same newspaper, one addressed to a specific reporter, one to a department or editor (e.g., the city editor), and another to the chief editor. Buy address labels which are made for photocopy machines. There are 33 labels to the page. If you have 33 or less names on your list, you need only one page of labels for an entire mailing. A press release sent to the United Press International (UPI) or the Associated Press (AP) may be sent over their wires to radio and television stations. Both the UPI and the AP keep local logs of press conferences and send them to their subscribers.

You can even draft an editorial in your own words, supporting the cause you espouse. Some newspapers will print the editorial with only minor revisions as its own editorial.

You may want to send a press kit. A kit may include fact sheets, photographs, brochures, and a press release. This will make it easy for the reporter to learn background material. You may even want to send a cassette tape recording to radio stations, or film or slides to television stations. Before you do, call the stations to see what format they need.

WRITING A PRESS RELEASE

A press release should read like a newspaper article. It should have an attention-grabbing headline. One of the best press releases that I recall involved a federal ruling that smokers should be restricted to the back seats on interstate buses. Action on Smoking and Health issued a press release praising the ruling with a banner headline: "Smokers Ordered to Back of Bus." Press releases are used to announce news, whether it is a new lawsuit being filed or a victory in one filed years earlier. But the release must hinge around a newsworthy event.

The event could be the formation of a new organization, a challenge to a mayor on a certain topic, a raffle, a lawsuit, a petition drive, or anything else that the media may be interested in.

The release must contain certain information. It must specify who is issuing the statement and have the name and phone number of a person to contact. The press release usually contains a release date, such as "FOR IMMEDIATE RELEASE," "EMBARGOED UNTIL MAY 1, 1982 AT 10:00 A.M.," or "RELEASE AT 9:00 A.M. JUNE 3, 1983." This instruction is used for your benefit. If you are holding a press conference and also issue a press release, you should give specific instructions in the release. These instructions usually appear in the upper-left portions of the release. The name of the contact should appear in the upper-right portion, for example:

"FOR MORE INFORMATION CONTACT SAM SMITH: 333-9990"

An actual press release is included in this chapter, along with a copy of an article which appeared in the *Washington Post* based on that press release. A release should start with the immediate news item, and later on give background information. Quotes are very appropriate in the middle of a press release. Make up your own quotes, for yourself, that is. Don't put words into anyone else's mouth.

HOLDING A PRESS CONFERENCE

If you want to hold a press conference, you must get reporters to attend. I once held a press conference that no one attended. It happened during the Watergate hearings in 1974, in Washington, and all of the reporters were busy with the Watergate crisis. Timing and luck are important.

You must make it convenient and newsworthy for reporters to make the trip. If you want television cameras to be there, you must make the event colorful and visually exciting. Otherwise a press release might be just as effective.

Don't make the conference too early in the morning. Make sure you know the deadlines of the papers from which you want a reporter sent. If they have a 1:00 P.M. deadline, don't call for a noon conference. Check to see if there are other confer-

ences scheduled. Both the UPI and the AP keep a log of press conferences. Check their list for the date you have in mind, and make sure that they put your conference on their list.

WHERE TO HOLD THE CONFERENCE

The conference should be held in a place that is convenient to reporters. Is there a room you can rent near the major paper? You can also hold a conference outdoors, if the setting is appropriate. Many lawsuits are announced at press conferences held on courthouse steps. If you are fighting the demolition of a building, hold the conference outside the threatened structure. Television crews will then be able to film your conference and the building simultaneously.

A notice of the press conference should be mailed or hand-delivered a week to 10 days before the conference. Use the press list that you have developed. Follow up with phone calls to the individual reporters who you want to attend.

Do something exciting at the press conference. Have a prominent politician, scientist, or both, make a statement. Use gadgets which will grab the camera's attention. A scientific gauge or meter may do the trick. You may want to stage a demonstration at the same time with placards, pickets, or banners. Make sure that something visual is going on.

It may sound phony, but a press conference is a pseudo-event. It only has to look good when the press is present and when the cameras are rolling. You are not using the press any more than they are using you to get a story.

INFORMAL MEETINGS

Take a newspaper reporter to lunch, if one will let you. Reporters may have instructions from their editors not to take "gifts" from anyone. A casual lunch engagement will let the reporter know who you are and will open the door for your cause or organization.

If you get along well with, and trust, a particular reporter, you may want to give him or her an exclusive. This may guarantee coverage in one newspaper, but it might hurt you with other publications. You will have to weigh the pros and cons of each.

FORM 3-1

Press Release Format

Embargoed until _____   FOR MORE INFORMATION
or for immediate release or   CONTACT: _____
for release _____

HEADLINE

Start with your lead to grab attention, just as a news story would. The first paragraph should tell the basic story. The second paragraph should be spiced with quotes.

The rest of the release should be background material saying who is involved, and what they have done previously.

FORM 3-2

Notice of Press Conference

FOR MORE INFORMATION
CONTACT: _____

PRESS CONFERENCE TO BE HELD

_____ will hold a press conference at _____ at _____
o'clock. (Give directions if it may be difficult to find.)
   The agenda for the conference is: _____ (Give a list of the speakers and their credentials.)

   The following information will be made available at the press conference: _____
_____
(Grab their attention, but don't tell everything, or else the media will not have to attend.)
   The conference should last until _____ o'clock.

4

How to Form a Non-Profit Organization

You may not have to form an organization. The right organization may already exist. However, an ad hoc organization addressed to the problem which concerns you may be the best chance for redress of your grievance.

It only takes two or three persons to form a non-profit corporation. I recommend that you incorporate for several reasons. First of all, you limit your personal liability for acts of the corporation. For example, say that the non-profit corporation files a lawsuit against Sears and the case is groundless. A judge dismisses the case and awards $2,000 in court costs against the corporation. Big deal. The corporation doesn't pay the court costs because it doesn't have any money. The founders of the corporation and the members of the corporation are not liable for the debts of the corporation, and the court costs are like any other debt.

The second major reason for incorporating is that the people you approach to join as members or to contribute will often feel that a corporation is more permanent and substantive than a group of three citizen activists.

Another reason for incorporating is that if you decide to seek tax-exempt status from the Internal Revenue Service you will need a corporate structure.

INVENT A CATCHY NAME

A recent group was formed in Maryland, called KISS. It stands for Kids In Safety Seats. Names like these are called acronyms, and they are very common for consumer organizations. It isn't necessary to have an acronymic name, but it does help in name-recognition. The American Civil Liberties Union (ACLU) has become so well-known that it is known by its initials, even though they don't spell anything. The same thing is true for the NAACP. However, both of these groups have names which immediately indicate the cause they espouse.

STATEMENT OF PURPOSE

When the initial nucleus of people get together they should agree on a short statement of the purposes and goals which they seek. This statement can be used in a brochure which describes the group. It can also be used in the Articles of Incorporation, the document which forms a non-profit corporation. There is a sample Articles of Incorporation at the end of this chapter.

THE ARTICLES OF INCORPORATION

The Articles of Incorporation is the basic document of a non-profit organization. It is filed with an official in your state, and the appropriate addresses for all the states and the District of Columbia is appended to this chapter. This official will be able to answer your specific questions concerning incorporation in your state. I have drafted a set of Articles of Incorporation designed to meet the requirements of all jurisdictions in the United States. While some states may only require one incorporator, none requires more than three. In a case like this, I provided that there be three incorporators. Some states require notarization, while others do not. It does not hurt to have your Articles notarized in any state, so I have included this in the form.

There are various provisions in the form agreement concerning membership. You can either have a membership or not have one. And it can be a voting or non-voting membership.

SHOULD YOU HAVE MEMBERS?

A Board of Directors runs every corporation. The Board can be self-perpetuating, or it can be elected by the members. If you form an organization and have a voting membership, you may later be voted out of control. For this reason, a non-voting membership may be a good compromise.

TAX-EXEMPT STATUS

You may not need tax-exempt status to be free from paying taxes. If the organization spends all of its donations and other income, it is not liable for tax in any event. Contributions to the corporation will not be tax deductions until the corporation has received tax-exempt status approval from the IRS.

The IRS procedure for applying for tax-exempt status is long and painful. At the initial stages, I usually advise against applying for tax-exempt status. This is because it is time-consuming, and because at the beginning you probably will not have large contributors.

TYPES OF TAX-EXEMPT STATUS

Entire books have been written on tax-exempt status. The purpose of this and the preceding sections is to give you a general idea of the type of organizations that can be formed.

The Internal Revenue Service allows two different types of tax-exempt organizations to exist: the "501 (c) (3)" and "501 (c) (4)." These names come from the federal statute that created them. Neither type of organization is liable for income tax on its contributions. However, the IRS must approve an organization before it can gain either tax-exempt status.

The difference between the two types of organizations is that contributors to (c) (3) organizations are allowed to deduct the amount of their contributions on the federal tax forms as a charitable deduction. Contributions to (c) (4) organizations are not tax deductions.

However, (c) (3) organizations are restricted in the amount of lobbying that they can perform, while (c) (4)s are not limited in their lobbying activities. A (c) (3) organization that spends less than $500,000 concerning its exempt purpose, can spend no more than 20% of this on lobbying activities. As the size of the non-profit organization increases the percentage allowed for lobbying declines. Above expenditures of $1.5 million concerning an organizations's exempt purpose, only 5% can be spent on lobbying activities.

LOCAL SOLICITATION PERMITS

Many cities have enacted solicitation laws which require you to register with the city hall before soliciting funds. Call the city hall to see what permits you need. Many of these statutes are horrendously burdensome, and occasionally the permit fee is excessive. In one case, I advised a group to ignore the statute since it required a large fee, and it required a form to be filled out which probably violated the First Amendment right to freedom of association and freedom of speech. In any event, before soliciting for funds, check to find out if you are required to obtain a permit. If it is relatively easy and inexpensive, get one. If not, you will have to decide whether it is worth the risk of being fined or prosecuted if the government finds out you solicited funds without a permit. The fine is usually small, and not many local prosecutors will waste their time on such a small matter—unless someone is out to get you.

FORM 4-1

Articles of Incorporation for Non-Profit Corporation

ARTICLES OF INCORPORATION

OF

_____

To: _____

_____

We, the undersigned natural persons of the age of twenty-one years or more, acting as incorporators of a corporation adopt the following Articles of Incorporation for such corporation pursuant to the _____ Non-profit Corporation Act:

FIRST: The name of the corporation is: _____

SECOND: The period of duration is perpetual.

THIRD: The purposes for which the corporation is organized are to:

_____

_____

_____

The corporation shall never be operated for the primary purpose of carrying on a trade or business for profit. No part of the earnings or assets of the corporation shall inure to the benefit of or be distributed to its directors, officers, members or any private person, except that it shall be authorized and empowered to pay reasonable compensation for services rendered and to make payments and distributions in furtherance of the purposes for which it is organized. No substantial part of the activities of the corporation shall be the carrying on of propaganda, or otherwise attempting to influence legislation, and it shall not participate in or intervene in (including the publishing and distribution of statements) any political campaign or on behalf of any candidate for public office. Notwithstanding any other provision of this Article, the corporation shall not carry on any activities not permitted to be carried on (1) by an organization exempt from Federal tax under Section 501(c) (3) of the Internal Revenue Code of 1954 (or the corresponding provision of any future United States Revenue Law), or (2) by an organization contributions to which are deductible under Section 170 of the Internal Revenue Code of 1954 (or the corresponding provision of any future United States Revenue Law). The corporation is organized for charitable, scientific, testing for public safety and educational purposes.

FOURTH: The corporation is to have members.

FIFTH: The corporation is to have one class of members. All members in good standing are entitled to vote at all meetings of the general membership.

SIXTH: The election or appointment of the Board of Directors shall be provided for in the bylaws.

SEVENTH: The bylaws shall provide for the regulation of the internal affairs of the corporation. Upon dissolution of the corporation, its assets shall be disposed of exclusively for the purpose of the corporation or distributed to such organization or organizations operating exclusively for charitable, educational, scientific, or testing for public safety as shall, at the time, qualify as an exempt organization or organizations under Section 501 (c) (3) of the Internal Revenue Code of 1954 (or the corresponding provision of any future United States Revenue Law).

EIGHTH: The address of the registered office of the corporation is:

_____

and the name of its initial registered agent at this address is:

_____

NINTH: The number of directors constituting the initial Board of Directors is three (3) and the names and addresses of the initial directors, who shall serve until their successors are elected and qualified are:

NAME   ADDRESS

_____   _____

_____   _____

_____   _____

TENTH: The name and address of each incorporator is:

NAME   ADDRESS

_____   _____

_____   _____

Dated: _____

I, _____, a notary public, certify that on the _____ day of _____, the incorporators listed above personally appeared before me, and subscribed and swore to this document as incorporators.

_____
NOTARY PUBLIC

(Signature of Incorporator) _____
NAME OF INCORPORATOR

(Signature of Incorporator) _____
NAME OF INCORPORATOR

(Signature of Incorporator) _____
NAME OF INCORPORATOR

Incorporators

5

The Basics of Litigation

Litigation is a formal term for "court proceedings." In Old England, disputes were settled in trials by battle, where one could hire a stand-in to physically fight his opponent or his opponent's stand-in. Since we are now civilized, we fight paper battles and our stand-ins are called attorneys.

Rule Number One: Anybody can sue anybody for anything. You can sue someone for $1,000,000 for stepping on your foot. But the key question is: can you win? Even if your chances of winning are slim, by filing suit you create what is known as "nuisance value." A company or an insurance carrier will often settle a case for its nuisance value, even if they feel that they will win. This is because even if they win, they will still incur attorneys' fees and expenses that may exceed the amount they could settle for. Governmental bodies will not usually settle a case for nuisance value, because the nuisance costs do not come out of their pockets, but out of the taxpayers' collective pocket.

Rule Number Two: Sue everybody. In law school, students are taught that if you are unsure about who is liable for something, sue everybody. For example, if a credit-reporting company is falsely reporting that you owe XYZ Company money, and you are not sure which company made the error, sue them both. After you sue them they will come running to you to correct the reporting error.

TYPES OF CLAIMS THAT YOU CAN RAISE

There are four different types of claims on which you can base a lawsuit. The four are:

1. Tort (car accidents and other personal injury)
2. Contract
3. Violation of a statute
4. Violation of a provision in the constitution

Types of torts include assault and battery, negligence, libel and slander. These are based on common law, and are not written into statutory law.

Contract claims are based on written or oral contracts. If someone agrees with you to paint your house for $500, you have a contract for that amount, and the painter can sue you if you fail to pay him.

Federal and state statutes create hundreds of types of claims. Some examples are: discrimination, environmental, and consumer credit cases.

Very few cases are brought solely based on constitutional rights. An example of a constitutional claim is: Your school refused to publish the school paper because of a critical article in it. The First Amendment right to freedom of the press may have been violated by this action, and a claim under that constitutional amendment would be appropriate.

WHO IS WHO? PARTIES TO A LAWSUIT

The plaintiff is the party doing the suing, and the defendant is the person who is being sued. When the defendant files a counterclaim against the plaintiff, the defendant is also a counterplaintiff, and the plaintiff a counterdefendant. Other parties can be brought into the lawsuit, but their names will only add confusion at this stage of the game.

Plaintiffs are sometimes called petitioners, and defendants are occasionally called respondents. If you file an appeal you are an appellant. If you file a motion you are a movant. Similarly, if you file a petition you are a petitioner; if you file a declaration you are a declarant. If you sign an affidavit you are an affiant.

WHAT COURT SHOULD YOU BE IN?

There are two types of courts in the United States: federal courts and state courts. Many state courts have subdivided their courts into small claims courts and other courts. Small claims courts ordinarily have jurisdiction up to $1,000 or $1,500.

Federal courts hear disputes between residents of different states if the claim exceeds $10,000. Federal courts also have jurisdiction over certain types of cases, such as bankruptcy (which is a special federal court), employment discrimination, environmental matters, and other claims based on federal statutes.

FILING DOCUMENTS

Before filing any document in court, make sure that you know the size of paper required and the number of copies that you must file. Also, certain documents have to be notarized; check with the court clerk concerning this. Most court documents should be typed and double-spaced.

Rule Number Three: Keep a copy of everything. Always get the clerk to stamp an extra copy of the document with a "filed" or "received" stamp, or to sign your copy of the document. This will give you proof of filing, in case the court loses the papers.

Every document filed at court should either be served or mailed to the other parties involved in the case. Most documents will have a "Certificate of Service" on the last page which will look like this:

CERTIFICATE OF SERVICE

I certify that I have mailed a copy of this document to _____ on the _____ day of _____, 19_____.

Signature
NAME

ANATOMY OF A LAWSUIT

There are four basic stages to a lawsuit. They are:

1. Pleadings
2. Motions
3. Discovery
4. Trial

These stages can overlap at times; many lawsuits, probably the majority, end at the first stage.

STAGE ONE

The first step in any lawsuit is the filing with a court of a complaint. Many courts also require a cover sheet to be filed with a complaint. The complaint is the document which sets forth the reasons that someone owes you money; or it is to obtain an injunction to get someone to do something. In some states a complaint is known as a "declaration" or as a "motion for judgment."

Filing a complaint at the courthouse will stop the statute of limitations from running. The statute of limitations is the time period for filing your claim. For example, if the statute of limitations concerning car accidents is two years,[1] you must file a complaint in court within two years from the date of the accident.

After filing the complaint, the defendant must be served with a summons. A federal summons is included at the end of this chapter as Form 5-2. A summons requires the defendant to respond to the complaint within a specified period, often 20 or 30 days. This service can be effected either by registered or certified mail, personal delivery, or by publication. Local court rules specify how service is to be obtained. The clerk at the local courthouse is usually very informative about these matters. In small claims courts the clerk will usually serve a summons and complaint for you.

After receiving a summons and complaint, the defendant can do one of three things.[2] He can (1)

---

1. Statutes of limitations vary from state to state. Depending on the nature of the claims involved, they vary from 30 days to 20 years. The first thing you should do is determine the appropriate statute of limitations.

2. A defendant could possibly file a petition for removal in federal court on the basis of diversity, that he is a federal official, or for civil reasons.

file an answer, (2) file a motion, or (3) do nothing.

If the defendant does nothing, you can ask the court to enter a judgment by default in your favor.

In most cases an answer will be filed. In the answer the defendant can file a counterclaim against the plaintiff. Together, the complaint and answer are referred to as the "pleadings" stage of the lawsuit.

MOTIONS

The different kinds of motions that can be filed are only limited by the creativity of those drafting them. In some courts you have to file a motion to do almost anything. If you must file something late, you will usually need a motion to permit it. This section will deal with the most common motions, the ones that you are likely to encounter.

In response to a complaint, the defendant may file a motion to dismiss. The motion may contend that the defendant was not properly served, that the court does not have jurisdiction, or that the complaint does not state a valid claim. Jurisdiction refers to the area of authority over which the court has power. For example, a small claims court may have jurisdiction over claims of $1,000 or less. A court in Connecticut would not have jurisdiction over a dispute between residents of Massachusetts which arose in Maine.

A motion for summary judgment is very common. This motion is filed when there are no disputed facts; or that based on the undisputed facts, one party or the other is entitled to win, according to the law.

DISCOVERY

Discovery is that part of a lawsuit where the parties can ask each other questions, and can ask each other for documents. Discovery by written questions is called interrogatories. Answers to interrogatories must be under oath. A failure to answer interrogatories within a specified time period can cause a dismissal of your case if you are a plaintiff, or a judgment against you if you are a defendant.

Certain courts, such as small claims courts, and landlord and tenant courts, often do not allow discovery, except by special permission of the court.

A deposition is a type of discovery where oral questions are asked in the presence of a court reporter, and a transcript is later prepared. Deposi-

tions can be very costly, since court reporters charge about $2.50 per page of transcript.

A request for the production of documents is exactly what it sounds like. All of these discovery techniques are conducted without a judge present. A judge will resolve discovery disputes only when they are brought to his or her attention by a motion. If a party refuses to answer questions during discovery, the other party can file a motion to compel them to. If a party feels he is being harassed by the other side, he can file a motion for a protective order to stop or limit discovery.

TRIAL

At the close of the discovery period there will often be a pretrial. Pretrial is when the parties exchange witness lists and lists of exhibits, and narrow the issues that will be tried.

If the trial will be before a jury, jury instructions may be settled upon during pretrial. *Voir dire* is the formal name for the questioning of potential jurors to determine their impartiality. *Voir dire* may be decided at the pretrial conference.

At the trial, evidence is introduced through the testimony of witnesses and the introduction of documents. If you want a person to be a witness and they are unwilling, or if you want to insure that they will attend a trial, you can issue a subpoena. A subpoena should be issued at least five days before a trial; local rules may require a longer period. A subpoena is a court order requiring a person to attend a hearing. The court clerk issues subpoenas which must then be served on the witness. When they are served, the witness must usually be paid a witness fee, plus their travel expenses to get to the hearing. The clerk in your area should tell you the proper witness fee and travel allowance.

COLLECTING A JUDGMENT

Winning a case at trial is not always the hard part. Often the hard part is collecting the judgment. If a defendant will not voluntarily pay a judgment, you have two major options available. One is to attach or seize the person's property or money. Another is to garnish the defendant's wages. To garnish someone's wages means to have the defendant's employer take money out of the defendant's paycheck to pay the judgment. The court clerk will help you file the proper forms to attach property or garnish salary.

FORM 5-1

UNITED STATES DISTRICT COURT

JS 44C
(Rev. 9/81)

CIVIL COVER SHEET

CO-913
Rev. 11/81

The JS-44 civil cover sheet and the information contained herein neither replace nor supplement the filing and service of pleadings or other papers as required by law, except as provided by local rules of court. This form, approved by the Judicial Conference of the United States in September 1974, is required for the use of the Clerk of Court for the purpose of initiating the civil docket sheet.

PLAINTIFFS	DEFENDANTS
COUNTY OF RESIDENCE OF FIRST LISTED PLAINTIFF_____ (EXCEPT IN U.S. PLAINTIFF CASES)	COUNTY OF RESIDENCE OF FIRST LISTED DEFENDANT_____ (IN U.S. PLAINTIFF CASES ONLY) NOTE: IN LAND CONDEMNATION CASES, USE THE LOCATION OF THE TRACT OF LAND INVOLVED
ATTORNEYS (FIRM NAME, ADDRESS, AND TELEPHONE NUMBER)	ATTORNEYS (IF KNOWN)

(PLACE AN ⊠ IN ONE BOX ONLY) **BASIS OF JURISDICTION**

☐ 1 U.S. PLAINTIFF ☐ 2 U.S. DEFENDANT ☐ 3 FEDERAL QUESTION (U.S. NOT A PARTY) ☐ 4 DIVERSITY

IF DIVERSITY, INDICATE CITIZENSHIP BELOW. (28 USC 1332, 1441)

CAUSE OF ACTION (CITE THE U.S. CIVIL STATUTE UNDER WHICH YOU ARE FILING AND WRITE A BRIEF STATEMENT OF CAUSE)

(PLACE AN ⊠ IN ONE BOX ONLY) **NATURE OF SUIT**

ACTIONS UNDER STATUTES

CONTRACT	TORTS	CIVIL RIGHTS	FORFEITURE/PENALTY	OTHER STATUTES
☐ 110 INSURANCE	**PERSONAL INJURY**	☐ 441 VOTING	☐ 610 AGRICULTURE	☐ 400 STATE REAPPORTIONMENT
☐ 120 MARINE			☐ 620 FOOD & DRUG	☐ 410 ANTI-TRUST
☐ 130 MILLER ACT	☐ 310 AIRPLANE	☐ 442 JOBS	☐ 630 LIQUOR LAWS	**BANKRUPTCY**
☐ 140 NEGOTIABLE INSTRUMENT	☐ 315 AIRPLANE PRODUCT LIABILITY	☐ 443 ACCOMMODATIONS	☐ 640 R.R. & TRUCK	☐ 420 TRUSTEE
☐ 150 RECOVERY OF OVERPAYMENT & ENFORCEMENT OF JUDGEMENT	☐ 320 ASSAULT, LIBEL & SLANDER		☐ 650 AIR LINE REGS.	☐ 421 TRANSFER (915b)
	☐ 330 FEDERAL EMPLOYERS' LIABILITY	☐ 444 WELFARE	☐ 660 OCCUPATIONAL SAFETY/ HEALTH	☐ 422 APPEAL (801)
☐ 151 MEDICARE ACT	☐ 340 MARINE	☐ 440 OTHER CIVIL RIGHTS	☐ 690 OTHER	☐ 430 BANKS AND BANKING
☐ 152 RECOVERY OF DEFAULTED STUDENT LOANS	☐ 345 MARINE PRODUCT LIABILITY			☐ 450 COMMERCE ICC RATES, ETC.
☐ 153 RECOVERY OF OVERPAYMENT OF VETERANS BENEFITS	☐ 350 MOTOR VEHICLE		**LABOR**	☐ 460 DEPORTATION
	☐ 355 MOTOR VEHICLE PRODUCT LIABILITY	**PRISONER PETITIONS**	☐ 710 FAIR LABOR STANDARDS	☐ 810 SELECTIVE SERVICE
☐ 160 STOCKHOLDERS SUITS	☐ 360 OTHER PERSONAL INJURY	☐ 510 VACATE SENTENCE (2255)	☐ 720 LABOR/MGMT. RELATIONS	☐ 850 SECURITIES COMMODITIES EXCHANGE
☐ 190 OTHER CONTRACT	☐ 362 PERSONAL INJURY-MED. MALPRACTICE		☐ 730 LABOR/MGMT. REPORTING & DISCLOSURE ACT	**SOCIAL SECURITY**
☐ 195 CONTRACT PRODUCT LIABILITY	☐ 365 PERSONAL INJURY PRODUCT LIABILITY	☐ 520 PAROLE COMMISSION REVIEW		☐ 861 HIA
			☐ 740 RAILWAY LABOR ACT	☐ 862 BLACK LUNG
REAL PROPERTY	**PERSONAL PROPERTY**	☐ 530 HABEAS CORPUS	☐ 790 OTHER LABOR LITIGATION	☐ 863 DIWC
☐ 210 CONDEMNATION	☐ 370 FRAUD OR TRUTH IN LENDING			☐ 863 DIWW
☐ 220 FORECLOSURE		☐ 540 MANDAMUS & OTHER	**PROPERTY RIGHTS**	☐ 864 SSID Title XVI
☐ 230 RENT LEASE & EJECTMENT	☐ 380 OTHER PERSONAL PROPERTY DAMAGE		☐ 820 COPYRIGHT	☐ 865 RSI
☐ 240 TORTS TO LAND		☐ 550 CIVIL RIGHTS	☐ 830 PATENT	**TAX SUITS**
☐ 245 TORT PRODUCT LIABILITY	☐ 385 PROPERTY DAMAGE PRODUCT LIABILITY		☐ 840 TRADEMARK	☐ 870 TAXES
☐ 290 ALL OTHER REAL PROPERTY				☐ 871 IRS-THIRD PARTY

OTHER STATUTES (continued)

☐ 875 CUSTOMER CHALLENGE 12 USC 3410
☐ 891 AGRICULTURAL ACTS
☐ 892 ECONOMIC STABILIZATION ACT
☐ 893 ENVIRONMENTAL MATTERS
☐ 894 ENERGY ALLOCATION ACT
☐ 895 FREEDOM OF INFORMATION ACT
☐ 900 APPEAL OF FEE DETERMINATION UNDER EQUAL ACCESS TO JUSTICE ACT
☐ 950 CONSTITUTIONALITY OF STATE STATUTES
☐ 970 NARA, TITLE III
☐ 890 OTHER STATUTORY ACTIONS

(PLACE AN ⊠ IN ONE BOX ONLY) **ORIGIN**

☐ 1 ORIGINAL PROCEEDING ☐ 2 REMOVED FROM STATE COURT ☐ 3 REMANDED FROM APPELLATE COURT ☐ 4 REINSTATED OR REOPENED ☐ 5 TRANSFERRED FROM (SPECIFY DIST.) ☐ 6 MULTIDISTRICT LITIGATION ☐ 7 APPEAL TO DISTRICT JUDGE FROM MAGISTRATE JUDGMENT

CITIZENSHIP OF PRINCIPAL PARTIES (IF DIVERSITY)

	PTF	DEF
CITIZEN OF THIS STATE	☐ 1	☐ 1
INCORPORATED THIS STATE	☐ 2	☐ 2
FOREIGN CORPORATION-PRINCIPAL PLACE OF BUSINESS IN _____ (STATE)	☐ 3	☐ 3
OTHER NON-CITIZEN OF THIS STATE	☐ 4	☐ 4

Check YES only if demanded in complaint:
JURY DEMAND: ☐ YES ☐ NO

Check/Fill in if demanded in complaint:

☐ CHECK IF THIS IS A CLASS ACTION UNDER F.R.C.P. 23 | DEMAND $ | OTHER

Pursuant to Local Rule, you must prepare an additional form when filing a civil action which is related to any pending cases or which involves the same parties and subject matter of any dismissed cases. Cases are deemed related if they relate to common property, involve common issues of fact, grow out of the same event or transaction, involve the validity or infringement of the same patent or are filed by the same pro se litigant. Ask New Case Clerk for this form.

DATE _____ SIGNATURE OF ATTORNEY OF RECORD _____

UNITED STATES DISTRICT COURT

FORM 5-2

United States District Court

_____

CIVIL ACTION FILE NO._____

Plaintiff

v.   SUMMONS

Defendant

To the above named Defendant :

　　You are hereby summoned and required to serve upon

plaintiff's attorney   , whose address

an answer to the complaint which is herewith served upon you, within   days after service of this

summons upon you, exclusive of the day of service. If you fail to do so, judgment by default will be

taken against you for the relief demanded in the complaint.

_____
Clerk of Court.

_____
Deputy Clerk.

Date: [Seal of Court]

NOTE:—This summons is issued pursuant to Rule 4 of the Federal Rules of Civil Procedure.

FORM 5-2 Continued

RETURN ON SERVICE OF WRIT

I hereby certify and return that on the _____ day of _____ , 19 ____ .

I received this summons and served it together with the complaint herein as follows:

(For service made by mail:

I hereby certify that I mailed this summons on _____ , 19 ____ .

at _____ ; and that such service was
place of mailing

☐ accepted   ☐ refused   ☐ returned but not refused.

Upon refusal of service, I certify that I made further service as follows:

.)

Fees for Service

Travel ____ $ _____

Service ____ $ _____   _____   or   _____
                                Authorized or Specially   *United States Marshal*
                                Appointed Process Server

____ _____   by   _____
____ _____   *Deputy United States Marshal*

I certify under penalty of perjury under the laws of the United States of America that the foregoing is true and correct.

_____   _____
Date   *Authorized or Specially Appointed Process Server*

Note: Certification required only if service is made by a person other than a United States Marshal or his deputy.

STATE SMALL-CLAIMS COURTS

State	Type of Court	Claim Limit	Informal Procedure?	Lawyers Permitted?
Alabama	Small-Claims Division of District Court	$500	Yes	Yes
Alaska	Small-Claims Proceeding in District Court	$1,000	Yes	Yes
Arizona	Justice Court (Arizona has no small-claims system except Boone County)	$999.99 (Boone Co. $500)	No	Yes
Arkansas	Municipal and Justice Courts	$300 ($100 if personal)	Yes	Yes
California	Small-Claims Court, part of Municipal or Justice Court	$1,500	Yes	No
Colorado	Small-Claims Division of County Court	$500	Yes	No
Connecticut	Small-Claims Proceeding in Court of Common Pleas	$750	Yes	Yes
Delaware	Justice of Peace Courts (Delaware has no small-claims system)	$1,500	Yes	Yes
District of Columbia	Small-Claims Division of the Superior Court	$750	Yes	Yes
Florida	Small-Claims Division of County Court	$1,500 (County cts. generally are $2,500)	Yes	Yes

STATE SMALL-CLAIMS COURTS (continued)

State	Type of Court	Claim Limit	Informal Procedure?	Lawyers Permitted?
Georgia	Justice of Peace Courts	$200	No	Yes
	Small-Claims Division (one third of the counties)	Varies from $100-$1,000 depending on county	Yes	Yes
Hawaii	Small-Claims Division of District Court	$300	Yes	Yes
Idaho	Small-Claims Dept. of Mag. Div. of Dt. Ct.	$500	Yes	No
Illinois	Small-Claims Division of Circuit Court	$1,000	Yes	Yes
	Cook County Pro Se Court	$300	Yes	No
Indiana	Small-Claims Docket of Sup. Ct., Circuit Ct., and County Ct. Small-Claims Court in Marion County	$3,000 ($1,500 in Marion County)	Yes	Yes
Iowa	Small-Claims Procedure in District Court	$1,000	Yes	Yes
Kansas	Small-Claims Procedure in County Courts	$300	Yes	Yes
Kentucky	Small-Claims Division of District Court	$500	Yes	Yes
Louisiana	Small-Claims Division of City Courts	$300 ($25 for City Court)	Yes	Yes
Maine	Small-Claims Procedure in District Courts	$800	Yes	Yes

STATE SMALL-CLAIMS COURTS (continued)

State	Type of Court	Claim Limit	Informal Procedure?	Lawyers Permitted?
Maryland	District Court	$500	Yes	Yes
Massachusetts	Small-Claims Procedure in District Court & Boston Mun. Court	$400 (except property damage by motor veh.)	Yes	Yes
Michigan	Small-Claims Division of District Court	$300	Yes	No
Minnesota	Conciliation Court in each county	$1,000 ($500 in Mpls./St. Paul)	Yes	No
Mississippi	Justice of the Peace Courts (Mississippi has no small-claims system)	$500	Yes	Yes
Missouri	Small-Claims Docket of Magistrate Cts.	$500	Yes	Yes
Montana	Small Claims, part of District Court (at option of county)	$1,500	Yes	Yes, if both P and D have lawyers
Nebraska	Small-Claims Division of Mun. or County Courts	$500	Yes	No
Nevada	Small-Claims Proceedings in Justice Courts	$300	Yes	Yes
New Hampshire	Small-Claims Proceedings in Municipal and District Courts	$500	Yes	Yes
New Jersey	Small-Claims Division of District Court	$500	Yes	Yes

STATE SMALL-CLAIMS COURTS (continued)

State	Type of Court	Claim Limit	Informal Procedure?	Lawyers Permitted?
New Mexico	Magistrate Courts	$2,000	No	Yes
	Small-Claims Court in Albuquerque	$2,000	Yes	Yes
New York	Small-Claims Court in Civil Court, District Court, and City Courts	$1,000	Yes	Yes
North Carolina	Small-Claims Procedure in District Court	$500	No	Yes
North Dakota	Small-Claims Procedure in Justice Court and County Court	$200 in Justice Ct. $500 in County Ct.	Yes	Yes
Ohio	Small-Claims Division of County and Municipal Courts	$300	Yes	Yes
Oklahoma	Small-Claims Procedure in District Court	$600	Yes	Yes
Oregon	Small-Claims Department in District and Justice Courts	$500	Yes	Only with consent of court
Pennsylvania	Justice of Peace	$1,000	No	Yes
	Philadelphia Small-Claims Ct.	$1,000	Yes	Yes
Rhode Island	Small-Claims Proceeding in District Ct.	$500	Yes	Yes
South Carolina	Magistrate Court	$500-3,000	Yes	Yes

STATE SMALL-CLAIMS COURTS (continued)

State	Type of Court	Claim Limit	Informal Procedure?	Lawyers Permitted?
South Dakota	Small-Claims Procedure in Magistrate Cts.	$1,000	No	Yes
Tennessee	Justice of Peace or General Sessions (No small-claims court in this state)	$3,000	No	Yes
Texas	Small-Claims Court	$150 ($200 for wages)	Yes	Yes
Utah	Small-Claims Department of City and Justice Courts	$400	Yes	Yes
Vermont	Small-Claims Procedure in District Court	$500	Yes	Yes
Virginia	General District Court (No state small-claims system)	$5,000	No	Yes
Washington	Small-Claims Department of District and Justice Courts	$300 ($200 if not proc. under ch. 3.30-374RCW)	Yes	Only with consent of court
West Virginia	Magistrate Courts	$1,500	No	Yes
Wisconsin	Small-Claims Proceedings in County Court	$1,000	Yes	Yes
Wyoming	Small-Claims Proceedings in Justice of Peace and County Courts	$200	Yes	Yes
Puerto Rico	Small-Claims Proceeding in District Court	$100	Yes	Yes

6

How to Protect and Enhance Your Credit Rating

Prevention in credit, like in health, is the best medicine. It may take you seven months to screw up your credit rating, and seven years to untangle it.

PAY OR EXPLAIN BEFORE YOU ARE ASKED TO DO SO

Creditors like regular monthly payments. They would rather have $10 each and every month, than $100 every three months. If you have a credit card with a minimum monthly payment of $10, keep paying at least that amount every month. If you pay more one month it will not improve your rating; but if you pay $100 and skip only a single month your credit rating will be harmed.

WHAT TO DO TO DISPUTE A BILL

If you think that a bill is incorrect, or if you need more information about a transaction on your statement, write the credit card company. Do not write a note on your statement. Write a separate letter (keep a copy for yourself), providing your name, account number, the dollar amount of the error, and the reason that the correction should be made.

You must write the creditor within 60 days after the bill was mailed to you. Do not telephone the company, as this will not preserve your rights under the Fair Credit Billing Act.

Under the Fair Credit Billing Act, the credit card company must acknowledge your letter within 30 days, unless the error has been corrected by then. Within two billing cycles, but not more than 90 days, the company must either correct the error or send you a written explanation as to why it believes that the bill was correct. If the company fails to comply with either requirement, even if it did not make an error, it must deduct $50 from your account.

After the credit card company receives your letter it cannot try to collect the disputed amount, or report you as delinquent. The creditor can continue to bill you for the disputed item and charge a finance charge. The company can also apply the disputed amount against your credit limit.

But you do not have to pay the disputed amount while the company is investigating the item or charge that you have questioned. You must continue to pay the undisputed portion of your bill.

If the credit company finds that it did make an error, you will not have to pay a finance charge on that portion of the statement. If the company insists that it did not err, it can charge you interest on the amount that you questioned. But that does not mean that the company's finding is final.

If you are not convinced by a company's explanation of a charge, write it and offer to settle the matter. Cite your account history, if it is good. If you cannot work out a compromise, write to the credit bureaus in your area *before* the company reports that you are delinquent. As usual, keep a copy of your letter. There are two national credit reporting agencies which keep files on most of us. They are the Credit Bureau, Inc. (CBI) and TRW Credit. Look up their address in the telephone directory, but do not call them, as you want to have a written record of all that transpires.

WHAT YOU SHOULD DO WHEN YOU ARE DENIED CREDIT

If you are denied credit you must be given a statement in writing on the reasons for the denial. The most common reason for the denial of credit is a poor credit rating on your credit report.

Under the Fair Credit Reporting Act, you are entitled to a copy of your own credit report. If you are seeking a loan, it is a good idea to get a copy of your credit report first. You will have to pay a few dollars for a copy, unless you have been denied credit within 30 days.

INTERPRETING YOUR CREDIT REPORT

Study your credit report, and learn what each symbol stands for. R-1 and 0-1 are the best credit ratings and mean that you pay your bills when they are due. R-2 means that you have paid late, but not more than one month late. R-9 means very serious problems, either a repossession or a lawsuit. A creditor may deny you credit because of your income, or because you were late on one payment, but it must be explained to you.

Your credit report must include any written statement that you have sent to the credit bureau concerning the dispute of a debt. Both sides of the story are supposed to be reported. However, a bank or other creditor may not see or care if you have an explanation. They often do not want troublemakers, and if you do not pay a bill you may be a bad risk in their minds.

CLEANING UP YOUR CREDIT REPORT

If a creditor is giving you a bad report, talk to them about it. Ask them what you can do to improve your credit rating with them. They may tell you that if you make six consecutive payments, then they will erase your bad marks. If the creditor has been paid off, ask them if they will stop reporting your old delinquency. If they refuse, ask them not to report anything, which they may be willing to do.

If a creditor refuses to do anything about your credit rating, you may have to file suit against them, or at least have a lawyer send them a letter threatening to do so.

WHAT YOU CAN DO ABOUT A JUDGMENT ON YOUR CREDIT RECORD

Say, for example, that a judgment against you was entered in a small claims case for $500. Even if you have paid or settled the case, the credit agency may still be reporting the judgment. You can get the judgment "vacated" or "dismissed" in several ways. This will require the credit-reporting agency to eliminate reference to the judgment.

To get a judgment removed, first talk to the attorney or the person who obtained the judgment against you. If you have not paid the judgment, agree to pay the amount, or a lesser amount if you can negotiate it, only when the other party signs an agreement as follows:

FORM 6-1

Settlement Agreement

Plaintiff and defendant are settling case number _____, for the sum of $_____. Upon payment of this sum, the judgment entered in this case will be vacated and the case dismissed.

(Signature) _____
PLAINTIFF'S NAME

(Signature) _____
DEFENDANT'S NAME

Both sides should sign the agreement and each should keep a copy. Send a certified copy to the credit agency with a letter explaining that the judgment has been vacated. If you cannot reach the other side to discuss the matter, you may have to file a motion in court to vacate the judgment. Forms are included at the end of this chapter for this purpose.

SUING YOUR LOCAL BANK FOR HARMING YOUR CREDIT

If, after attempting negotiations, you find the creditor to be stubborn and unwilling to compromise, you may have to sue. If they have reported false information to the credit bureau, they have defamed you. Defamation is either libel (written), or slander (spoken). A form is included at the end of this chapter for suing a creditor who has falsely reported information concerning your credit (Form 6-2).

SUING THE CREDIT REPORTING AGENCY

If the credit bureau refuses to supply you with a copy of your report, fails or refuses to correct a copy of your report, or fails or refuses to correct an incorrect report, you have the right to sue them in court under the Fair Credit Reporting Act. Two sample lawsuits are included as follows:

FORM 6-2

Complaint for Libel Regarding Erroneous Credit Report

Name of Court

_____,

Plaintiff,

v.   Civil Action No.

_____,

Defendant.

COMPLAINT FOR DAMAGES AND INJUNCTIVE RELIEF

I. NATURE OF THE CASE

1. Plaintiff is suing the defendant for libel.

II. JURISDICTION

2. Defendant libeled plaintiff in the state of _____.

(If plaintiff and defendant reside in the state where the court is located, state that here).

III. PARTIES

3. Plaintiff, is a resident of _____.
4. Defendant is a resident of _____ and is in the business of _____ _____.

IV. FACTUAL ALLEGATIONS

5. Plaintiff was/is a customer of defendant.

6. Defendant submitted a written report to _____ concerning the plaintiff. The report stated that plaintiff _____ .

V. CAUSE OF ACTION: Libel

7. Plaintiff incorporates by reference paragraphs one through six, inclusive.

8. Plaintiff notified defendant that the statement mentioned in paragraph 6 was false.

9. The statement in paragraph 6 is false and in fact plaintiff_____ .

10. Defendant knowingly and willfully defamed plaintiff.

11. Plaintiff has suffered the following damages on account of the libelous statements made by defendant: _____

_____ .

VI. REQUEST FOR RELIEF

WHEREFORE, plaintiff requests judgment against defendant in the amount of $_____ for actual damages and $_____ as punitive damages.

Respectfully submitted,

(Signature)
_____
PLAINTIFF'S NAME
ADDRESS
TELEPHONE NUMBER

FORM 6-3

Complaint Under Fair Credit Reporting Act

UNITED STATES DISTRICT COURT
FOR THE _____ DISTRICT OF _____
_____ DIVISION

_____,
Plaintiff,

v. _____ Civil Action No.

_____,
Defendant.

COMPLAINT FOR ACTUAL AND PUNITIVE DAMAGES

I. NATURE OF THE CASE

1. This is an action brought under the Fair Credit Reporting Act against a consumer reporting agency for violating that act.

II. JURISDICTION

2. Jurisdiction is conferred on this court by 15 U.S.C. §1681p.

III. PARTIES

3. Plaintiff is a resident of _____.

4. Defendant is a consumer credit reporting agency whose office is located at _____ _____.

IV. FACTUAL ALLEGATIONS

6. (State the facts, including how and when you learned of violations, and state if agency failed to give you your report, failed to correct an inaccurate report, or failed to provide information to creditors about a dispute that you have about a bill or service.)

7. Plaintiff has been harmed by defendant's actions and failure to act as follows:

V. CAUSE OF ACTION: Violations of the Fair Credit Reporting Act

8. Plaintiff incorporates by reference paragraphs one through 7, inclusive.

9. Defendant's willful refusal to disclose (or correct) the information described above in paragraph 6, violates to Fair Credit Reporting Act, 15 U.S.C. §1681 *et. seq.* This willful violation subjects defendant to liability for punitive damages under 15 U.S.C. §1681n.

10. Plaintiff has suffered actual damages caused by defendant's violations of law, in the amount of $_____.

VI. REQUEST FOR RELIEF

WHEREFORE, plaintiff requests judgment against defendant for actual damages in the amount of $_____, with interest of _____% from _____ (date), punitive damages in the amount of $_____, court costs, attorney's fees and such other relief as this court deems just and proper.

(Signature) _____

PLAINTIFF'S NAME
ADDRESS
TELEPHONE NUMBER

7

How to Stop a Foreclosure Sale

Have you fallen behind in your mortgage payments? If so, you have plenty of company. In September of 1982, the Mortgage Bankers Association reported that a record-high 5.56% of all home loans were delinquent. During the second quarter of 1982, 150,000 homeowners were in the foreclosure process. Half of those homeowners lost their homes at foreclosure auctions. The long housing recession, record-high interest rates, and "creative" financing have teamed up to cause these undesirable records.

The Census Bureau reported that the median price of a home went from $42,200 in 1976, to $66,400 in 1982. During the same period mortgage rates skyrocked from 8.9% to 15.4%; even though personal income rose from $15,000 to $21,000, and average monthly mortgage payments nearly tripled from $276 to $745, rising from 22% of family income to 43%. It's no wonder that mortgage delinquencies are higher now than at any other time since 1932.

Balloon payment loans present the most difficult foreclosure problem. When the balloon is due, often the expectation of ones being able to refinance or to get a windfall does not materialize and the bubble bursts. I will address the easier problems first.

NEGOTIATE FIRST

Talk to your lender before you become delinquent. If you have a good reason for being late, such as illness or unemployment, the bank may be flexible with you. Do not stonewall when the bank calls. Be forthright with them.

If you have an FHA-insured loan, you have a good chance of avoiding foreclosure. Under federal law, a bank or savings and loan cannot foreclose on an FHA-insured loan until you are at least three months behind on your payments. If you are three months late you can apply to the U.S. Department of Housing and Urban Development for financial assistance. Write to:

Federal Housing Administration
Homeowner Assistance Program
451 7th St., S. W.
Washington, DC 20410
(202) 755-5995

If the FHA approves your application, it can agree to take over the bank loan and allow you to work out a new payment plan. However, in 1982 only about one in five applications was accepted by FHA.

A Veterans Administration insured loan (VA) offers similar protection under federal law. If a VA homeowner falls behind in mortgage payments and he or she can come up with 50% of the delinquent amount in a lump sum, the mortgage lender is required to negotiate for the repayment of the remainder.

Conventional lenders are not required by federal

legislation to negotiate with you. If you are one day delinquent, the foreclosure process could be started. Bad publicity is one of the things that is stopping banks from initiating foreclosure for minor transgressions. However, some lenders loaded down with old, low interest loans, are starting to get tough with payments only a few days late. If you have a 6% or 7% loan, make sure that all your payments are on time. If it is a choice between paying on your credit cards or your house, make the house payment. A credit card company cannot repossess your clothing, or a meal you charged. It is always wise to pay your mortgage first and if necessary let other payments ride.

REFINANCING WITH ANOTHER LENDER

If you anticipate that trouble is ahead and your credit is still good, you can refinance your mortgage loan to prevent a foreclosure. Often, after refinancing you can have your first payment due in two months to give you time to get back on your feet. If you refinance, you can get a loan larger than needed to pay off the old mortgage holder, so that you have a cushion. Put the extra money in a money market account and use it only for emergencies. Unfortunately, banks and other lenders will lend money only to those who appear not to need it.

If you can't refinance on your own, you can possibly find a friend or parent who has good credit to co-sign for you. It may be embarrassing to ask someone to co-sign, but it is certainly less embarrassing than losing your home at a foreclosure sale.

Equity-sharing is another possibility. Investors will lend you money for a share of the future appreciation of your house. Equity-sharing deals vary considerably. At one extreme, the investor does not expect you to make monthly payments to him; such an investor would want a large share of appreciation when you sell the property. You would have to sign a detailed contract with such an investor, and may be required to sell the house within a specified period or buy out the investor by that time. At the other extreme of equity-sharing you may have to make large monthly payments for interest and still have to pay the investor a part of your appreciation. All of these variables depend on whether an investor believes that your property will appreciate, your credit rating, and the prevailing interest rates. In any event, sharing appreciation with an investor

may be preferable to the alternatives, such as losing all of the equity that you have built up over the years. A foreclosure sale is likely to wipe out all of the equity you have in a property, and may even leave you in debt.

FILING FOR BANKRUPTCY AUTOMATICALLY STOPS FORECLOSURE

Under the current bankruptcy laws, you will not necessarily lose your house if you file for personal bankruptcy. You can keep a maximum of $7500 in equity in your house when you file for a complete bankruptcy.

If your assets exceed your debts, you may want to consider filing a "Chapter 13" petition. Chapter 13 is a reorganization of debt rather than a complete bankruptcy.

Either petition filed in bankruptcy court will cause an automatic stay of foreclosure proceedings. Any other civil legal proceedings against you will also be stayed or held in abeyance.

Filing a petition in bankruptcy is a last resort. If you file a "Chapter 13" petition, your creditors may seek a complete bankruptcy. A bankruptcy judge or trustee will make decisions concerning your finances and take away your financial discretion and control.

An attorney who specializes in bankruptcy should be consulted before you consider the alternative of bankruptcy. Bankruptcy attorneys expect to be paid in advance because of the nature of the proceeding. Even if you choose to file a petition in bankruptcy by yourself, either by using a how-to book or by asking the court clerk for forms, a half hour discussion with an attorney–specialist is well worth the $50 or so that it may cost.

SELL THE HOUSE BEFORE FORECLOSURE

If you want to sell your house anyway, a quick sale before a foreclosure can save your equity in the property. Some real estate brokers will pay cash for your property, but they pay much less than the market rate.

If you want to stay in your house, you may want to consider selling to an investor and letting him lease it back to you. Businesses use the sale and lease-back technique when they are in need of cash, and a homeowner can do the same thing. Investors know that the property will be rented to a reliable tenant, and that a vacancy will be unlikely. Or you can sell part of the property to an investor. See the section in this chapter on refinancing.

You can sell your home with or without a real estate broker. Whenever a contract for a sale without contingencies is signed, a proposed foreclosure sale can be stopped in its tracks. The lender will be pleased because it will be paid off.

If your foreclosure is scheduled for a certain date, you can hold an auction sale several days before. A firm contract at the auction will also stop the foreclosure sale.

BID AT THE FORECLOSURE SALE

Often the only bidders at a foreclosure sale are the lender and the homeowner. The terms of the sale are usually a cash or certified check deposit on the day of the sale. Depending on the amount of the loan in question, a reasonable deposit for a $50,000 loan is from $5,000 to $10,000. Usually the purchaser will have 20–30 days, or possibly more to pay the balance.

Often the lender does not really want your property; he wants to get his money out of it. But the lender will bid to protect his interest; he will bid to drive up the bidding.

If you are the high bidder and can't come up with the balance due, you stand a chance of losing your deposit. But the deposit will be credited toward your payment of the mortgage loan, so all is not lost if you can't complete the deal.

You may have a friend who will bid on the property, either for you, or as your partner. An equity-sharing arrangement can be worked out with a foreclosure bidder.

THE RIGHT OF REDEMPTION

The "right of redemption" is the right of a homeowner to reclaim his house, even after it is lost at foreclosure. Some states do not have a right of redemption. A table of the right of redemption for every state is included at the end of this chapter.

COURT INJUNCTIONS AGAINST FORECLOSURE

If you have a legal defense for your late payments, a court can grant an injunction against the foreclosure while your case is proceeding. One court has held that the continued acceptance of late payments is a defense to a foreclosure and has granted an injunction[1]. Other defenses which can be raised are: (1) violations of the truth-in-lending law, (2) usury law violations (interest higher than the legal limit), (3) fraud or misrepresentation, (4) violations of other statutes, such as those limiting balloon payment loans, (5) violations of FHA or VA requirements discussed in this chapter, and (6) the trustees of the deed of trust are not truly independent trustees, and are really acting only in the interests of the lender.

To get an injunction, most courts require four criteria to be met:

(1) That you are likely to win your lawsuit. A motion for an injunction *must* be a part of a lawsuit or complaint.

(2) That the homeowner is likely to be harmed irreparably. If you own and live in the same home it is to your advantage. If you, with or without a lawyer, file a motion for an injunction in court, be sure to specify how long you have lived in the home, how many children you have, what schools they attend, and how all of your lives would be disrupted if you were forced to move by a foreclosure sale.

(3) That the lender will not suffer great harm. Offer to pay interest to the lender while the suit is progressing. This will minimize harm to the lender.

(4) The last criteria is on whose side the public interest is stronger. The public interest does not lie with throwing long-term homeowners on the street, but neither does it lie on the side of those who refuse to make monthly payments.

---

1. *Greene* v. *Gibralter Mortgage Corp.*, 488 F. Supp. 177 (D.C. 1980).

RIGHT OF REDEMPTION AFTER FORECLOSURE SALE

State	Yes/No	If Yes, Period for Redemption
Alabama	Yes	One Year
Alaska	No	
Arizona	Yes	If Abandoned, 30 Days; If Not, 6 Months
Arkansas	Yes	One Year
California	Only For Deficiency Judgments	One Year
Colorado	Yes	75 Days
Connecticut	No	
Delaware	No	
District of Columbia	No	
Florida	No	
Georgia	No	
Hawaii	No	
Idaho	Yes	Not Specified
Illinois	No	
Indiana	Yes	One Year
Iowa	No	
Kansas	Yes	One Year
Kentucky	Yes, But Only if Sale Does Not Bring ⅔ Value	One Year
Louisiana	No	
Maine	Yes	One Year
Maryland	No	
Massachusetts	No	
Michigan	No	
Minnesota	Yes	One Year
Mississippi	Yes	Ten Years
Missouri	Yes	One Year
Montana	Yes	One Year
Nebraska	Yes	Until Sale Confirmed by Court
Nevada	Yes	One Year
New Hampshire	Yes	One Year
New Jersey	Yes	10 Days
New Mexico	Yes	9 Months

RIGHT OF REDEMPTION AFTER FORECLOSURE SALE (Continued)

State	Yes/No	If Yes, Period for Redemption
New York	Yes	10 Years
North Carolina	No	
North Dakota	Yes	6 Months or One Year
Ohio	Yes	Before Confirmation
Oklahoma	Yes	6 Months
Oregon	Yes	One Year
Pennsylvania	No	
Rhode Island	Yes	3 Years
South Carolina	No	
South Dakota	Yes	One Year
Tennessee	Yes	2 Years
Texas	No	
Utah	Yes	6 Months
Vermont	Yes	6 Months
Virginia	No	
Washington	Yes	One Year
West Virginia	No	
Wisconsin	Yes	Prior to Transfer
Wyoming	Yes	3 Months

8

How to Fight the Internal Revenue Service

Disputes with the Internal Revenue Service are unlike any dispute that you may have with a private company. Private companies have to file suit against you and obtain a judgment (often after years of court delays), before they can have your property seized to pay a debt. But the IRS can have your property seized when it determines that you owe Uncle Sam tax money.

You should know it when the IRS claims that you owe them taxes. But if you have moved and the IRS notices don't reach you, you can be in for a rude awakening. You cannot avoid the IRS by failing to give the post office your new address. By running away you only worsen your tax problems.

The IRS will agree to installment payments if you cannot afford to pay your tax liability in one payment. If you dispute your tax liability, you can appeal within the IRS, and if that fails, you can take the IRS to court.

APPEAL WITHIN IRS

If you have been audited, and you do not agree with the auditor's proposed assessment of your taxes, there are two appeal routes you can take within the IRS. First, the proposed assessment can be discussed informally with the auditor's supervisor. To the IRS, an *auditor* is one who conducts a desk audit, and his superior is called a *supervisor*.

On the other hand, *revenue agents* conduct field audits and their supervisors are called *group managers*. Therefore, if you have suffered through a field audit, discuss the revenue officer's proposed assessment with his or her group manager. A phone call to the IRS is enough to set up this informal appeals process.

After the informal process has been exhausted, the taxpayer can make his appeal formal. After your audit, you will receive in the mail a copy of the audit report containing proposed adjustments of your tax liability, and a letter advising you of your right to appeal within 30 days. This is known as a "30-day letter," or a "Preliminary Notice." You must request an appeals conference within this 30-day period. After 30 days a conference will no longer be available, but you may appeal to the U.S. Tax Court, or pay the tax and appeal to a federal court.

The request for an appeals conference is sent to the local IRS district office. You can make this request by telephone, or by sending a short letter in three situations:

1. If the examination was conducted by correspondence (known as a limited contact audit)

2. If the audit was conducted at an IRS office (desk audit)

3. If the assessment after a field audit does not exceed $2,500 for any one year

DIAGRAM OF THE IRS APPEAL AND REVIEW PROCESS

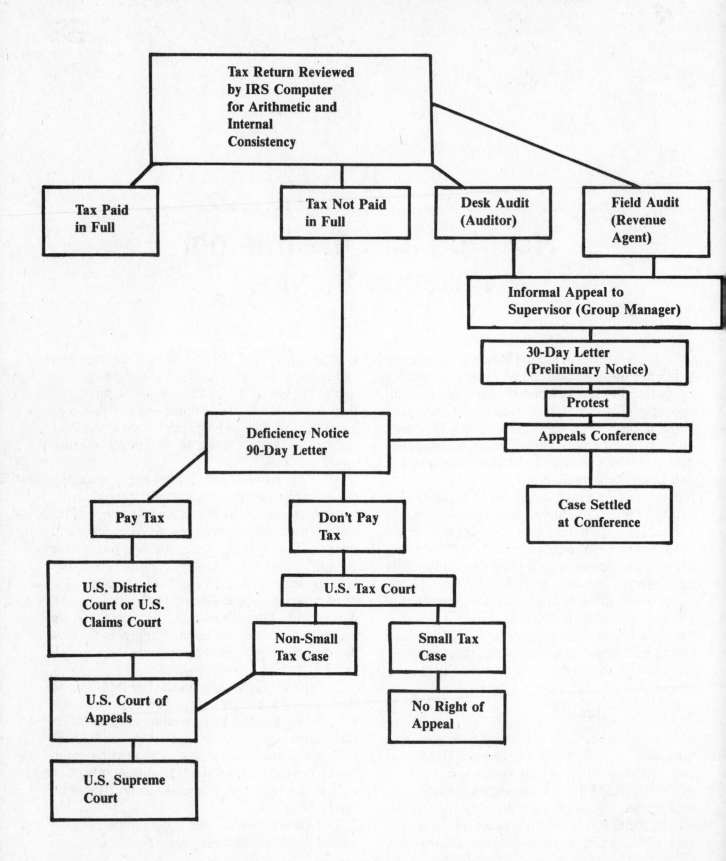

FORMAL PROTESTS

If more than $2,500 is involved, a formal written protest must be filed with the district director within the 30-day period specified in the Preliminary Notice. The form for a protest letter is shown in Form 8-1 at the end of this chapter.

THE APPEALS CONFERENCE

The regional director of appeals will schedule a conference when an appeal is requested within the 30-day period specified in the Preliminary Notice letter. At this conference the IRS will be represented by a "conferee." The taxpayer may present his or her own case or may be accompanied by a lawyer, CPA, or someone enrolled to practice before the IRS. A signed power-of-attorney form (IRS form 2848) must be filed for this representative. The conferee will refer to the auditor's report, and will consider evidence that the taxpayer presents. You can submit affidavits from third parties, copies of receipts, live witnesses, and other evidence. The conferee will attempt to settle the case with a compromise agreement with the taxpayer. About two-thirds of the appeals conferences are settled, and usually the IRS will compromise by reducing the tax assessment. If an agreement is not reached, a 90-day letter (a Notice of Deficiency) will be sent.

NOTICE OF DEFICIENCY

Before your property can be seized, the revenue service must send you a Notice of Deficiency. This is also known as a 90-day letter because you are given 90 days to take action—to either pay up or take the IRS to court: the United States Tax Court.

There are three general classes of taxpayers who receive deficiency notices. The first type is the taxpayer who makes an arithmetic error in the tax return. This is the most common starting point for a deficiency notice as about five million taxpayers annually err on the side of underpayment. All tax returns are checked by computer for arithmetic and internal consistency.

The other common starting point for a deficiency notice is the failure to pay the tax as computed on your tax form. It is very important that tax forms be filed on time, even if you cannot afford to pay the tax. The failure to file a tax form is a criminal offense, and it is one of the only offenses which does not have a statute of limitations. If you don't pay your taxes in one lump sum, the IRS will usually allow you to make monthly installment payments, over one or more years. Never ignore calls or letters from the IRS—it can lead to the seizure of your property, attachment of your wages, or both. Politely go into an IRS office and explain your financial circumstances. By doing so you show your good faith and your intent to pay taxes, and you make it more likely that the IRS will allow you to pay monthly installment payments. The IRS will ask you for details of your financial affairs; be honest with them, and the IRS will usually be fair about allowing installment payments.

Deficiency notices also result from the IRS audits. There are two types of audits: the office audit and the field audit. Regarding an office audit, the IRS will send you a notice requesting that you bring certain records to its office. Often this will only involve one or two items on your return. For example, if you took a fairly large deduction for gifts to charity, the IRS computer may have targeted your return for an audit of this deduction.

The IRS also conducts field audits, where examiners are sent to your home or office for a more detailed examination of your records. After either type of audit has been completed, the examiner will decide if you were entitled to the deductions that you claimed. If he or she finds that you overstated your deductions, or under-reported your income, you will receive a deficiency notice.

OPTIONS AVAILABLE AFTER RECEIVING A DEFICIENCY NOTICE

Don't panic when you receive a deficiency notice. It is a scary document to receive in the mail, but it can be dealt with properly without much difficulty. If you have a valid basis for believing that the IRS is wrong (and it is often wrong), you do not have to pay the taxes if you file a petition with the United States Tax Court within 90 days of the date on the notice. The Tax Court has a small tax case procedure which makes filing a petition relatively easy. Form 8-2 is the Tax Court's approved form for filing a petition in Tax Court. The use of this form will be explained in greater detail later in this chapter.

Another option that you have after receiving a notice of a deficiency is to pay the tax, and then sue for a refund. Before filing suit for a refund, you must request a refund from the IRS, and have this request denied. Form 8-3 is enclosed for this purpose (IRS form 843). Suits for a refund of taxes can be brought either in the United States Claims Court or in a United States District Court. In a district court you have the right to a trial by jury; in the claims court you do not. Neither the Claims Court nor the district courts are geared toward small tax cases, and neither of these courts like to deal with citizens who are not represented by counsel.

In summary, it is usually to your advantage to file a petition in the U.S. Tax Court. The major advantage is that you do not have to pay the tax while your case is pending. You also have a small tax case option for claims of $5,000 and less, per tax year. Small claims cases are less formal, and the filing fee is only $10 as opposed to $60, but you give up your right to appeal if you lose (the government cannot appeal if you win)!

SMALL TAX CASE PROCEDURE AT THE TAX COURT

You have the right to bring a case to the United States Tax Court by paying the filing fee and filing a petition with the court in Washington, D.C. Your petition must be filed no later than 90 days after the Notice of Deficiency was mailed to you. Ninety days is not the same as three months. A petition filed one day late will not be considered, and you will be out of luck. If the Notice of Deficiency was addressed to you outside of the United States, you have an additional 60 days to file your petition. The petition must be received at the court by the 90th day after the date postmarked on the envelope you received containing the Notice of Deficiency. Form 8-2 is the proper form to use for your petition. Mail the original and two copies of the petition by certified mail—return receipt requested—to:

Clerk
United States Tax Court
400 Second Street, N.W.
Washington, DC 20217

Enclose the appropriate filing fee with the petition. If you want to proceed with a small tax case, the filing fee is $10. If you want the full-blown treatment, including the right to appeal, the filing fee is $60. If you do not want small tax case treatment, you must check the block at the bottom of

Form 8-1. Your check should be made payable to "Clerk, United States Tax Court."

Filing out the petition form is a relatively simple matter. You must attach a copy of the notice of deficiency and include in your petition the name of the IRS office that issued the notice. You must also provide your social security number or your taxpayer identification number, whichever was on the notice of deficiency. Corporations, estates, and trusts, as well as individuals, can use the small tax case procedure.

Your petition must include the year and the amount of tax that you dispute. If you dispute only part of the deficiency, make this clear in your petition. If a taxpayer files a frivolous case without any basis whatsoever, he or she can be fined up to $5,000. State the reasons for your dispute, and attach additional pages to the petition explaining the reasons. For example, if the IRS determined that your gift of artwork to charity was worth $1,000 and you claimed a $7,500 deduction for it, you should state: "I disagree with the IRS determination of fair market value for the painting that I donated to charity."

Be certain that you have documentation for your point of view. In small tax cases the technical rules of evidence are relaxed, so you can use and introduce as evidence, appraisals and receipts. Under non-small tax cases, this type of evidence would only be admissible if a witness testified about the document; and an appraisal could only be used if an expert appraiser testified, supporting the reasonability of the appraisal.

If both husband and wife are disputing a deficiency on a joint return, both names should be entered into the blank space above the word "Petitioner(s)." When there is more than one petitioner, all of them must sign the petition and date it.

Make sure that you provide the court with your correct address and telephone number, as the court has about 50,000 cases pending before it at any given time. On all other correspondence, provide the case number and your name. Small tax cases take about one year to be resolved.

PLACE OF TRIAL

You have the right to designate the city where you want your tax case to be heard. Small tax cases are heard in many smaller cities. Tax cases are heard in the following cities:

Alabama
Birmingham
Mobile
*Montgomery

Alaska
Anchorage

Arizona
Phoenix
*Tucson

Arkansas
*Fort Smith
Little Rock

California
*Fresno
Los Angeles
San Diego
San Francisco

Colorado
Denver

Connecticut
Hartford

Delaware
*Wilmington

**District of
   Columbia**
Washington

Florida
Jacksonville
Miami
*Tallahassee
Tampa

Georgia
Atlanta
*Macon
*Savannah

Hawaii
Honolulu

Idaho
Boise
*Pocatello

Illinois
Chicago
*Danville
*Peoria
*Springfield

Indiana
*Evansville
*Fort Wayne
Indianapolis

Iowa
*Cedar Rapids
Des Moines

Kansas
*Witchita

Kentucky
Louisville

Louisiana
New Orleans
*Shreveport

Maine
*Portland

Maryland
Baltimore

Massachusetts
Boston
*Springfield

Michigan
Detroit
*Grand Rapids

Minnesota
*Duluth
Minneapolis
St. Paul

Mississippi
*Greenville
Jackson
Biloxi

Missouri
Kansas City
St. Louis

Montana
*Billings
Helena

Nebraska
Omaha

Nevada
Las Vegas
Reno

New Hampshire
*Concord

New Jersey
*Atlantic City
Newark

New Mexico
Albuquerque

New York
*Albany
Buffalo
New York City
*Syracuse

North Carolina
*Asheville
Greensboro
*Raleigh
Winston-Salem

North Dakota
*Bismarck

Ohio
Cincinnati
Cleveland
Columbus
*Toledo

Oklahoma
Oklahoma City
Tulsa

Oregon
Portland

Pennsylvania
*Harrisburg
Philadelphia
Pittsburgh
*Scranton

Rhode Island
*Providence

South Carolina
*Charleston
Columbia

South Dakota
*Aberdeen

Tennessee
Knoxville
Memphis
Nashville

Texas
Dallas
El Paso
Houston
Lubbock
San Antonio

Utah
Salt Lake City

Vermont
*Burlington

Virginia
*Norfolk
Richmond
*Roanoke

Washington
Seattle
Spokane

West Virginia
Charleston
*Clarksburg
Huntington

Wisconsin
*Eau Claire
*Green Bay
Milwaukee

Wyoming
*Cheyenne

---

*Cities where only small tax cases are heard.

Form 8-4 is the proper form for requesting a specific place for trial. The original and two copies of this form should be filed with your petition.

Your case will be listed for trial at a trial session regularly scheduled for the city you request. Trial sessions will be announced, and a notice of trial will be sent to you at least 60 days before the trial date. You will ordinarily have a trial within less than one year after you file your petition.

REMOVAL OF SMALL TAX CASE DESIGNATION

At any time before the trial you may ask the court to remove the small case designation so that your case can be handled as a regular case. The court does not have to approve your request, but ordinarily it will do so if you give a valid reason for your request. One valid reason would be that you filed the petition without benefit of an attorney, that you have since hired or consulted an attorney, and that the attorney has recommended that the case be treated as a regular case. Concerning this example, it would be appropriate if the attorney made the request. If the designation of a case is changed to a regular tax case, you must then pay an additional $50 filing fee.

The government will have an attorney assigned to your case. Before filing a request with the court, it is advisable to ask the government attorney to consent to it. The government attorney may be willing to consent to a procedural matter, such as changing the designation of a case or changing the time or place of hearing.

SETTLEMENT BEFORE TRIAL

The government settles many of the small tax cases pending before the tax court. Because there are 50,000 cases pending before the court at any given time, the attorneys handling these cases for the government are each burdened with hundreds of them. If you are willing to compromise with the government, write the attorney and make a suggested settlement. Leave some room for negotiation. If you would agree to pay 60 percent of the tax deficiency, offer to pay 40 percent. You may wind up with a 50/50 settlement, as long as you have some basis for your claim. Even if you have very little basis for your claim, the overburdened gov-

ernment attorney may settle the matter for 70 percent of the deficiency just to get the case off his or her docket.

TRIAL PROCEDURE

You may represent yourself before the Tax Court, or you may hire an attorney to do so. Most petitioners in small tax cases are not represented by an attorney. Small tax cases are conducted informally. Any evidence that you offer which the judge thinks has value as proof will be admissible. If you have receipts or other documents which support your claim, bring them with you when you come to the court for trial. The judge will try to help you develop the facts in your case, and will often ask you and your witnesses questions. You have the right to subpoena documents which are in someone else's custody. If you have supplied documents to the IRS, ask the government attorney to bring them to court for trial. The clerk of the tax court will explain how you can subpoena witnesses or force someone to produce documents. The clerk's office can be reached by calling (202) 376-2754. Employees of the clerk's office are very helpful, and are an invaluable aid to taxpayers and lawyers.

It is usually best to use the original of a document for evidence, but copies are acceptable. After all of the evidence and testimony have been given, you have the right to make an oral statement to the court. If you want to submit a written statement to the court after the hearing, advise the judge of this and he or she will give you a deadline for submitting such a statement or "post-trial brief." If you do not want to submit any arguments after trial the judge may issue a decision at once. Often the judge will take the case under advisement and issue a decision after he or she has had a chance to think it over.

If you have elected to have your case tried as a small tax case, the decision of the tax court judge is final and cannot be appealed. Thus, if the decision is in your favor, the government cannot appeal to a higher court. Similarly, if the court finds that you owe taxes, you have no right of appeal.

ATTORNEY FEES AND FRIVOLOUS CASES

When the IRS loses in the tax court it may have to pay your attorney's fees. You can recover these fees if you can show that the government's position was unreasonable. This is a new law that went into effect on March 1, 1983, so there have been few court decisions defining what is reasonable. The same law increased from $500 to $5,000 the maxi- mum penalty for taking a delaying, frivolous, or groundless case to the tax court. Congress gives with one hand and takes with the other. But the law gives fair warning to both sides not to bring unnec- essary disputes before the tax court.

FORM 8-1

Protest Letter to Internal Revenue Service

Name
Address
Social Security Number/or
Taxpayer Identification Number

Date

District Director
Internal Revenue Service

PROTEST LETTER

Dear District Director:

I want to appeal the findings of the examining officer to the Regional Director of Appeals. This appeal comes within the 30-day period specified in the preliminary notice letter dated _____, and included the identifying symbol _____. Tax years _____ and _____ are the subject of this appeal.

I do not agree with the schedule of adjustments because _____ _____.

(Insert your reasoning, supporting facts, and provisions of law that you rely on.)

Sincerely,

[Signature(s)] _____
NAME(S)

(Include your spouse's name if a joint return was involved.)

Under penalties of perjury, I (we) declare that I (we) have examined the statement of facts con- tained in this letter, and in accompanying schedules and statements and, to the best of my knowledge the belief, they are true, correct and complete.

(Signature) _____
NAME

FORM 8-2: Tax Court Petition

UNITED STATES TAX COURT

(FIRST)   (MIDDLE)   (LAST)

(PLEASE TYPE OR PRINT)   Petitioner(s)

V.

COMMISSIONER OF INTERNAL REVENUE
                        Respondent   Docket No.

PETITION

1. Petitioner(s) disagree(s) with the tax deficiency(ies) for the year(s)
_____ , as set forth in the NOTICE OF DEFICIENCY
dated _____ , A COPY OF WHICH IS ATTACHED. The notice
was issued by the Office of the Internal Revenue Service at
_____
                        (CITY AND STATE)

2. Petitioner(s) taxpayer identification (e.g. social security) number(s) is (are)
_____ .

3. Petitioner(s) dispute(s) the following:

Year	Amount of Deficiency Disputed	Addition to Tax (Penalty) if any, Disputed	Amount of Over-payment Claimed
_____	_____	_____	_____
_____	_____	_____	_____
_____	_____	_____	_____

4. Set forth those adjustments, i.e. changes, in the NOTICE OF DEFICIENCY
with which you disagree and why you disagree.

_____

_____

Petitioner(s) request(s) that this case be conducted under the "small tax case" procedures authorized by Congress to provide the taxpayer(s) with an informal, prompt, and inexpensive hearing at a reasonably convenient location. Consistent with these objectives, a decision in a "small tax case" is final and cannot be appealed to higher Courts (the Courts of Appeals and the Supreme Court) by the Internal Revenue Service or the Petitioner(s). *

| SIGNATURE OF PETITIONER | DATE | PRESENT ADDRESS—STREET, CITY, STATE, ZIP CODE—TELEPHONE NO. |

| SIGNATURE OF PETITIONER (SPOUSE) | DATE | PRESENT ADDRESS—STREET, CITY, STATE, ZIP CODE—TELEPHONE NO. |

| SIGNATURE AND ADDRESS OF COUNSEL, IF RETAINED BY PETITIONER(S) | DATE |

* If you do not want to make this request, you should place an "X" in the following box.

T.C. Form 2
(Rev. Feb. 1979)

Form **843**
(Rev. October 1981)
Department of the Treasury
Internal Revenue Service

FORM 8-3: Request for Tax Refund
Claim
▶ **See Instructions on back**

OMB No. 1545–0024
Expires 12–31–83

If your claim is for an overpayment of income taxes, do NOT use this form (see Instructions)

Please print or type

Name of taxpayer or purchaser of stamps

Number and street

City or town, State, and ZIP code

Fill in applicable items—Use attachments if necessary

1 Your social security number	**2** Employer identification number

3 Internal Revenue Service Center where return (if any) was filed

4 Name and address shown on return, if different from above

5 Period—prepare separate form for each tax period From _____ , 19___ , to _____ , 19___	**6** Amount to be refunded or abated $

7 Dates of payment

8 Type of tax
☐ Employment ☐ Estate ☐ Excise ☐ Gift ☐ Stamp

9 Kind of return filed
☐ 706 ☐ 709 ☐ 720 ☐ 940 ☐ 941 ☐ 990–PF ☐ 4720 ☐ Other (specify) ▶

10 If this claim involves refund of excise taxes on gasoline, special fuels or lubricating oil, please indicate your tax year for income tax purposes

11 Explain why you believe this claim should be allowed and show computation of tax refund or abatement

Under penalties of perjury, I declare that I have examined this claim, including accompanying schedules and statements, and to the best of my knowledge and belief it is true, correct, and complete.

Signed .... Dated .... 19..........

Director's Stamp
(Date received)

For Internal Revenue Service Use Only
☐ Refund of taxes illegally, erroneously, or excessively collected.
☐ Refund of amount paid for stamps unused, or used in error or excess.
☐ Abatement of tax assessed (not applicable to estate or gift taxes).

For Paperwork Reduction Act Notice, see instructions on back.

Form **843** (Rev. 10–81)

FORM 8-4

Request for Place of Tax Court Trial

United States Tax Court

_____
                           Petitioner(s),
                  v.   Docket No.
COMMISSIONER OF INTERNAL REVENUE,
                           Respondent.

REQUEST FOR PLACE OF TRIAL
Petitioner(s) hereby request(s) that trial of this case be held at _____.
                                        (City and State)

_____
(Signature of Petitioner or Counsel)

Dated: _____, 19____

9

What You Should Do When Your Employer Underpays You

This chapter explains your rights under the federal Fair Labor Standards Act. This act establishes the national minimum wage and overtime pay requirements. More than fifty million full-time and part-time workers are covered by this law.

WHO IS COVERED

Approximately half of the workers in the United States are covered by the Fair Labor Standards Act: anyone engaged in laundering, dry cleaning, construction, hospitals, schools, retail businesses with annual sales of $362,580 per year or more, or any other businesses with annual sales of $250,000 or more. Domestic workers, such as maids, housekeepers, or babysitters are covered if they receive at least $50 in wages in a calendar quarter, or work more than eight hours a week from one or more employers.

WHO IS NOT COVERED BY THE ACT

In general, salaried employees are not covered by the overtime requirements of the law, as long as they are paid the minimum wage. Independent contractors, who usually provide services outside of the workplace without supervision, are not covered. An independent contractor is not an employee; he is a separate business entity. For example, if you send your typing to a secretarial service, the service and its employees are not your employees. The service is an independent contractor. Apprentices or students may be paid less than minimum wages when a special certificate is issued by the Labor Department.

Farm workers are not covered by the law if their employer used no more than 500 man-days of farm labor in any quarter of the preceding year. Casual babysitters and persons employed as companions are usually exempt from the overtime requirements of the law. There are many other minor exceptions. Call or write your nearest Department of Labor, Employment Standards Administration Wage and Hour Division. A list of addresses is included at the end of this chapter.

BASIC WAGE STANDARDS

As of January 1, 1981, the minimum wage for covered workers is $3.35 per hour. Work after 40 hours in a week must be compensated at one and one-half times the regular wage. Deductions made from wages for items like cash shortages or merchandise shortages are not legal if they reduce wages below the minimum or overtime rates. Hospitals and residential case facilities may adopt, by agreement with their employees, a 14-day overtime period, instead of the usual seven-day work week, if the employees are paid time-and-a-half for work over eight hours in a day, or 80 hours in a 14-day period.

The value of food or overnight lodging may be considered part of your wages, if the acceptance of the food or sleeping quarters is voluntary on your part.

TIPPED EMPLOYEES

Tipped employees are those who regularly receive more than $30 per month in tips. The employer may consider tips a part of wages, but the credit for tips cannot exceed 40 percent of the minimum wage. For example, a waitress in a restaurant must be paid by her employer 60 percent of minimum wage or $2.01 per hour (when this book was written). But this waitress must actually receive at least an average of $1.34 per hour in tips which she is allowed to keep.

LARGEST WAGE AND HOUR SETTLEMENT

In the largest settlement ever obtained under the federal wage and hour law, the United States Postal Service agreed to pay $400 million in back wages to 800,000 employees, an average of $500 per employee. The Labor Department brought suit after receiving complaints from postal workers that they were not paid time-and-a-half for working more than 40 hours in a week. Employees also complained that they were not paid for required training time. The case was settled in 1982. A postal service spokesman said that the settlement would not increase postal rates because the money had been held in an escrow account in anticipation of the agreement.

ENFORCEMENT

The Wage and Hour Division of the United States Department of Labor enforces the law concerning private employees, postal employees, and certain other government employees. The Office of Personnel Management is responsible for enforcement concerning most federal employees. The Wage and Hour Division has compliance officers throughout the United States. If you want the Wage and Hour Division to investigate your employer, you must file a complaint with them. Your complaint can be confidential, if you so choose. A complaint form is included at the end of this chapter as Form 9-1. The Division may supervise the payment of back wages. The Secretary of Labor can bring suit against your employer for twice the amount your employer owes you for paying you less than minimum wage, and less than time-and-a-half for overtime work.

YOU HAVE A RIGHT TO SUE YOUR EMPLOYER DIRECTLY

The law gives you the right to sue your employer directly for twice the amount of unpaid wages that your employer owes you. You are permitted to ask for attorneys' fees and court costs. Ordinarily, you must have an attorney represent you before you can recover attorneys' fees. But if there isn't much money involved, you may not want to hire an attorney, and few attorneys are interested in very small cases.

Form 9-2 is included at the end of this chapter for filing your case against your employer. You must fill in all of the blanks and file it with a court in your area. Small claims courts have exclusive jurisdiction in many states for claims under $1,500.[1] However, you may file your complaint in federal court. Even if you are owed only a small amount, the federal court will hear your case because it is based on a federal law. There are federal courts in every state of the United States and in most major cities.

---

1. This amount varies from state to state. Most small-claims limits range from $750 to $1500; these amounts are changed frequently. Call the small claims court in your area to determine the limits of its jurisdiction.

FORM 9-1: Labor Department Complaint Form for Underpayment of Wages

Form Approved
Budget Bureau No. 44-R0304

U.S. DEPARTMENT OF LABOR EMPLOYMENT STANDARDS ADMINISTRATION WAGE AND HOUR DIVISION	EMPLOYMENT INFORMATION FORM

This report is authorized by Section 11 of the Fair Labor Standards Act. While you are not required to respond, submission of this information is necessary for the Division to schedule any compliance action. Your identity will be kept confidential to the maximum extent possible under existing law.

1. PERSON SUBMITTING INFORMATION

A. Name (Print first name, middle initial, and last name)

Mr.
Miss
Mrs.
Ms.

B. Date

C. Telephone number:
(Or No. where you
can be reached)

D. Address: (Number, Street, Apt. No.)

_____

(City, County, State, ZIP Code)

E. Check one of these boxes

☐ Present employee
of establishment

☐ Former employee
of establishment

☐ Other_____
(Specify: relative, union, etc)

2. ESTABLISHMENT INFORMATION

A. Name of establishment

B. Telephone Number

C. Address of establishment: (Number, Street)

_____

(City, County, State, ZIP Code)

D. Estimate number of employees

E. Does the firm have branches?   ☐ Yes   ☐ No   ☐ Don't know

If "Yes", name one or two locations: _____

_____

F. Nature of establishment's business: (For example; school, farm, hospital, hotel, restaurant, shoe store, wholesale drugs, manufactures stoves, coal mine, construction, trucking, etc.)

_____

G. If the establishment has a Federal Government or federally assisted contract, check the appropriate box(es).

☐ Furnishes goods   ☐ Furnishes services   ☐ Performs construction

H. Does establishment ship goods to or receive goods from other States?
☐ Yes   ☐ No   ☐ Don't know

3. EMPLOYMENT INFORMATION

(Complete A, B, C, D, E, & F if present or former employee of establishment; otherwise complete F only)

A. Period employed (month, year)

From: _____

To: _____
(If still there, state present)

B. Date of birth if under 19

Month _____ Day_____Year _____

C. Give your job title and describe briefly the kind of work you do

_____

_____

(Continue on other side)

Form WH-3 (Rev. Oct. 1980)

FORM 9-1 Continued

D. Method of payment

$_____ per_____
   (Rate)   (Hour, week, month, etc.)

E. Enter in the boxes below the hours you usually work each day and each week (less time off for meals)

M	T	W	T	F	S	S	TOTAL

F. CHECK THE APPROPRIATE BOX(ES) AND EXPLAIN BRIEFLY IN THE SPACE BELOW the employment practices which you believe violate the Wage and Hour laws. (If you need more space use an additional sheet of paper and attach it to this form.)

☐ Does not pay the minimum wage

☐ Does not pay proper overtime

☐ Does not pay prevailing wage determination for Federal Government or federally assisted contract

   Approximate date of alleged discrimination

   _____

☐ Discharged employee because of wage garnishment (explain below)

☐ Excessive deduction from wages because of wage garnishment (explain below)

☐ Employs minors under minimum age for job

☐ Other (explain below)

_____

_____

_____

_____

_____

_____

_____

_____

_____

_____

_____

_____

_____

(NOTE: If you think it would be difficult for us to locate the establishment or where you live, give directions or attach map.)

COMPLAINT TAKEN BY:

_____

_____

FORM 9-2

Complaint by Employee Against Employer for Unpaid Minimum or Overtime Wages

UNITED STATES DISTRICT COURT
FOR THE _____ DISTRICT OF _____
_____ DIVISION

(Note: You may file in federal court or in a state or small claims court; some federal courts have divisions such as Eastern Division, some do not.)

_____,
                                                    Plaintiff,

        v.   Civil Action No.

_____,
                                                    Defendant.

COMPLAINT

I. NATURE OF THE CASE

1. Plaintiff is suing his (her) employer to recover unpaid minimum wages, unpaid overtime compensation, liquidated damages, attorneys' fees and costs.

II. JURISDICTION

2. Jurisdiction is conferred on this court by 28 U.S.C. § 1337 and 29 U.S.C. § 216(b). (If your case is not in federal court, omit the preceding sentence and add: "Jurisdiction is conferred on this court because defendant is a resident of this state.")

III. PARTIES

3. Plaintiff is a resident of the city of _____, State of _____.
4. Defendant conducts business in the city of _____, State of _____ _____. (Make sure that this city and state is within the jurisdiction of the court.)

IV. FACTUAL ALLEGATIONS

5. The defendant is in the business of _____
_____.
6. On _____ (date) defendant hired plaintiff as a _____ at a rate of pay of _____ per hour.
7. Defendant pays plaintiff $_____ per hour less than the minimum wage. Plaintiff has worked _____ hours for the defendant and was paid a total gross amount of $_____.
8. Plaintiff worked more than 40 hours per week during the following weeks: _____.
9. Defendant failed and refuses to pay plaintiff time and one-half for overtime work.

V. CAUSE OF ACTION: Violations of the Fair
Labor Standards Act

10. Plaintiff incorporates by reference paragraphs one through nine, inclusive.

11. Defendant is engaged in interstate commerce and is subject to the provision of the Fair Labor Standards Act.

12. Defendant paid plaintiff less than $3.35 per hour in violation of 29 U.S.C. § 206(a).

13. Defendant paid plaintiff less than one and one-half times his normal hourly pay for the work he performed over forty hours per week in violation of 29 U.S.C. § 207(a).

VI. REQUEST FOR RELIEF

WHEREFORE, plaintiff requests judgment against defendant for:

A. Two times the amount of the underpayment of wages;

B. Two times the amount of the underpayment of overtime wages;

C. Attorneys' fees;

D. Court costs; and

E. Such other relief as this court deems appropriate.

(Signature) _____

PLAINTIFF'S NAME
ADDRESS
TELEPHONE NUMBER

REGIONAL OFFICES FOR WAGE AND HOUR DIVISION DEPARTMENT OF LABOR

Region I: Boston
Connecticut, Maine, Massachusetts,
New Hampshire, Rhode Island,
Vermont

Employment Standards Administration
U.S. Department of Labor
JFK Federal Building
Government Center
Room 1612C
Boston, MA 02203

Region II: New York
Division of Labor Standards
2 World Trade Center
New York, NY 10047

Region III: Philadelphia
Delaware, District of Columbia
Maryland, Pennsylvania, Virginia,
West Virginia

Employment Standards Administration
U.S. Department of Labor
Gateway Building
Room 15230
3535 Market Street
Philadelphia, PA 19104

Region IV: Atlanta
Alabama, Florida, Georgia, Kentucky,
Mississippi, North Carolina, South
Carolina, Tennessee

Employment Standards Administration
U.S. Department of Labor
1371 Peachtree Street, N.E.
Room 105
Atlanta, GA 30367

Region V: Chicago
Illinois, Indiana, Michigan,
Minnesota, Ohio, Wisconsin

Employment Standards Administration
U.S. Department of Labor
230 South Dearborn Street
8th Floor
Chicago, IL 60604

Region VI: Dallas
Arkansas, Louisiana, New Mexico,
Oklahoma, Texas

Employment Standards Administration
U.S. Department of Labor
555 Griffin Square Building
Room 800
Young and Griffin Streets
Dallas, TX 75202

Region VII: Kansas City
Iowa, Kansas, Missouri, Nebraska

Employment Standards Administration
U.S. Department of Labor
Federal Office Building
Room 2000
911 Walnut Street
Kansas City, MO 64106

Region VIII: Denver
Colorado, Montana, North Dakota,
South Dakota, Utah, Wyoming

Employment Standards Administration
U.S. Department of Labor
Federal Office Building
Room 1442
1961 Stout Street
Denver, CO 80294

Region IX: San Francisco
Arizona, California, Hawaii, Nevada

Employment Standards Administration
U.S. Department of Labor
450 Golden Gate Avenue
Room 10353
San Francisco, CA 94102

Region X: Seattle
Alaska, Idaho, Oregon, Washington

Employment Standards Administration
U.S. Department of Labor
Federal Office Building
Room 4141
909 First Avenue
Seattle, WA 91874

AREA WAGE AND HOUR DIVISION OFFICES

Alabama
1931 Ninth Avenue, South
Birmingham, AL 35256
(205) 254-1305

Aronov Building
Room 130
474 South Court Street
Montgomery, AL 36104
(205) 832-7450

Alaska
Federal Building & Courthouse
701 C Street
Anchorage, AK 99513
(907) 271-5019

Arizona
2120 North Central Avenue
Suite G-130
Phoenix, AZ 85004
(602) 261-4223

Arkansas
Federal Office Building
Room 3519
700 West Capitol Avenue
Little Rock, AR 72201
(501) 378-5292

California
115 North Central Avenue
Glendale, CA 91203
(213) 240-5274

Federal Building
Room 3251
300 North Los Angeles Street
Los Angeles, CA 90012
(213) 688-4957,
(213) 688-4958

2800 Cottage Way
Room E-1603
Sacramento, CA 95825
(916) 484-4447

211 Main Street
Room 341
San Francisco, CA 94105
(415) 556-6815,
(415) 556-6816

1600 North Broadway
Suite 440
Santa Ana, CA 92706
(714) 863-2156

Colorado
U.S. Customs House
Room 228
721 19th Street
Denver, CO 80202
(303) 837-4405

Connecticut
Federal Building
Room 305
135 High Street
Hartford, CT 06103
(203) 244-2660

Delaware
Federal Building
Room 1318 E
844 King Street
Wilmington, DE 19801
(302) 571-6112

District of Columbia
(See Hyattsville, Maryland)

Florida
Federal Building
Room 307
299 East Broward Boulevard
Fort Lauderdale, FL 33301
(305) 527-7262

3947 Boulevard Center Drive
Suite 121
Jacksonville, FL 32207
(904) 791-2489

1150 Southwest First Street
Room 202
Miami, FL 33130
(305) 350-5767

700 Twiggs Street
Suite 617
Tampa, FL 33602
(813) 228-2154

Georgia
Citizens' Trust Building
Room 1100
75 Piedmont Avenue, N.E.
Atlanta, GA 30303
(404) 221-6401

415 West Broughton Street
Room 104
Savannah, GA 31401
(912) 944-4222

Hawaii
300 A La. Moana
Room 5108
Honolulu, HI 96850
(808) 546-8363

Idaho
250 Owyhee Plaza
Suite 250
1109 Maine Street
Boise, ID 83702
(208) 334-1029

Illinois
Summit First Federal Savings and
   Loan Association Building
3rd Floor
8020 South Harlem
Bridgeview, IL 60455
(312) 238-8832

6035 North Northwest Highway
Room 203
Chicago, IL 60631
(213) 775-5733,
(312) 775-5734

524 South 2nd Street
Room 630
Springfield, IL 62701
(217) 492-4060,
(217) 492-4061

Indiana
U.S. Court House
Room 465
Ohio & Pennsylvania Streets
Indianapolis, IN 46204
(317) 269-7163

Sherland Building
Suite 428
105 East Jefferson Boulevard
South Bend, IN 46601
(219) 234-4045

Iowa
Federal Building
Room 643
210 Walnut Street
Des Moines, IA 50309
(515) 284-4625

Kansas
Federal Office Building
Room 299
444 S.E. Quincy Street
Topeka, KS 66683
(913) 295-2526

Kentucky
Federal Building
Room 187-E
600 Federal Place
Louisville, KY 40202
(502) 582-5226

Louisiana
Federal Building
Room 703
600 South Street
New Orleans, LA 70130
(504) 589-6171

Maine
Court Square Professional Building
Room 211
66 Pearl Street
Portland, ME 04101
(207) 780-3344

Maryland
Federal Office Building
Room 913
31 Hopkins Plaza, Charles Center
Baltimore, MD 21201
(301) 962-2265

Presidential Building
Suite 904
6525 Belcrest Road
Hyattsville, MD 20782
(301) 436-6767

Massachusetts
Park Square Building
Room 462
31 St. James Avenue
Boston, MA 02116
(617) 223-6751

Michigan
U.S. Courthouse & Federal
    Building
Room 647
West Lafayette
Detroit, MI 48226
(313) 226-7447,
(313) 226-7448,
(313) 226-7449

Federal Building & U.S. Courthouse
Room 134
110 Michigan Street, N.W.
Grand Rapids, MI 49503
(616) 456-2337

Minnesota
Federal Building
100 North Sixth Street
Minneapolis, MN 55401
(612) 725-6106

Mississippi
Federal Building
Suite 1414
100 West Capitol Street
Jackson, MS 39201
(601) 960-4347

Missouri
Federal Office Building
Room 2900
911 Walnut Street
Kansas City, MO
64106
(816) 374-5721

210 North Tucker Boulevard
Room 563
St. Louis, MO 63101
(314) 425-4706

Montana
U.S. Post Office Building
Room 213
2602 First Avenue, North
Billings, MT 59103
(406) 657-6356

Nebraska
110 North 14th Street
Room 436
Omaha, NE 68102
(402) 221-4682

New Hampshire
120 Hanover Street
Room 216
Manchester, NH 03101
(603) 666-7716

New Jersey
Peter W. Rodino, Jr. Federal Building
Room 836
970 Broad Street
Newark, NJ 07102
(202) 645-2279

New Mexico
505 Marquette Avenue, N.W.
Suite 1130
Albuquerque, NM 87102
(505) 766-2477

New York
Leo W. O' Brien Federal Building
Room 822
Albany, NY 12202
(518) 472-3596

271 Cadman Plaza East
Room 631
Brooklyn, NY 11201
(212) 330-7662

400 East Fordham Road
Room 302
Bronx, NY 10458
(212) 289-9472

Federal Building
Room 617
111 West Huron Street
Buffalo, NY 14202
(716) 846-4891

159 North Franklin Street
Hempstead, NY 11550
(516) 481-0582

26 Federal Plaza
Room 2946
New York, NY 10278
(212) 264-8185

North Carolina
Federal Building
Room 408
310 New Bern Avenue
Raleigh, NC 27611
(919) 755-4190

North Dakota
Federal Building & U.S. Post
    Office
Room 252
657 2nd Avenue
North Fargo, ND 58102
(701) 237-5771

Ohio
Federal Office Building
Room 3525
550 Main Street
Cincinnati, OH 45202
(513) 684-2942,
(513) 684-2943

1240 East Ninth Street
Cleveland, OH 44199
(216) 522-3892,
(216) 522-3893

646 Federal Office Building
200 North High Street
Columbus, OH 43215
(614) 469-5677

Oklahoma
Center Mall Professional Building
Suite 306
717 South Houston
Tulsa, OK 74127
(918) 581-7695

Oregon
540 New Federal Building
1220 Southwest 3rd Avenue
Portland, OR 97204
(503) 221-3057

Pennsylvania
Federal Building
Room 774
228 Walnut Street
Harrisburg, PA 17108
(717) 782-4539

600 Arch Street
Room 4244
Philadelphia, PA 19106
(215) 597-4950

Federal Building
Room 1429
1000 Liberty Avenue
Pittsburgh, PA 15222
(412) 644-2996

Puerto Rico
F. Degetau Federal Office Building
Room 152
Carlos Chardon Street
Hato Rey, PR 00918
(809) 753-4463

Rhode Island
John E. Fogarty Federal Building
Room 103
24 Weybosset Street
Providence, RI 02903
(401) 528-4378

South Carolina
Federal Building
Room 1072
1835 Assembly Street
Columbia, SC 29201
(803) 765-5981

South Dakota
Federal Building & U.S. Courthouse
Room 256
515 Ninth Street
Rapid City, SD 57701
(605) 342-1884

Tennessee
608 South Gay Street
Room 202
Knoxville, TN 37902
(615) 627-9300

1720 West End Avenue
Room 610
Nashville, TN 37203
(615) 251-5452

Texas
The Six Hundred Building
Room 714
600 Leopard Street
Corpus Christi, TX 78473
(512) 888-3156

Suite 200
1607 Main Street
Dallas, TX 75201
(214) 767-6294

Area Director: Curtis L. Poer
Assistant Area Director: Robert
    Fortman
819 Taylor Street
Room 7A12
Fort Worth, TX 76102
(817) 334-2678

2320 LaBranch
Room 2101
Houston, TX 77004
(713) 226-4304

U.S. Federal Building
Room A-621
727 East Durango
San Antonio, TX 78206
(512) 229-6125

Utah
Federal Building
Room 4311
125 South State Street
Salt Lake City, UT 84138
(801) 524-5706

Vermont
Burlington Square
96 College Street
Building 1
Burlington, VT 05402
(802) 951-6283

Virginia
Federal Building
Room 7000
400 N. 8th Street
Richmond, VA 23240
(804) 771-2995

Seattle
Century Building
Suite 510
1520 Third Avenue
Seattle, WA 98101
(206) 442-4482

Wisconsin
Federal Center Building
Room 309
212 East Washington Avenue
Madison, WI 53703
(608) 264-5221

Federal Building
Room 601
517 E. Wisconsin Avenue
Milwaukee, WI 53202
(414) 291-3585

West Virginia
Hoyer Building
Suite 100
22 Capitol Street
Charleston, WV 25301
(304) 343-6181, Ext. 448

Wyoming
100 East B Street
Casper, WY 82601
(307) 365-5550

10

What You Can Do If Your Employer Discriminates Against You

Congress passed the Civil Rights Act of 1964 to outlaw discrimination in employment, housing, and other areas. Title VII of that act was concerned with employment discrimination based on race, religion, and national origin. However, other laws were concerned with discrimination in employment. The Age of Discrimination in Employment Act covers age discrimination. The Equal Pay Act of 1963 is concerned with discrimination based on sex.

These three laws have subtle differences. For example, the age law applies to private employers with 20 or more employees. Title VII applies to employers with 15 or more employees. The Equal Pay Act covers those employees covered by the Fair Labor Standards Act, which is discussed in Chapter 8. At one time, three different federal agencies handled these three statutes. That is where the differences are derived. However, now only one agency handles all three discrimination laws. That agency is the Equal Employment Opportunity Commission.

The laws generally provide that employers and labor unions cannot refuse to hire, fire, fail to promote, or treat employees differently because of their age, sex, race, religion, or national origin.

REVERSE DISCRIMINATION

The discrimination laws are written neutrally. They do not mention discrimination against blacks or women specifically; white persons and males can be protected by these anti-discrimination laws also. The key is that the employee was treated differently because of his or her sex, race, age, or religion. Many people refer to discrimination cases brought by whites and males to be "reverse discrimination" cases. The law does not call one type of discrimination "forward" and one type "reverse." All types of discrimination are unlawful, and none should be referred to as "reverse."

AGE DISCRIMINATION

The age discrimination law protects workers aged 40 to 70 from arbitrary discrimination in hiring, firing, pay, promotions, fringe benefits, and conditions of employment. The law applies to employers with 20 employees or more. There are a few exceptions in the law. You can be forced into involuntary retirement at age 65, if you are an executive making $27,000 per year or more. Similarly, college professors can be forced into retirement at age 65.

THE EQUAL PAY ACT

The Equal Pay Act protects men and women against pay discrimination based on sex. Men and women who perform substantially the same work must be paid the same. In addition to the claims that can be made under the Civil Rights Act for back wages, attorneys' fees, and costs, under Equal Pay Act an employee must recover double the amount of salary that was wrongly withheld. An equal pay complaint can be filed on the same form as a civil rights charge at the EEOC.

HOMOSEXUALS

Discrimination in employment against homosexuals is illegal statewide only in Pennsylvania and Wisconsin. However, various cities and counties outlaw discrimination in employment against gays. They are: Tucson, Arizona; Los Angeles, San Francisco, and San Mateo County, California; Aspen, Colorado; Hartford, Connecticut; Champaign and Urbana, Illinois; Bloomington, Indiana; Iowa City, Iowa; Howard County, Maryland; Amherst, Massachusetts; Ann Arbor, Detroit, and East Lansing, Michigan; Marshall and Minneapolis, Minnesota; Alfred, New York; Yellowsprings, Ohio; Austin, Texas; Seattle, Washington; and Washington D.C.

PREGNANCY

The Civil Rights Act was amended in 1978 to specify that discrimination based on pregnancy, childbirth, or related medical conditions would be considered sex discrimination. Two years earlier the United States Supreme Court ruled that discrimination against pregnant women was legal, even though only women can become pregnant.[1] Congress rapidly (two years is rapid for Congress) reversed the Supreme Court ruling to specifically include pregnancy protection in the Civil Rights Act. The Equal Employment Opportunity Commission is responsible for enforcing this provision of the law.

If you become pregnant and have to miss work because of your condition, or because of childbirth, you must be treated the same way as an employee who became injured or disabled. This means you are allowed to take sick leave for the time that you miss work, or any other type of leave which would be granted to you if you were ill. You cannot be demoted, fired, or transferred because you are or were pregnant.

SEX-PLUS

The Martin-Marietta Company had a policy of refusing to hire women with young children, while they would hire men with young children. An appeals court held that this was not discrimination based solely on sex, but was discrimination based on "sex-plus" another factor (young children). Luckily, Mrs. Ida Phillips appealed to the United States Supreme Court, which reversed the appeals court ruling, and held that Martin-Marietta's policy did indeed discriminate against women.[2] There are several lessons to be learned from this story. The first lesson is that courts and judges make mistakes. The second is that a person must persevere, and appeal, and appeal again if necessary, to vindicate his or her rights. If Mrs. Ida Phillips had failed to appeal to the United States Supreme Court, thousands of other women would have been hurt by the unfortunate ruling of the appeals court. We need more people like Ida Phillips in this world.

ALIENS

The Supreme Court has ruled that an employer may discriminate based on citizenship.[3] However, if an employer hires aliens from one country but not from another, the law against discrimination based on national origin may have been violated.

AMERICAN INDIANS

The law prohibits discrimination against American Indians, because they are protected under both race and color categories. But the law specifically allows discrimination against non-Indians when an employer is on or near an Indian reservation.

RELIGION

The provisions against discrimination based on a person's religion protects those in small religions, atheists, cults, and major religions as well. It is illegal religious discrimination to fire a person who refuses to work on his or her sabbath. If a religion requires someone to wear particular clothing, it is illegal to fire or refuse to hire such a person. In these situations an employer must make a reason-

1. *Gilbert* v. *General Electric Co.*, 429 U.S. 125 (1976).

2. *Phillips* v. *Martin Marietta Corp.*, 400 U.S. 542 (1971).
3. *Espinosa* v. *Farah Mfg. Co.*, 414 U.S. 86 (1973).

able accommodation of business practices to respect the employee's religious practices.

PROCEDURES FOR NON-FEDERAL EMPLOYEES

Victims of discrimination are not entitled to file a law suit until they have pursued certain administrative procedures. Often this means only filing a charge of discrimination with the Equal Employment Opportunity Commission, waiting, and waiting some more. After sitting on a charge of discrimination for six months or more, the EEOC will send you a "right to sue" letter upon request.

FILING THE CHARGE

The document called "Charge of Discrimination" starts the legal process rolling. Unless a charge is filed within 180 days from the act of discrimination, you may be out of luck. In states with their own equal employment laws, you may have 300 days in which to file a charge with the federal EEOC.

The best practice is to file a charge simultaneously with both the state or local agency, and with the EEOC. A list of addresses of all state EEOC offices and all state and local equal employment agencies is included at the end of this chapter.

In all cases the charge must be (1) written, (2) sworn to before a notary public, and (3) signed. The local agency will have exclusive jurisdiction over your case for 60 days. This means that if you file with a state agency and the EEOC at the same time, the EEOC cannot do anything with it for 60 days. If you file only with the EEOC, it will first refer the charge to the appropriate local agency for 60 days. Similarly, most state and local agencies will refer cases to the EEOC. I emphasize that the preferred method is to file simultaneously with both agencies. Mail your charge in by certified mail, return receipt requested. Agencies have been known to lose charges; a return receipt will give you proof of when you filed yours. A standard charge form is included at the end of this chapter as Form 10-1.

Once the charge has been filed with the EEOC, excluding the 60-day period when the case was at the state or local agency, the EEOC has exclusive jurisdiction for 180 days. The employer or union named in the charge is notified by the agency, and the EEOC starts an investigation. In less than one percent of the cases where the employment practice complained of is grossly discriminatory and many employees are affected, the EEOC goes directly into federal court to correct the situation. In cases against a state or local government, the attorney general of the United States would be responsible for bringing suit. If either the attorney general or the EEOC files suit, the individual who filed the charge cannot file a separate case, but can join in the lawsuit as an "intervenor."

Because of the large backlog of cases, the EEOC usually does little, if anything, within the 180-day period. If you want to file suit promptly, you should ask the EEOC to issue a "right to sue" letter. Otherwise, you may have to wait five years for an EEOC hearing. Upon receipt of the right-to-sue letter, you have 90 days to file suit in a federal district court. Every state has at least one federal district court; many have more than one. A suit is filed by filing a complaint. A complaint form, including paragraphs for age, race, sex, pregnancy, and national origin discrimination, is included at the end of this chapter as Form 10-4. Before filing suit, read Chapter 5 which explains the basics of litigation. If you can afford an attorney, you should consult one before filing suit. A short consultation with an attorney specializing in employment matters could mean the difference between success and failure. If you cannot afford an attorney, but feel that you need one, the court has the authority to appoint one for you. Form 10-3 is a motion to be filed with the court for the appointment of an attorney. If you file this form within the 90-day period specified in your right-to-sue letter, your right to sue will be preserved.[4]

FEDERAL EMPLOYEES

The procedure for federal employees who feel that they have been discriminated against is different than for other employees. The federal employee must consult with an Equal Employment Opportunity counselor at his or her agency within 30 days of the alleged wrongful action. The EEO counselor has 21 days to attempt to resolve the dispute. If the counselor is unable to resolve the dispute, which is common, the employee has 15 days to file a formal

---

4. *Huston* v. *General Motors Corp.*, 477 F.2d 1003 (8th Cir., 1973).

written complaint with the Equal Employment Opportunity Commission.[5] A copy of the form for filing a federal formal complaint of discrimination is included at the end of this chapter as Form 10-2.

AT THE HEARING

At the hearing, whether at the EEOC or in court, you will have to prove that you were discriminated against. You will first have to establish a "prima facie case." This legal phrase really means that you have to present the bare bones of the case, or a case "on its face." The elements of a prima facie case are:

1. Are you a member of a minority group, or within a protected age classification? For example, if you claim you were discriminated against because you were pregnant, you must prove that you were pregnant.
2. You must prove that you met the basic qualifications for the job that you sought.
3. You must show that you did not get the position despite your qualifications.

If you do not prove these three things, your case could be dismissed. Cases that do not involve hiring or promotion are treated somewhat differently. For example, if you claim you are being paid less than someone else because of your sex, you must prove that you are paid differently and that you were performing substantially the same work as someone of the opposite sex. Statistics showing discrimination alone are sometimes enough to prove a prima facie case.

Once you have proved a prima facie case, the burden of proof shifts to the employer. The employer must prove that he had a valid reason for not promoting or hiring you. If the employer introduces evidence of valid reasons, you have the right to show that the reason or reasons given have been concocted by the employer as an excuse. This is known as "pretext." Once all the evidence has been heard, the hearing examiner or judge will make a decision. No jury trials are held in employment discrimination cases, except in age discrimination cases. The judge can award you attorneys' fees and costs if you win your case.

EMPLOYERS' DEFENSES TO CLAIM OF DISCRIMINATION

The most typical defense to an employment discrimination case is to attack the ability of the person who filed the charge or complaint. Employers will claim that the employee was often late to work, had poor work habits, came to work drunk or under the influence of drugs, was sloppy, careless, or any number of things. If you came to work late on occasion, but not any more than most employees, a claim that you were fired for tardiness is not a good defense to your discrimination case. Be prepared to prove that you are a good employee by lining up fellow workers, supervisors, and clients that you call on to be witnesses on your behalf.

The law also allows employers to discriminate because of a business necessity, or if sex, religion, or national origin are "bona fide occupational qualifications" (BFOQ). One BFOQ may be that only women are hired to be attendants in a female washroom. Another BFOQ could be a requirement of a Chinese restaurant that employees be Chinese. Other requirements, such as height or weight limits, could discriminate against men or women. If such a requirement truly relates to the job function, it may be permissible. However, arbitrary height or weight requirements will not hold up in court.

---

5. Some agencies, such as the Library of Congress, have their own internal procedures.

FORM 10-1: EEOC Charge of Discrimination

(PLEASE PRINT OR TYPE)

APPROVED BY GAO B—180541 (RO512)	CHARGE OF DISCRIMINATION IMPORTANT This form is affected by the Privacy Act of 1974, see Privacy Act Statement on reverse before completing it	CHARGE NUMBER(S) (AGENCY USE ONLY) ☐ STATE/LOCAL AGENCY ☐ EEOC

_____ and Equal Employment Opportunity Commission

(State or Local Agency)

NAME (Indicate Mr, Ms or Mrs)	HOME TELEPHONE NUMBER (Include area code)
STREET ADDRESS	
CITY, STATE, AND ZIP CODE	COUNTY

NAMED IS THE EMPLOYER, LABOR ORGANIZATION, EMPLOYMENT AGENCY, APPRENTICESHIP COMMITTEE, STATE OR LOCAL GOVERNMENT AGENCY WHO DISCRIMINATED AGAINST ME. (If more than one list below).

NAME	TELEPHONE NUMBER (Include area code)
STREET ADDRESS	CITY, STATE, AND ZIP CODE
NAME	TELEPHONE NUMBER (Include area code)
STREET ADDRESS	CITY, STATE, AND ZIP CODE

CAUSE OF DISCRIMINATION BASED ON MY (Check appropriate box(es))

☐ RACE ☐ COLOR ☐ SEX ☐ RELIGION ☐ NATIONAL ORIGIN ☐ OTHER (Specify)

DATE MOST RECENT OR CONTINUING DISCRIMINATION TOOK PLACE (Month, day, and year)

THE PARTICULARS ARE:

☐ I also want this charge filed with the EEOC. I will advise the agencies if I change my address or telephone number and I will cooperate fully with them in the processing of my charge in accordance with their procedures.	I swear or affirm that I have read the above charge and that it is true to the best of my knowledge, information and belief. SIGNATURE OF COMPLAINANT SUBSCRIBED AND SWORN TO BEFORE ME THIS DATE (Day, month, and year)
I declare under penalty of perjury that the foregoing is true and correct.	NOTARY — (When necessary to meet State and Local Requirements)
DATE: CHARGING PARTY (Signature)	

EEOC FORM 5C MAR. 79   PREVIOUS EDITIONS OF ALL EEOC FORM 5'S ARE OBSOLETE AND MUST NOT BE USED

CHARGE FILE COPY

FORM 10-2: Federal Employee EEOC Complaint Form

EQUAL EMPLOYMENT OPPORTUNITY COMMISSION	COMPLAINT NUMBER(S)
STATEMENT OF ALLEGATIONS MADE IN A FEDERAL FORMAL COMPLAINT	EEOC AGENCY

NAME	HOME TELEPHONE NUMBER

STREET ADDRESS

CITY, STATE AND ZIP CODE

THE FOLLOWING AGENCY DISCRIMINATED AGAINST ME:

NAME OF AGENCY	TELEPHONE NUMBER

STREET ADDRESS

CITY, STATE AND ZIP CODE

CAUSE OF DISCRIMINATION BASED ON MY (Check appropriate box(es))

☐ RACE   ☐ COLOR   ☐ SEX   ☐ RELIGION   ☐ NATIONAL ORIGIN   ☐ OTHER (Specify)

DATE MOST RECENT DISCRIMINATION TOOK
PLACE (Month, day, and year)

THE PARTICULARS ARE:

I will advise the agency if I change my address or telephone number and I will cooperate fully with it in the processing of my complaint..

I declare under penalty of perjury that the foregoing is true and correct.

DATE   COMPLAINANT (Signature)

EEOC FORM 368
JUL 79

Motion for Appointment of Attorney

UNITED STATES DISTRICT COURT

FOR THE _____ DISTRICT OF _____

_____ DIVISION

_____

                   Plaintiff,

      v.   Civil Action No.

_____

                   Defendant.

MOTION FOR APPOINTMENT OF AN ATTORNEY

_____, Plaintiff, moves the court to appoint an attorney to represent him/her in the above-captioned case.

Plaintiff received a Notification of Right to Sue from the Equal Employment Opportunity Commission on _____ (date).

Plaintiff is unable to afford an attorney to represent him/her in this case because: (insert statement that you are unemployed, or that your income is $_____ per month, under the poverty line, or whatever the truth is).

Plaintiff has a meritorious claim against _____, defendant, because: (Insert detail indicating that claim is not frivolous and has merit.)

Plaintiff has made a reasonable effort to retain an attorney by _____, but has been unable to find an attorney who will represent him/her in this matter.

WHEREFORE, plaintiff respectfully requests that this court enter an order, pursuant to the provisions of Section 706(f)(I) of the Civil Rights Act of 1964, as amended, appointing an attorney to represent plaintiff in this matter.

                   Signature of Plaintiff _____

                   NAME OF PLAINTIFF
                   Pro Se
                   Address
                   Telephone Number

Subscribed and sworn to before me this _____ day of _____, 19_____.

                   _____

                   NOTARY PUBLIC

CERTIFICATE OF SERVICE

I certify that I mailed a copy of this motion to _____, attorney for the defendant, this _____ day of _____, 19_____.

                   (Signature of Plaintiff) _____

                   NAME OF PLAINTIFF

Federal Court Complaint Including Age, Race, Sex, and Religion Claims

UNITED STATES DISTRICT COURT

FOR THE _____ DISTRICT OF _____

_____ DIVISION

_____

Plaintiff,

v.   Civil Action No.

_____

Defendant.

COMPLAINT FOR DECLARATORY, INJUNCTIVE AND COMPENSATORY
RELIEF; JURY TRIAL DEMANDED

I. PRELIMINARY STATEMENT

1. This is an action for declaratory, injunctive, and compensatory relief to redress the deprivation of plaintiff's civil rights on account of his race (black), sex (male), religion (atheist), and age (52).

II. JURISDICTION

2. Jurisdiction is conferred on this court by 28 U.S.C. Section 1331, 1343, 1202, 2202 and by 42 U.S.C. Section 2000e-16; (race, religion, sex) and 29 U.S.C. § 633(a)(c) (age).

III. PLAINTIFF

3. _____ is a black male atheist citizen of the United States, age 52.

IV. DEFENDANT

4. Defendant _____ is the plaintiff's employer.

V. ADMINISTRATIVE PROCEDURE

5. On _____ (date) plaintiff filed a charge/complaint of discrimination with the Equal Employment Opportunity Commission (or Equal Employment Office) who conducted an inquiry into plaintiff's charges of discrimination. The efforts of the EEO investigator did not resolve this dispute and more than 180 days have passed since the complaint was filed.

VI. FACTUAL ALLEGATIONS

6. Plaintiff is employed as a _____ for the defendant.

7. Plaintiff applied for a promotion to a position which was announced in _____ _____.

8. Plaintiff was better qualified than any of the persons selected for the _____ position. This selection was announced on or about _____.

9. Plaintiff is paid less for performing the same work as female employees of defendant.

VII. FIRST CAUSE OF ACTION: Discrimination of the
basis of race and sex in
violation of Title VII
of the Civil Rights Act
of 1964, as amended.

10. Plaintiff incorporates by reference paragraphs one (1) through nine (9), inclusive.

11. The defendant discriminated against plaintiff on account of his race, religion, and sex by promoting a less-qualified female, non-black, non-atheist for the vacant position.

VIII. SECOND CAUSE OF ACTION: Violation of the Age
Discrimination in
Employment Act.

12. Plaintiff incorporates by reference paragraphs one (1) through eleven (11), inclusive.

13. The defendant discriminated against plaintiff on account of his age, by promoting a less-qualified person, younger than plaintiff, for the vacant position.

IX. THIRD CAUSE OF ACTION: Violations of the Equal
Pay Act.

14. Plaintiff incorporates by reference paragraphs one (1) through thirteen (13), inclusive.

15. Defendant has violated the Equal Pay Act by paying plaintiff less than females who are performing substantially the same work.

X. REQUEST FOR RELIEF

WHEREFORE, plaintiff requests this court to:

A. Issue a declaratory judgment that the defendant violated plaintiff's rights, secured by Title VII of the Civil Rights Act of 1964, as amended; the Age Discrimination in Employment Act and the Equal Pay Act;

B. Order defendant to promote plaintiff immediately with back pay, attorneys' fees and costs;

C. Order defendant to pay plaintiff unpaid wages and liquidated damages for underpaying his wages, under the Equal Pay Act.

D. Retain jurisdiction to assure full compliance with the orders of this court.

E. Order such other relief as this court deems just and proper.

Respectfully submitted,

_____
PLAINTIFF'S NAME
ADDRESS
TELEPHONE NUMBER

STATE AND LOCAL EQUAL EMPLOYMENT OPPORTUNITY OFFICES

Alabama
(No State or Local Agencies)

Alaska
Alaska State Commission for Human Rights
431 W. 7th Avenue
Suite 105
Anchorage, AK 99501
(907) 276-7474

Anchorage Equal Rights Commission
Pouch 6-650
Anchorage, AK 99501
(908) 264-4342

Arizona
Arizona Civil Rights Division
1645 West Jefferson Street
Phoenix, AZ 85007
(602) 255-5263

Arkansas
(No State or Local Agencies)

California
The Department of Fair Employment and Housing
1201 I Street, 2nd Floor
Suite 211
Sacramento, CA 95814
(916) 323-5256 (Sacramento)
(415) 557-2934 (San Francisco)

Colorado
Colorado Civil Rights Division
1525 Sherman Street
Room 600c
Denver, CO 80203
(303) 866-2621

Colorado State Personnel Board
1525 Sherman Street
Room 617
Denver, CO 80203
(303) 839-3244

Connecticut
Connecticut Commission on Human Rights and
  Opportunities
90 Washington Street
Hartford, CT 06106
(203) 566-4895

Delaware
Delaware Department of Labor
Anti-Discrimination Section
820 North French Street
6th Floor
State Office Building
Wilmington, DE 19801
(302) 571-2900

Florida
Clearwater Community Relations Department
P.O. Box 4748
Clearwater, FL 33518
(813) 462-6884

Broward County Human Relations Division
Governor's Club #602
236 S.E. 1st Avenue
Fort Lauderdale, FL 33301
(305) 765-5260

Jacksonville Equal Employment Opportunity
  Commission
220 East Bay Street
Room 701
Jacksonville, FL 32202
(904) 633-2010

Dade County Fair Housing and Employment Appeals
  Board
1515 N.W. 7th Street
Room 205
Miami, FL 33125
(305) 547-7840

Orlando Human Relations Department
400 South Orange Avenue
Suite 103
Orlando, FL 32801
(305) 849-2122

St. Petersburg Office of Human Relations
P.O. Box 2842
St. Petersburg, FL 33731
(813) 893-7345

Florida Commission on Human Relations
2562 Executive Center Circle, East
Suite 100
Tallahassee, FL 32301
(904) 488-7082

Georgia
Georgia Office of Fair Employment Practices
Executive Department
2 Martin Luthur King Jr., Drive
Atlanta, GA 30334
(404) 656-1736

Richmond County Human Relations Commission
Suite 400/500 Building
Augusta, GA 30901
(404) 724-2246

Hawaii
Hawaii Department of Labor and Industrial Relations—
    Enforcement Division
888 Mililani Street
Room 401
Honolulu, HI 96813
(808) 548-7625

Idaho
Idaho Human Rights Commission
Statehouse
Boise, ID 83720
(208) 334-2873

Illinois
Bloomington Human Relations Commission
City Hall Building
109 E. Olive Street
P.O. Box 3157
Bloomington, IL 61701
(309) 828-7361 ext. 218/219

Illinois Department of Human Rights
32 W. Randolph Street
Room 890
Chicago IL 60601
(312) 793-6200

Indiana
Bloomington Human Rights Commission
P.O. Box 100 Municipal Building
Bloomington, IN 47402
(812) 339-2261

East Chicago Human Rights Commission
City Hall
Room 9
4525 Indianapolis Boulevard
East Chicago, IN 46312
(219) 392-8236

Evansville Human Relations Commission
Civic Center Complex
Room 133
Evansville, IN 47708
(812) 426-5474

Fort Wayne Metropolitan Human Relations
    Commission
City-County Building
Room 680
One Main Street
Fort Wayne, IN 46802
(219) 423-7664

Gary Human Relations Commission
475 Broadway
Rooms 108-109-110
Gary, IN 46402
(219) 944-6541

Indiana Civil Rights Commission
311 West Washington Street
Fair Building 3rd Floor
Suite 319
Indianapolis, IN 46204
(317) 232-2623

Michigan City Human Rights Commission
City Hall
100 East Michigan Boulevard
Michigan City, IN 46360
(219) 879-8117

South Bend Human Rights Commission
1200 County-City Building
227 W. Jefferson Boulevard
South Bend, IN 46601
(219) 284-9355

Iowa
Iowa Civil Rights Commission
Colony Building
507 Tenth Street
8th Floor
Des Moines, IA 50319
(515) 281-4478

Kansas
Kansas City Human Relations Department
Municipal Office Building
One Civic Center Plaza
Kansas City, KS 66101
(913) 371-2000 Ext. 373

Kansas Commission on Civil Rights
535 Kansas Avenue
5th Floor
Topeka, KS 66603
(913) 296-3206

Witchita Commission on Civil Rights
City Hall
2nd Floor
455 North Main
Witchita, KS 67202
(316) 268-4488

Kentucky
Lexington-Fayette Human Rights Commission
207 N. Upper Street
Lexington, KY 40507
(606) 252-4931

Kentucky Commission on Human Rights
701 W. Mohammed Ali Boulevard
P.O. Box 60
Louisville, KY 40201
(502) 588-4024

Louisville & Jefferson
  County Human Relations Commission
200 S. 7th Street
Louisville, KY 40202
(502) 587-3631

Louisiana
(No State or Local Agencies)

Maine
Maine Human Rights Commission
Statehouse
Station 51
Augusta, ME 04333
(207) 868-2326

Maryland
Maryland Commission on Human Relations
20 E. Franklin Street
Baltimore, MD 21202
(301) 659-1700

Baltimore Community Relations Commission
100 North Eutaw Street
Baltimore, MD 21201
(301) 396-3141

Montgomery County Human Relations Commission
6400 Democracy Boulevard
Bethesda, MD 20817
(301) 468-4260

Howard County Human Rights Commission
John Lee Carol Building
3450 Courthouse Drive
Ellicott City, MD 21043
(301) 922-2162

Rockville Human Rights Commission
City of Rockville
Rockville City Hall
Maryland Avenue and Vinsin Street
Rockville, MD 20850
(301) 424-8000

Prince George's County Human Relations Commission
County Administration Building
Room 1136
14741 Governor Oden Bowie Drive
Upper Marlboro, MD 20772
(301) 952-3070

Massachusetts
Massachusetts Commission Against Discrimination
One Ashburton Place
Room 601
Boston, MA 02108
(617) 727-7319

Michigan
Michigan Department of Civil Rights
Michigan Plaza Building
1200 Sixth Avenue
Detroit, MI 48226
(313) 256-2578

Minnesota
Minneapolis Department of Civil Rights
2649 Park Avenue South
Minneapolis, MN 55407
(612) 348-7736

Minnesota Department of Human Rights
Bremer Tower 5th Floor
7th Place and Minnesota Street
St. Paul, MN 55101
(612) 296-5665

St. Paul Department of Human Rights
515 City Hall
St. Paul, MN 55102
(612) 298-4288

Mississippi
(No State or Local Agencies)

Missouri
Missouri Commission on Human Rights
P.O. Box 1129
Jefferson City, MO 65102
(314) 751-3325

Kansas City, Human Relations Department
City Hall 4th Floor
Kansas City, MO 64106
(816) 274-1432

St. Louis Civil Rights Enforcement Agency
Civil Courts Building
3rd Floor
St. Louis, MO 63101
(314) 622-3301

Montana
Montana Human Rights Division
Cogswell Building
Room C-317
Helena, MT 59620
(406) 449-2884

Nebraska
Nebraska Equal Opportunity Commission
301 Centennial Mall South
5th Floor
Lincoln, NB 68509
(402) 471-2024

Lincoln Commission of Human Rights
129 North 10th
Room 323
Lincoln, NB 68508
(402) 471-7624

Omaha Human Relations Department
1819 Farnam Street
Suite 502
Omaha, NB 68183
(402) 444-5050

Nevada
Nevada Equal Rights Commission
1515 E. Tropicana Avenue
Suite 590
Las Vegas, NV 89158
(702) 386-5304

New Hampshire
New Hampshire State Commission for Human Rights
61 South Spring Street
Concord, NH 03301
(603) 842-2767

New Jersey
New Jersey Division on Civil Rights
1100 Raymond Boulevard
Newark, NJ 07112
(201) 648-2700

New Mexico
New Mexico Human Rights Commission
303 Bataan Memorial Building
Santa Fe, NM 87503
(505) 827-6420

New York
New York City Commission on Human Rights
52 Duane Street
New York, NY 10007
(212) 566-5588

New York State Division of Human Rights
2 World Trade Center
New York, NY 10047
(212) 488-7617

North Carolina
North Carolina State Personnel Commission
State Administrative Building
116 W. Jones Street
Raleigh, NC 27611
(919) 733-7108

New Hanover Human Relations Commission
320 Chestnut
Room 409
Wilmington, NC 28401
(919) 763-0194

North Dakota
North Dakota Department of Labor
State Capitol Building
Bismarck, ND 58505
(701) 224-2660

Ohio
Ohio Civil Rights Commission
220 Parsons Avenue
Columbus, OH 43215
(614) 466-6715

Springfield Human Relations Department
76 East High Street
City Hall
Springfield, OH 45502
(513) 324-7380

Oregon
Oregon Bureau of Labor and Industries, Civil Rights
    Division
1400 Southwest 5th
Portland, OR 97201
(503) 229-6619

Pennsylvania
Allentown Human Relations Commission
City Hall
Room 315
Allentown, PA 18101
(215) 437-7600

Pennsylvania Human Relations Commission
101 South Second Street
Suite 300
P.O. Box 3145
Harrisburg, PA 17105
(717) 787-4410

Philadelphia Commission on Human Relations
601 City Hall Annex
Philadelphia, PA 19107
(215) 686-4673

Pittsburgh Commission on Human Relations
908 City–County Building
Pittsburgh, PA 15219
(412) 255-2600

York City Human Relations Commission
225 East Princess Street
York, PA 17403
(717) 846-2926

Puerto Rico
Puerto Rico Department of Labor and Human
    Resources
Anti-Discrimination Unit
Commonwealth of Puerto Rico
505 Munoz Rivera Avenue, Guyama Street
Hato Rey, PR 00918
(809) 754-5294

Rhode Island
Rhode Island Commission for Human Rights
334 Westminster Mall
Providence, RI 02903
(401) 277-2661

South Carolina
South Carolina Human Affairs Commission
P.O. Box 11300
Columbia, SC 29211
(803) 758-2748

South Dakota
South Dakota Division of Human Rights
State Capitol
Pierre, SD 57501
(605) 773-3803

Sioux Falls Human Relations Commission
224 W. 9th Street
City Hall
Sioux Falls, SD 57102
(605) 339-7039

Tennessee
Tennessee Commission for Human Development
208 Tennessee Building
535 Church Street
Nashville, TN 37219
(615) 741-5825

Texas
Austin Human Relations Commission
P.O. Box 1088
Austin, TX 78767
(512) 472-9168

Corpus Christi Human Relations Commission
P.O. Box 9277
110 N. Shoreline
Corpus Christi, TX 78408
(512) 884-5011 ext. 897

Fort Worth Human Relations Commission
600 Texas Street
Fort Worth, TX 76102
(817) 870-7534

Utah
Utah Industrial Commission
Anti-Discrimination Division
560 South 300 East
Salt Lake City, UT 84111
(801) 533-5971,
(801) 533-5552

Vermont
Vermont Attorney General's Office—Public Protection
    Division
109 State Street
Montpelier, VT 06502
(802) 828-3171

Virginia
Alexandria Human Rights Commission
110 North Royal
Suite 501
Alexandria, VA 22313
(703) 838-4955

Fairfax County Human Rights Commission
4085 Chain Bridge Road
Equity Building
Suite 300
Fairfax, VA 22030
(703) 691-2953

Virgin Islands
Virgin Islands Department of Labor
P.O. Box 148, Charlotte Amalie
St. Thomas, VI 00801
(809) 775-3224

Washington
Washington State Human Rights Commission
402 Evergreen Plaza Building (SJ-41)
Olympia, WA 98504
(206) 464-6500—Seattle
(206) 755-6770—Olympia

Seattle Human Rights Department
105 14th Avenue
Suite C
Seattle, WA 98122
(206) 625-4384

Tacoma Human Relations Commission
740 St. Helens Avenue
Room 1420
Tacoma, WA 98402
(206) 591-5151

West Virginia
West Virginia Human Rights Commission
215 Professional Building
1036 Quarrier Street
Charleston, WV 25301
(304) 348-2616

Charleston Human Rights Commission
P.O. Box 2749
Charleston, WV 25330
(304) 348-6880

Huntington Human Relations Commission
City Hall
P.O. Box 1659
Huntington, WV 25717
(304) 696-5592

Wheeling Human Rights Commission
City-County Building
Wheeling, WV 36003
(304) 234-3609

Wisconsin
Wisconsin Equal Rights Division—Department of
    Industry, Labor and Human Relations
201 E. Washington Avenue
Madison, WI 53702
(608) 266-0946

Wisconsin Personnel Commission
131 W. Wilson Street
Room 803
Madison, WI 53702
(608) 266-9571

Madison Equal Opportunities Commission
210 Monona Avenue
Room 500
City-County Building
Madison, WI 53703
(608) 266-4910

Wyoming
Wyoming Fair Employment Practices Commission
Hathaway Building
Cheyenne, WY 82002
(307) 777-7261

11

How to Protect Your Right to a Safe Workplace

Federal law requires employers to provide you with a safe and healthful place to work. The law providing this requirement was passed by Congress in 1970 as the Occupational Safety and Health Act, known as OSHA. The agency responsible for enforcing OSHA is known by the same initials. It is the Occupational Safety and Health Administration.

OSHA, the agency, has very few inspectors to inspect the hundreds of thousands of workplaces in the United States. If you find an unsafe work condition at your place of employment, it is your responsibility to see that it is made safe.

When you find an unsafe condition, notify your union if you have one. It is better for you if the union pursues the complaint of an unsafe condition. Let them take the credit if the plant is made safe. There are risks involved if you pursue the safety issue yourself. As I have said before, there is safety in numbers, and the union provides those numbers. While the company can fire you, it is unlikely that the entire union will be terminated.

The OSHA law provides that you cannot legally be fired for filing even an inaccurate complaint with the agency. But laws do not enforce themselves. You may have to sue your employer to win your job back if you are improperly fired.

OSHA STANDARDS

Under the Occupational Safety and Health Act every employer has a general duty to provide a workplace which is free from recognized hazards. This requirement is in addition to all the specific standards of the agency. These standards are provided in the regulations of OSHA. Statutes, such as the OSH Act were passed by Congress. Regulations are passed by the agency and have the full force of law, as if they were passed by Congress.

Your employer has a legal obligation to keep you informed of the standards that apply to your industry, and he must make these regulations available to you, upon your request.

Certain standards require your employer to measure your exposure to dangerous substances, such as carbon monoxide. You or your union representative (or other representative) have the right to observe these measurements and to examine test results. If the levels of these substances are higher than the limit set by the agency, then your employer must inform the workers of his plans to reduce exposure to the dangerous substance.

FILING AN OSHA COMPLAINT

If your employer maintains an unsafe plant, or otherwise endangers employees' safety or health, you have the right to file a complaint with the Occupational Safety and Health Administration. OSHA maintains area offices in every state and the District of Columbia. These offices receive complaints and send inspectors to investigate complaints. OSHA's form for filing a complaint is included at the end of this chapter as Form 11-1. You do not have to use this standard form, but using it will speed its processing. If you can, it is useful to type on the form. Handwritten and illegible complaints are often put aside. The more professional your complaint looks, the better it will be received. A list of all OSHA area offices is included in the appendix to this chapter. If your OSHA area office has moved, you can look it up in the United States Government listings in your telephone directory, under Department of Labor, Occupational Safety and Health Administration, Area Office.

It is useful to make reference to OSHA regulations in your complaint. As I have mentioned, your employer must make these available to you. However, it is often better to obtain the proper standards from the OSHA area office because your employer will not be tipped off in advance, and because you can be certain that you get up-to-date standards. After receiving your complaint, OSHA will send an inspector to the plant.

THE OSHA INSPECTION

Under federal law, a worker's representative has the right to accompany an OSHA inspector (known as a compliance officer) during the inspection. The representative must be paid at the normal rate of pay, including overtime for time spent with the OSHA officer. The representative must be chosen by the union (if there is one), the employees, or the inspector. Under no circumstances can the employer choose the worker's representative. If there is more than one union, each may choose a representative to monitor the inspection.

Usually the OSHA compliance officer will meet with both employer and employee representatives in a pre-inspection conference to discuss procedures for the inspection. If a joint conference is not possible, separate conferences can be held. If separate conferences are held, OSHA will provide a written summary of each conference upon request. Workers have the right to talk to the inspector privately and confidentially, during or after the inspection.

AFTER AN OSHA INSPECTION

At the end of the inspection the inspector will meet with the employer and employee representa-

tives to discuss hazards that have been found. You have the right to provide the inspector with information concerning other hazards that you believe may exist. The inspector will file a report with the area office. The director of the area office will decide what citations for violations will be issued, what dates will be set for correcting hazards, and what penalties, if any, will be proposed. A citation must be prominently posted for three workdays, at or near each place a violation has occurred. A copy of the citation is required to be provided to the worker's representative.

APPEAL FROM CITATION

If your employer challenges OSHA's citation, proposed penalty, or deadline for correcting hazardous conditions, the case will be reviewed on appeal by the Occupational Safety and Health Review Commission. Your employer must post a notice at your workplace and inform the employee representative if a "contest" has been filed with the Review Commission. You or your employee representative has a right to participate in this case before the Commission. The address for the Commission is:

Executive Secretary
Occupational Safety and
Health Review Commission
1825 K Street, N.W.
Washington, DC 20006
(202) 634-7950

RECORDS OF ILLNESS AND INJURIES

If there are more than ten employees in your workplace, your employer must maintain records of all work-related illnesses and injuries. Employers and employees' representatives have the legal right to inspect and copy those records. An injury must be recorded if it results in death, lost workdays, restriction of work or movement, loss of consciousness, transfer to another job, or medical treatment (except minor first aid treatment).

DISCRIMINATION FOR EXERCISING RIGHTS

You have the right to demand job safety and

cannot legally be fired for complaining about dangerous work conditons. But employers have been known to create "reasons" for firing people who complain about safety. Before you make your complaint public, make sure your time records and other employment records are beyond dispute. The law protects your right to complain to your employer, your union, and any government agency about job safety and health hazards. You are also protected if you participate in inspections, hearings, or other activities relating to a safe work environment.

If you exercise your rights, your employer cannot discriminate against you in any way. He cannot fire you, demote you, take away seniority or other benefits, transfer you, or otherwise harass you. If most workers come in five minutes late, your employer cannot single you out because you complained about job safety.

If you feel you have been punished for exercising your rights, you must file a complaint within 30 days after you find out action has been taken against you. If you have a union representative, he or she can file a complaint for you. This type of complaint is called an "11 (c)" complaint, named after the section of the health and safety law which provides for it. This is also known as a reprisal, or retaliation complaint. A form for filing this type of complaint is included at the end of this chapter (Form 11-2). The complaint should be filed at an OSHA area office. A list of area offices is also included at the end of this chapter. Your complaint should be sent by certified mail, return receipt requested, so that you have a written receipt to prove when and where your complaint was filed. Your complaint will be considered more seriously if it is sent by certified mail. If may be a good idea to send a copy of the complaint to OSHA's national and regional offices. These addresses are included in the appendix to this chapter.

If an extremely dangerous condition exists at your workplace which you fear will cause serious injury if not corrected immediately, ask your employer to correct it at once, or ask your union representative to do so. If your employer fails to take immediate steps to correct this dangerous condition, contact the nearest OSHA area office. OSHA can order a prompt inspection and corrective action. You and your union have the right to bring suit to correct the dangerous condition. While OSHA has a duty to bring suit to correct immediate hazards, it does not always have the resources to do so. If OSHA has not done anything to correct the dangerous situation, and if you can afford a lawyer,

you should file suit on your own. Form 11-3, at the end of this chapter, is a complaint which is designed to correct serious hazards. When your file this complaint in the federal district court in the area where the dangerous condition exists, you should also file a motion for a temporary restraining order (TRO) and a brief or memorandum in support of the motion. These are included with Form 11-4. Court clerks will often help you. When you file, ask to have a hearing time and date set at once. If you know who the company's attorney is, you should notify him or her by telephone that you are seeking a TRO and that the judge has set a hearing time and date.

REFUSAL TO WORK IN A DANGEROUS PLACE

According to a 1980 Supreme Court ruling, you can refuse to work in an unsafe workplace, and your employer must still pay you.[1] Employees in that case worked for the Whirlpool Corporation in Marion, Ohio. They were required to walk on wire mesh which was suspended 20 feet above the plant floor to pick up parts that had fallen on the mesh. One worker had already fallen through the meshing and died from his injuries. The other workers complained to the Occupational Safety and Health Administration and refused to work on the mesh. The company placed reprimands on the workers' files. OSHA regulations provide that a worker faced with a hazardous workplace may refuse to work[2]. This government agency filed suit against Whirlpool because it had reprimanded employees who had refused to work in a hazardous workplace. The United States Supreme Court ruled in favor of the workers' right to refuse to work in an unsafe condition and upheld the OSHA regulations.

If you are confronted with a choice between not performing assigned work, and working at a hazardous work site, you can refuse to do the hazardous work. If you refuse to do dangerous work and your employer fires you, transfers you, docks you pay, demotes you, or takes other action against you, you must file a complaint against your employer with the Occupational Safety and Health Administration. You should use the reprisal com-

---

1. *Whirlpool* v. *Marshall*, 445 U.S. 1 (1980).

2. 29 CFR (Code of Federal Regulations) §1977.12 (1979) provides in part: "(2) However, occasions might arise when an employee is confronted with a choice between not performing assigned tasks or subjecting himself to serious injury or death arising from a hazardous condition at the workplace. If the employee, with no reasonable alternative, refuses in good faith to expose himself to the dangerous condition, he would be protected against subsequent discrimination."

plaint form, which is included at the end of this chapter as Form 11-2. The complaint should be filed at the nearest area office of OSHA. A list of area offices in each state is included in the appendix to this chapter. Your complaint should be sent by certified mail with a return receipt requested. This will provide you with proof of mailing and will make the area office take notice. Your use of certi-

fied mail will demonstrate that you believe your complaint is urgent, and that it should be taken seriously. It is a good idea to send a copy of the complaint to the regional office of OSHA; and if the problem has national implications, you should send a copy to the national OSHA office. These addresses are also included in the appendix to this chapter.

FORM 11-1: Complaint of Unsafe Working Conditions for OSHA

Occupational Safety and Health Adn. .stration   **U.S. Department o.   .bor**
Complaint

This form is provided for the assistance of any complainant and is not intended to constitute the exclusive means by which a complaint may be registered with the U.S. Department of Labor.	Form Approved O.M.B. No. 044R1449

Sec. 8(f) (1) of the Williams-Steiger Occupational Safety and Health Act, 29 U.S.C. 651, provides as follows: Any employees or representative of employees who believe that a violation of a safety or health standard exists that threatens physical harm, or that an imminent danger exists, may request an inspection by giving notice to the Secretary or his authorized representative of such violation or danger. Any such notice shall be reduced to writing, shall set forth with reasonable particularity the grounds for the notice, and shall be signed by the employees or representative of employees, and a copy shall be provided the employer or his agent no later than at the time of inspection, except that, upon request of the person giving such notice, his name and the names of individual employees referred to therein shall not appear in such copy or on any record published, released, or made available pursuant to subsection (g) of this section.   If upon receipt of such notification the Secretary determines there are reasonable grounds to believe that such violation or danger exists, he shall make a special inspection in accordance with the provisions of this section as soon as practicable, to determine if such violation or danger exists. If the Secretary determines there are no reasonable grounds to believe that a violation or danger exists he shall notify the employees or representative of the employees in writing of such determination.

NOTE: Section 11 (c) of the Act provides explicit protection for employees exercising their rights, including making safety and health complaints.

	For Official Use Only		
	Area	Date Received	Time
	Region	Received By	Formal ☐ Non Formal ☐

The undersigned *(check one)*

☐ Employee   ☐ Representative of Employees   ☐ Other *(specify)* _____

believes that a violation at the following place of employment of an occupational safety or health standard exists which is a job safety or health hazard.

Employer's Name _____

Employer's Address *(Street)* _____   *(City)* _____

(State) _____   *(Zip Code)* _____   Telephone _____

1. Kind of business _____

2. Specify the particular building or worksite where the alleged violation is located, including address. _____

3. Specify the name and phone number of employer's agent(s) in charge. _____

4. Describe briefly the hazard which exists there including the approximate number of employees exposed to or threatened by such hazard. _____

OSHA-7 (Rev. October 1977)   **CONTINUED ON REVERSE SIDE**

FORM 11-1 Continued

_____
_____
_____
_____
_____
_____
_____
_____
_____
_____
_____
_____
_____
_____
_____
_____
_____
_____
_____

5. (a)   To your knowledge is this condition being considered by any other Government agency, or has it been considered by any other Government agency?

Yes ☐   No ☐

5. (b)   If yes, and you know, which Government agency?

6. Has this condition been brought to the attention of the employer?

Yes ☐   No ☐   Don't know ☐

7. Please indicate your desire:

☐ I _do not_ want my name revealed to the employer.   ☐ My name _may be_ revealed to the employer.

NOTE: It is unlawful to make any false statement, representation or certification in any document filed pursuant to the Occupational Safety and Health Act of 1970. Violations can be punished by a fine of not more than $10,000, or by imprisonment of not more than six months, or by both. (Section 17(g))

Signature _____   _____ Date _____

Typed or Printed Name _____

Address _(Street)_ _____   _(City)_ _____

(State) _____ _(Zip Code)_ _____ Telephone _____

If you are an authorized representative of   _____
employees affected by this complaint, please   _____
state the name of your organization and your title   _____   _____

FORM 11-2

Complaint of Reprisal Under the Occupational Safety and Health Act

Section 11(c) of the Occupational Safety and Health Act provides protection for employees exercising their rights under that act, including those making safety and health complaints.

	For Official Use Only		
	Area	Date Received	Time
	Region	Received By	Formal ☐ Non Formal ☐

The undersigned *(check one)*

☐ Employee   ☐ Representative of Employees   ☐ Other *(specify)*_____
believes that a violation of Section 11(c) of the Act has occurred.

Employer's Name
_____

Employer's Address *(Street)* _____ *(City)* _____

(State) _____ *(Zip Code)* _____ Telephone _____

1. Kind of business
_____

2. (Specify the discrimination which took place (firing, lack of promotion, transfer, denial of benefits, etc.)
_____
_____
_____

3. Specify the name and phone number of employer's agent(s) in charge.
_____
_____

4. (Describe briefly the hazard which exists, whether it still exists, and when and to whom you complained about it. Attach a copy of your safety complaint to this complaint, if it was made in writing.)
_____
_____
_____
_____
_____
_____
_____
_____
_____

5. (a) To your knowledge is this condition being considered by any other Government agency, or has it been considered by any other Government agency?

Yes ☐   No ☐

5. (b) If yes, and you know, which Government agency?

6. Has this condition been brought to the attention of the employer?

Yes ☐   No ☐   Don't know ☐

7. Please indicate your desire:

☐ I *do not* want my name revealed to the employer.   ☐ My name *may be* revealed to the employer.

NOTE: It is unlawful to make any false statement, representation or certification in any document filed pursuant to the Occupational Safety and Health Act of 1970. Violations can be punished by a fine or not more than $10,000, or by imprisonment of not more than six months, or by both. (Section 17(g))

Signature _____ Date _____

Typed or Printed Name _____

Address *(Street)* _____ *(City)* _____

(State) _____ *(Zip Code)* _____ Telephone _____

If you are an authorized representative of
employees affected by this complaint, please
state the name of your organization and your title. _____

FORM 11-3

Lawsuit to Correct Dangerous Working Conditions

IN THE _____ COURT
(Name of Court,
such as District,
Superior, Supreme,
or Circuit Court)

FOR _____
(Location of Court, City
County and/or State)

_____,
Plaintiff,

v.   Case or Civil Action Number.

_____,
Defendant.   (A number will be assigned when case is
filed)

COMPLAINT

(Some states will call this document a
declaration or a motion for judgment; ask the
court clerk)

I. NATURE OF THE CASE

1. This case is brought by an employee(s) of _____ company because a dangerous condition exists at its workplace located at _____. Plaintiffs seek an injunction to correct this dangerous condition and damages for harm that has been suffered.

II. JURISDICTION

2. Jurisdiction is conferred on this court by _____ (the clerk of court can tell you the statute creating jurisdiction, or allow you to look at cases filed.

III. PARTIES

3. Plaintiff(s) is _____, who lives at _____ and is currently employed by defendant at _____ as a _____.

4. Defendant is a _____

_____.

IV. FACTUAL ALLEGATIONS

5. State all of the facts concerning the dangerous condition, such as when it began, that you brought this to the attention of your employer, an office of the Occupational Safety and Health Administration, or a state agency concerned with occupational conditions, and that the employer failed to correct the dangerous condition. Also state whether you refused to work under these conditions, or whether you continue to work in order to provide for your family. Break these statements into short paragraphs and number them in sequence.

V. IRREPARABLE INJURY

6. State why money cannot compensate you for the dangerous condition. For example, you could state that in order to provide food and shelter for your family you are required to work in an unhealthy environment and that this unhealthy environment has already caused you certain physical and mental harm. Then explain the harm that you are suffering or may suffer.

VI. CAUSE OF ACTION: Breach of duty to
(OR CLAIM)   provide reasonably
safe workplace.

7. Plaintiff incorporates by reference paragraphs one (1) through (provide number of last paragraph), inclusive.

8. Defendant owes plaintiff a duty to provide a workplace which is reasonably safe and free of recognized hazards.

9. Defendant breached this duty by providing a dangerous workplace by _____.

VII. REQUEST FOR RELIEF

WHEREFORE, plaintiff(s) requests judgment against defendant and requests the court to:

A. Enjoin defendant from continuing to allow to exist the dangerous condition complained of by the plaintiff(s);

B. Order defendant to correct the dangerous condition within _____ (days or hours);

C. Award plaintiff the sum of $_____ as compensatory damages;

D. Award plaintiff the sum of $_____ as punitive damages for willfully allowing the dangerous condition to exist;

    E. Order defendant to pay plaintiff's costs and attorneys' fees; and

    F. Order such other relief as are in the interests of justice.

(Signature)

PLAINTIFF'S NAME
ADDRESS

Subscribed and sworn to before me this _____ day of _____.

NOTARY PUBLIC

FORM 11-4

Motion for a Temporary Restraining Order to Correct Dangerous Working Conditions

[This form can only be used when a complaint has been filed. It can be filed at the same time a complaint is filed or shortly thereafter. The heading of the document (Court, plaintiffs, and so forth) should be the same as the complaint.]

MOTION FOR A TEMPORARY RESTRAINING ORDER

    Plaintiffs move this court for a temporary restraining order to restrain the defendant from operating (explain dangerous condition). In the alternative, plaintiffs ask the court to order defendant to continue to pay plaintiffs' salaries and not require plaintiffs to work in the hazardous condition.

Respectfully submitted,

(Signature)

PLAINTIFF'S NAME
ADDRESS

CERTIFICATE OF SERVICE

    I certify that I have hand-delivered a copy of this motion, a copy of the complaint, a copy of the brief in support of this motion, and a proposed order to _____, attorney for defendant, at _____ (address) at _____ (time and date).

(Signature)

PLAINTIFF or AGENT

FORM 11-5

Brief in Support of Motion for a Temporary Restraining Order

BRIEF IN SUPPORT OF MOTION FOR A TEMPORARY RESTRAINING ORDER

(In the first paragraph, explain the nature of the imminently dangerous condition, and how plaintiffs are threatened with harm.)

The employer has a common law duty to provide a safe place to work which has been recognized in every state of the United States. *See* W. Prosser, *The Law of Torts,* 4th Ed. at 526; *Kreigh* v. *Westinghouse,* 214 U.S. 249 (1909).

The requirements for the issuance of a temporary restraining order are: (1) that plaintiffs are likely to prevail on their case; (2) that if the restraining order is not granted, plaintiffs will suffer irreparable injury; (3) that the defendant will not suffer greatly if the order is granted; and (4) that the public interest lies on the side of plaintiffs. We will now discuss these criteria.

I. PLAINTIFFS ARE LIKELY TO PREVAIL

The condition complained of is so dangerous that all plaintiffs are risking their lives by working at the _____. See the affidavit of _____ an expert of plant safety, who confirms the severity of the health hazard.

II. IRREPARABLE INJURY

Plaintiffs need income from their job to pay the basic necessities of life: rent (or mortgage), food, utilities, and so forth. Attach an affidavit to confirm need. If this income is cut off, plaintiffs and their children will suffer irreparable harm. If plaintiffs are forced to work in a hazardous plant, they may injure themselves, or they may be killed. Plaintiffs are on the horns of a dilemma and need this court's assistance to avoid irreparable injury to themselves and their families. The court can order the defendant to correct the dangerous condition immediately. Or the court can order the defendant to continue to pay salaries for plaintiffs while not requiring plaintiffs to work in the dangerous condition.

III. HARM TO DEFENDANT

Any harm that will be suffered by defendant will be economic and not irreparable. As previously stated, defendant has a legal duty to provide plaintiffs a safe place in which to work. Any costs that defendant incurs to make the workplace safe are requirements of law, so defendant would only be doing what is required by law.

IV. PUBLIC INTEREST

The public interest is on plaintiffs' side. The United States Supreme Court recently upheld regulations of the Occupational Safety and Health Administration which permit employees to refuse to work in unsafe workplaces: *Whirlpool Corp.* v. *Marshall,* 445 U.S. 1

(1980). Under the Occupational Safety and Health Act, employers are required to maintain safe and healthful workplaces. 29 U.S.C. § 651, *et seq.* The public interest lies with plaintiffs who are seeking that defendant comply with the laws of this state, and federal laws concerning safety and health.

CONCLUSION

For all these reasons the motion of plaintiffs for a temporary restraining order should be granted.

Respectfully submitted,

(Signatures) _____
PLAINTIFFS
ADDRESSES
TELEPHONE NUMBERS

FORM 11-6

Proposed Court Order

(Most courts require a proposed order with a motion. The heading should be the same as the motion and brief.)

ORDER

Upon consideration of plaintiffs' motion for a temporary restraining order and defendant's opposition, it is ordered as follows:

1. Defendant is ordered to correct the unsafe condition at _____ immediately;

2. Until this condition is corrected, plaintiffs are not required to work; however, defendant is required to continue to pay plaintiffs their usual salary and benefits. Defendant may require plaintiffs to report to work at another location, as long as the location is reasonably close and as long as the work required is not unduly burdensome or degrading.

3. This order continues in effect until the unsafe condition is corrected or until further order of this court.

_____
JUDGE

APPENDIX TO CHAPTER 11: LIST OF ADDRESSES

NATIONAL

Occupational Safety and Health Administration
   (OSHA)
Washington, DC 20210
(202) 523-6091

National Institute for Occupational Safety and Health
   (NIOSH)
5600 Fishers Lane
Rockville, MD 20857
(301) 496-4000

Health Research Group
(A Ralph Nader Affiliate)
2000 P Street, N.W.
Washington, DC 20036
(202) 872-0320

REGIONAL OFFICES FOR OCCUPATIONAL SAFETY AND HEALTH ADMINISTRATION

Region I
Connecticut, Maine, Massachusetts, New Hampshire,
Rhode Island, Vermont

JFK Federal Building
Room 1804
Government Center
Boston, MA 02203
(617) 223-6712

Region II
Canal Zone, New Jersey, New York, Puerto Rico, Virgin
   Islands

1 Astor Plaza
Room 3445
1515 Broadway
New York, NY 10036
(212) 399-5754

Region III
Delaware, District of Columbia, Maryland,
Pennsylvania, Virginia, West Virginia

Gateway Building
Suite 2100
3535 Market Street
Philadelphia, PA 19104
(215) 596-1201

Region IV
Alabama, Florida, Georgia, Kentucky, Mississippi,
North Carolina, South Carolina, Tennessee

1375 Peachtree Street, N.E.
Suite 587
Atlanta, GA 30309
(404) 881-3573

Region V
Illinois, Indiana, Michigan, Minnesota, Ohio,
Wisconsin

230 South Dearborn Street
32nd Floor, Room 3263
Chicago, IL 60604
(312) 353-2220

Region VI
Arkansas, Louisiana, New Mexico, Oklahoma, Texas

555 Griffin Square
Room 602
Dallas, TX 75202
(214) 767-4731

Region VII
Iowa, Kansas, Missouri, Nebraska

911 Walnut Street
Room 3000
Kansas City, MO
64106
(816) 374-5861

Region VIII
Colorado, Montana, North Dakota, South Dakota,
Utah, Wyoming

Federal Building
Room 1554
1961 Stout Street
Denver, CO 80294
(303) 837-3883

Region IX
American Samoa, Arizona, California, Guam,
Hawaii, Nevada, Trust Territory of the Pacific Islands

450 Golden Gate Avenue
Box 36017
San Francisco, CA 94102
(415) 556-0586

Region X
Alaska, Idaho, Oregon, Washington

Federal Office Building
Room 6003
909 First Avenue
Seattle, WA 98174
(206) 442-5930

U.S. DEPARTMENT OF LABOR AREA OFFICES FOR OCCUPATIONAL SAFETY AND HEALTH ADMINISTRATION

Alabama
2047 Canyon Road—Todd Mall
Birmingham, AL 35216
(205) 822-7100

Commerce Building
Room 600
118 North Royal Street
Mobile, AL
(205) 690-2131

Alaska
Federal Building U.S. Courthouse
701 "C" Street
P.O. Box 29
Anchorage, AK 99513
(907) 271-5152

Arizona
Amerco Towers
Suite 300
2721 North Central Avenue
Phoenix, AZ 85004
(602) 261-4858

Arkansas
West Mark Building
Suite 212
4120 West Markham
Little Rock, AR 72205
(501) 378-6291

California
400 Oceangate
Suite 530
Long Beach, CA 90802
(213) 432-3434

211 Main Street
San Francisco, CA 94105
(415) 556-7260

Colorado
Office Building "Y"
Room 102
10597 W. 6th Avenue
Lakewood, CO 80215
(303) 234-4471

Connecticut
555 Main Street
2nd Floor
Hartford, CT 06103
(203) 244-2294

Delaware
Ninth and King Streets
Wilmington, DE 19801
(302) 573-6115

District of Columbia
400 First Street, N.W.
Room 602
Washington, DC 20215
(202) 523-5224

Florida
299 East Broward Boulevard
Room 302
Fort Lauderdale, FL 33301
(305) 527-7292

Art Museum Plaza
Suite 4
2809 Art Museum Drive
Jacksonville, FL 32207
(904) 791-2895

700 Twiggs Street
Room 624
Tampa, FL 33602
(813) 228-2821

Georgia
152 New Street
Macon, GA 31201
(912) 746-5143

Enterprise Building
Suite 210
6605 Abercom Street
Savannah, GA 31405
(912) 354-0733

Building 10, Suite 33
La Vista Perimeter Office Park
Tucker, GA 30084
(404) 221-4767

Hawaii
300 Ala Moana Boulevard
Suite 5122
Honolulu, HI 96805
(808) 546-3157

Idaho
1315 West Idaho Street
Boise, ID 83702
(208) 384-1867

Illinois
1400 Torrence Avenue
2nd Floor
Calumet City, IL 60409
(312) 631-8200

6000 W. Touhy Avenue
Niles, IL 60648
(312) 631-8200

344 Smoke Tree Business Park
North Aurora, IL 60542
(312) 896-8700

228 N.E. Jefferson
3rd Floor
Peoria, IL 61603
(309) 671-7033

Indiana
U.S. Post Office and Courthouse
46 East Ohio Street
Room 423
Indianapolis, IN 46204
(317) 269-7290

Iowa
210 Walnut Street
Room 815
Des Moines, IA 50309
(515) 284-4794

Kansas
216 N. Waco
Suite B
Wichita, KS 67202
(316) 267-6311, ext. 644

Kentucky
600 Federal Place
Suite 554-E
Louisville, KY 40202
(502) 582-6111

Louisiana
2156 Wooddale Boulevard
Hoover Annex
Suite 200
Baton Rouge, LA 70806
(504) 923-0718, ext. 474

600 South Street
Room 337
New Orleans, LA 70130
(504) 589-2451

Maine
40 Western Avenue
Augusta, ME 04330
(207) 622-8417

Maryland
Federal Building
Room 1110
Charles Center, 31 Hopkins Plaza
Baltimore, MD 21201
(301) 962-2840

Massachusetts
1200 Main Street
Suite 513
Springfield, MA 01103
(413) 781-2420, ext. 522

400-2 Totten Pond Road
2nd Floor
Waltham, MA 02154
(617) 890-1239

Michigan
231 West Lafayette
Room 628
Detroit, MI 48226
(313) 226-6720

Minnesota
Butler Square
Room 801
100 N. 6th Street
Minneapolis, MN 55403
(612) 725-2571

Mississippi
57601-55 North Frontage Road East
Jackson, MS 39211
(601) 969-4606

Missouri
1150 Grand Avenue
6th Floor
12 Grand Building
Kansas City, MO 64106
(816) 374-2756

210 North 12th Boulevard
Room 520
St. Louis, MO 63101
(314) 425-5461

Montana
Petroleum Building
Suite 525
2812 1st Avenue North
Billings, MT 59101
(406) 657-6649

Nebraska
113 West 6th Street
2nd Floor
North Platte, NE 69101
(308) 534-9450

Overland-Wolf Building
Room 100
6910 Pacific Street
Omaha, NE 68106

Nevada
1100 E. William Street
Suite 222
Carson City, NV 89701
(702) 883-1226

New Hampshire
P.O. Box 178
55 Pleasant Street
Concord, NH 03301
(603) 224-1995

New Jersey
Belle Mead GSA Depot
Building T3
Belle Mead, NJ 08502
(201) 359-2777

2101 Ferry Avenue
Room 403
Camden, NJ 08104
(609) 757-5181

2 East Blackwell Street
Dover, NJ 07801
(201) 361-4050

Teterboro Airport Professional
    Building
377 Route 17
Room 206
Hasbrouck Heights, NJ 07604
(201) 288-1700

970 Broad Street
Room 1435C
Newark, NJ 07102
(201) 645-5930

New Mexico
Western Bank Building
Room 1125
505 Marquette Avenue, N.W.
Albuquerque, NM 87102
(505) 766-3411

New York
Leo W. O'Brien Federal Building
Clinton Avenue & N. Pearl Street
Room 132
Albany, NY 12207
(518) 472-6085

185 Montague Street
2nd Floor
Brooklyn, NY 11201
(212) 330-7667

111 W. Huron Street
Room 1305
Buffalo, NY 14202
(716) 846-4881

136-21 Roosevelt Avenue
3rd Floor
Flushing, NY 11354
(212) 445-5005

90 Church Street
Room 1405
New York, NY 10007
(212) 264-9840

Federal Office Building
Room 608
100 State Street
Rochester, NY 14614
(716) 263-6755

100 S. Clinton Street
Room 1267
Syracuse, NY 13260
(315) 423-5188

990 Westbury Road
Westbury, NY 11590
(516) 334-3344

200 Mamaroneck Avenue
Room 403
White Plains, NY 10601
(914) 946-2510

North Carolina
Federal Office Building
Room 406
310 New Bern Avenue
Raleigh, NC 27601
(914) 755-4770

North Dakota
Russel Building
Highway 83 North, Rt. 1
Bismarck, ND 58501
(701) 255-4011, ext. 521

Ohio
Federal Office Building
Room 4028
550 Main Street
Cincinnati, OH 45202
(513) 684-2354

Federal Office Building
Room 847
1240 East Ninth Street
Cleveland, OH 44199
(216) 522-3818

Federal Office Building
Room 634
200 N. High Street
Columbus, OH 43215
(614) 259-7542

Oklahoma
50 Penn Place
Suite 408
Oklahoma City, OK 73118
(405) 231-5351

717 S. Houston
Suite 304
Tulsa, OK 74127
(918) 581-7676

Oregon
1220 S.W. Third Street
Room 640
Portland, OR 97204
(503) 221-2251

Pennsylvania
147 W. 18th Street
Erie, PA 16501
(814) 453-4351

Progress Plaza
49 N. Progress Avenue
Harrisburg, PA 17109
(717) 782-3902

Wm. J. Green, Jr., Federal Building
Room 4256
600 Arch Street
Philadelphia, PA 19106
(215) 597-4955

Suite 600
400 Penn Center Boulevard
Pittsburgh, PA 15235
(412) 644-2905

Penn Place
Room 3107
20 North Pennsylvania Avenue
Wilkes-Barre, PA 18701
(717) 826-6538

Puerto Rico
U.S. Courthouse & FOB
Carlos Chardon Avenue
Room 555
Hato Rey, PR 00918
(809) 753-4457

Rhode Island
Federal Building & U.S. Post Office
Room 204
Providence, RI 02903
(401) 528-4466

South Carolina
Kittrel Center
Suite 102
2711 Middleburg Drive
Columbia, SC 29204
(803) 765-5904

South Dakota
Court House Plaza Building
Room 408
300 North Dakota Avenue
Sioux Falls, SD 57102
(605) 336-2980, ext. 425

Tennessee
1600 Hayes Street
Suite 302
Nashville, TN 37203
(615) 251-5313

Texas
American Bank Tower
Suite 310
221 W. 6th Street
Austin, TX 78701
(512) 397-5783

Fort Worth Federal Center
4900 Hemphill Building 24
Room 145
P.O. Box 6477
(817) 334-5274

Riverview Professional Building
1325 S. 77 Sunshine Strip
Suite 9
Harlingen, TX 78550
(512) 425-6811

1100 NASA Road I
Suite 505
Houston, TX 77004
(713) 226-4357

1425 W. Pioneer Drive
Irving, TX 75061
(214) 749-7555

Federal Building
Room 421
1205 Texas Avenue
Lubbock, TX 74901
(806) 762-7681

FOB-USPO & Courthouse
Room 208
211 W. Ferguson Street
Tyler, TX 75702
(214) 595-1404

Utah
U.S. Post Office Building
Room 451
350 South Main Street
Salt Lake City, UT 84101
(801) 524-5080

Vermont
Montpelier, VT 05602
(802) 828-2765

Virginia
Federal Building
Room 6226
400 North 8th Street
Richmond, VA 23240
(804) 782-2864

Washington
121 107th Avenue, N.E.
Bellevue, WA 98004
(804) 782-2886

West Virginia
Charleston National Plaza
Room 1726
700 Virginia Street
Charleston, WV 25301
(304) 343-6181, ext. 420

Wisconsin
2618 North Ballard Road
Appleton, WI 54911
(414) 734-4521

Clark Building
Room 400
633 West Wisconsin Avenue
Milwaukee, WI 53203
(414) 291-3315

Wyoming
605 East 25th Street
Cheyenne, WY 82001
(307) 277-7786

12

How to Fight the Social Security Administration

Before you can take the Social Security Administration (SSA) to court, you must apply for benefits and pursue a series of internal administrative appeals. If you dispute the amount, or were denied benefits for retirement, disability, survivors benefits, or Supplemental Security Income (SSI), you have a right to challenge the Social Security Administration.

First, you must apply for benefits at one of the SSA's more than 800 district and branch offices or more than 3,300 smaller offices. The list is too numerous to print in this book, but every major city and many smaller cities have social security offices. Look in the telephone directory under: Federal Government, Department of Health and Human Services, Social Security Administration. There are many types of forms for applying for benefits. The SSA personnel will help you fill them out at the offices.

ELIGIBILITY FOR RETIREMENT BENEFITS

Before you can get a Social Security retirement check, you must have worked for certain minimum periods of time. If you reached age 62 in 1978, you need to have worked for 6½ years. No one ever needs to have worked more than ten years to be eligible for retirement benefits.

HOW TO APPLY FOR RETIREMENT BENEFITS

The Social Security Administration requires that you be entitled to benefits before it will approve payment of them. To expedite your claim you will need to produce the following documents at a Social Security office:

1. Social Security card or number
2. Proof of your date of birth
3. W-2 statements of self-employment returns for 2 years
4. Marriage certificate
5. Childrens' birth certificates (if they are eligible for benefits)

Proof of your birth date is the most important item. If you have a birth certificate, it must be certified by the agency who issued it. If you do not have a birth certificate, you can use some other official record confirming your date of birth, such as a religious record, a passport, immigration records, military records, or other official documents which have your birth date on them. You must submit the original document. Make photocopies of the documents before giving them to the agency.

If you were self-employed you must bring proof that you filed your self-employment returns. Can-

**MONTHLY RETIREMENT BENEFITS FOR WORKERS WHO
REACHED 62 BEFORE 1979 (EFFECTIVE JUNE 1982)**

Average Yearly Earnings	Worker at 65	Spouse[1] at 65 or child	at 64	at 63	at 62	Family[2] benefits
1,200	235	117	107	98	88	353
2,000	305	152	140	127	114	459
2,600	345	172	158	143	129	517
3,000	377	188	173	157	141	577
3,400	405	202	185	168	151	652
4,000	444	222	203	185	166	759
4,400	476	238	218	198	178	844
4,800	504	252	231	210	189	919
5,200	530	265	242	220	198	994
5,600	556	278	254	231	208	1,030
6,000	582	291	267	242	218	1,068
6,400	608	304	278	253	228	1,106
6,800	636	318	291	265	238	1,143
7,200	669	334	306	278	250	1,183
7,600	698	349	320	291	261	1,222
8,000	724	362	331	301	271	1,267
8,400	739	369	338	308	277	1,294
8,800	757	378	347	315	284	1,325
9,200	774	387	354	322	290	1,354
9,600	787	393	360	328	295	1,377
10,000	802	401	367	334	300	1,403
10,400	817	408	374	340	306	1,430
10,800	830	415	380	345	311	1,452
11,400	851	425	390	354	319	1,490

[1] If a person is eligible for both a worker's benefit and a spouse's benefit, the check actually payable is limited to the larger of the two.

[2] The maximum amount payable to a family is generally reached when a worker and two family members are eligible.

celled checks are an excellent way to prove this.

If your husband or wife is applying for benefits, he or she will need the same documentation. You may need to prove that you are married, so bring your marriage certificate or license with you. If either of you were married before, you may have to prove the date of your divorce. A certified copy of the divorce decree is the best proof of divorce.

DISABILITY CLAIMS

When you apply for disability benefits, your earnings record will be reviewed to determine if you meet the basic requirements for eligibility. The younger you are, the less time you need to have worked to be eligible for disability benefits. For example, if you are under 24, you need to have worked one and a half years during the previous three years to be eligible. If you are age 24 to 31 you must have worked one-half of the time between your 21st birthday and the date you became disabled for eligibility benefits. Between the ages of 31 and 42 you need to have worked five years to qualify for benefits.

If you are uncertain whether you qualify for disability benefits, you should apply anyway. You cannot receive benefits until you have been unable to work for six months, but you can apply in advance

TABLE OF ELIGIBILITY FOR DISABILITY BENEFITS

Born after 1929, become disabled at age	Born before 1930, become disabled before 62 in	Years of work credit you need
42 or younger		5
44		5½
46		6
48		6½
50		7
52	1981	7½
53	1982	7¾
54	1983	8
55	1984	8¼
56	1985	8½
58	1987	9
60	1989	9½
62 or older	1991 or later	10

if, because of your condition, it is unlikely that you will work again in the near future. Even if you do not qualify for disability benefits, you may be eligible under another program such as the SSI program. It generally takes the SSA two to three months to process a disability claim.

In order to process your disability claim, you will need to provide the SSA with the following:

1. Social Security card or number
2. names and addresses of those who treated you: doctors, hospitals and clinics
3. list of employers for the past 15 years
4. W-2 forms for the past two years, or self-employment returns
5. military service dates
6. marriage license if your spouse is also applying

If your request for benefits is denied you have a right to ask that the decision be reconsidered. At this point you should discuss the matter with an attorney experienced in social security cases. You have the right to proceed without an attorney, but a legal consultation usually will be worthwhile. You have 60 days to request that the adverse decision be reconsidered.

A form for requesting reconsideration is included at the end of this chapter as Form 12-1

HEARING BEFORE AN ADMINISTRATIVE JUDGE

If you disagree with the reconsidered decision, you have the right to ask for a hearing before an administrative law judge (ALJ). Again, you have 60 days to ask for a hearing after receiving the reconsidered decision.

Form 12-2 is a request for a hearing. The hearing will be held in a city near you. The ALJ reviews all the evidence that had earlier been submitted, and questions you and witnesses that you bring to the hearing. All testimony is given under oath. You and your representative have the right to ask witnesses questions, and to present new evidence. If you choose, you may request that the ALJ review the case without you being present. In that case, the ALJ will base his or her decision on the evidence previously submitted.

REVIEW BY THE APPEALS COUNCIL

If you believe that the ALJ's decision was incorrect, you have the right to appeal to the Appeals Council. Its address is:

Appeals Council
Bureau of Hearings and Appeals
Social Security Administration
P.O. Box 2518
Washington, DC 20013

The form for requesting the Appeals Court for review is Form 12-3. The Appeals Council may decide not to hear your appeal. If so, you have the right to file suit in federal district court within 60 days.

If the Appeals Council decides to hear your case, you have the right to submit a written statement or brief as to why you feel that the ALJ made a mistake. You have the right to request an oral hearing, but the Council does not have to hear oral arguments.

FEDERAL COURT

You case will become final if you do not file a complaint in a federal district court within 60 days after receiving the decision of the Appeals Council. Your complaint must be filed in the proper U.S. District Court. It can be filed in the District Court where you live, do business, or in the District of Columbia. A complaint form is included at the end of this chapter as Form 12-4.

If you have been proceeding without an attorney up to this point, it is advisable to discuss the case with an attorney. An attorney cannot charge you a fee unless it is approved by the SSA. The maximum fee which the agency will approve is 25 percent of the benefits that are recovered for you. Once the case is properly filed in the District Court, the case is appealable to a circuit court judge of appeals, and then to the United States Supreme Court. About one social security case per year is heard by the Supreme Court.

FORM 12-1: Request for Reconsideration of Social Security Decision

DEPARTMENT OF HEALTH, EDUCATION, AND WELFARE
SOCIAL SECURITY ADMINISTRATION

TOE 710

Form Approved
OMB No. 72-R0552

REQUEST FOR RECONSIDERATION

(Do not write in this space)

The information on this form is authorized by law (20 CFR 404.910 – 404.914). While your responses to these questions is voluntary, the Social Security Administration cannot reconsider the decision on this claim unless the information is furnished.

NAME OF CLAIMANT	NAME OF WAGE EARNER OR SELF-EMPLOYED PERSON *(If different from claimant.)*
SOCIAL SECURITY CLAIM NUMBER	SUPPLEMENTAL SECURITY INCOME CLAIM NUMBER

SPOUSE'S NAME AND SOCIAL SECURITY NUMBER *(Complete ONLY in Supplemental Security Income Case)*

CLAIM FOR *(Specify type, e.g., retirement, disability, hospital insurance, supplemental security income, etc.)*

I do not agree with the determination made on the above claim and request reconsideration. My reasons are:

_____
_____
_____

NOTE: If the notice of the determination on your claim is dated more than 65 days ago, include your reason for not making this request earlier. Include the date on which you received the notice of the determination.

I am submitting the following additional evidence (If none, write "None,"):

_____
_____
_____
_____

Signature *(First name, middle initial, last name) (Write in ink)*	Date *(Month, day, year)*
SIGN HERE ➡	Telephone Number

Mailing Address *(Number and street, Apt. No., P.O. Box, or Rural Route)*

City and State	ZIP Code	Enter Name of County (if any) in which you now live

Witnesses are required ONLY if this request has been signed by mark (X) above. If signed by mark (X), two witnesses to the signing who know the person requesting reconsideration must sign below, giving their full addresses.

1. Signature of Witness	2. Signature of Witness
Address *(Number and street, City, State, ZIP Code)*	Address *(Number and street, City, State, ZIP Code)*

FOR SOCIAL SECURITY OFFICE USE ONLY

SOCIAL SECURITY OFFICE ADDRESS

ROUTING INSTRUCTIONS *(Check one)*

☐ State Agency *(Route with disability folder)*
☐ Program Service Center
☐ BDI, Balto.

☐ District Office Reconsideration
☐ Division of International Operations, Balto.
☐ BDP, Attn: ACB, Balto.

FORM SSA-561-U2 (1-79) (FORMERLY SSA-561)
PRIOR EDITIONS MAY BE USED UNTIL SUPPLY IS EXHAUSTED

NOTE: Take or mail completed copies to your Social Security Office.

FORM 12-2: Request for a Hearing (Social Security Case)

DEPARTMENT OF HEALTH AND HUMAN SERVICES
SOCIAL SECURITY ADMINISTRATION
OFFICE OF HEARINGS AND APPEALS

REQUEST FOR HEARING

Take or Mail original and all copies to your local Social Security Office.

CLAIMANT	
	(Check One) ☐ Termination or other ☐
WAGE EARNER *(Leave blank if same as above)*	Initial Entitlement Post-Entitlement Action

Type Claim (Check ONE)

Retirement or Survivors . . . . Only ☐ (RSI)
Disability, Worker or Child . . . . Only ☐ (DIWC)
Disability, Widow or Widower . . . . Only ☐ (DIWW)

SOCIAL SECURITY NUMBER

SPOUSE'S NAME AND SOCIAL SECURITY NUMBER
(Complete ONLY in Supplemental Security Income Case)

SSI, Aged . . . . Only ☐ (SSIA) | SSI, Aged . . . . With Title II Claim ☐ (SSAC)
SSI, Blind . . . . Only ☐ (SSIB) | SSI, Blind . . . . With Title II Claim ☐ (SSBC)
SSI, Disability . . Only ☐ (SSID) | SSI, Disability . . With Title II Claim ☐ (SSDC)
Other (Specify)_____

I disagree with the determination made on the above claim and request a hearing. My reasons for disagreement are:

_____
_____

Check one of the following:

☐ I have additional evidence to submit (Attach such evidence to this form or forward to the Social Security Office within 10 days.)

☐ I have no additional evidence to submit.

Check ONLY ONE of the statements below:

☐ I wish to appear in person.

☐ I do not wish to appear at a hearing. I request that a decision be made on the basis of the evidence in my case.

Signed by: (Either the claimant or representative should sign. Enter addresses for both. If claimant's representative is not an attorney, complete Form SSA-1696.)

SIGNATURE OR NAME OF CLAIMANT'S REPRESENTATIVE	CLAIMANT'S SIGNATURE
☐ ATTORNEY ☐ NON ATTORNEY	
ADDRESS	ADDRESS
CITY, STATE, AND ZIP CODE	CITY, STATE, AND ZIP CODE
TELEPHONE NUMBER DATE:	TELEPHONE NUMBER

(Claimant should not fill in below this line)

TO BE COMPLETED BY SOCIAL SECURITY ADMINISTRATION

Is this request timely filed? ☐ YES ☐ NO
If "No" is checked: (1) Attach claimant's explanation for delay, (2) Attach any pertinent letter, material, or information in the Social Security Office.

Interpreter Needed_____
(Language)

ACKNOWLEDGMENT OF REQUEST FOR HEARING

This request for hearing was filed on_____at_____
The Administrative Law Judge will notify you of the time and place of the hearing at least 10 days in advance of the hearing.

		For the Social Security Administration:
HEARING OFFICE COPY	TO: ☐ Hearing Office_____ (Location) ☐ _____ (Location) (Claims Involving SSI or combined SSI-RSDI) ☐ Supplemental Security Income File Attached	By:_____ (Signature) _____ (Title)
CLAIM FILE COPY	TO: ☐ Hearing Office ☐ Claim File(s) Requested by Teletype to_____ (Location) ☐ RDS (OCRO)	_____ (Street Address) _____ (City, State, and Zip Code) Servicing Social Security Office Code_____

Form HA-501 U5 (2-81)

CLAIM FILE

FORM 12-3: Request for Appeals Council Review (Social Security Case)

DEPARTMENT OF HEALTH, EDUCATION, AND WELFARE
SOCIAL SECURITY ADMINISTRATION
BUREAU OF HEARINGS AND APPEALS

REQUEST FOR REVIEW OF HEARING DECISION/ORDER

Take or mail original and all copies to your local social security office.

CLAIMANT	CLAIM FOR
	☐ Entitlement to Disability Benefits
WAGE EARNER (Leave blank if same as above)	☐ Continuance of Disability Benefits
SOCIAL SECURITY NUMBER	☐ Other (Specify) _____
SPOUSE'S NAME AND SOCIAL SECURITY NUMBER (Complete ONLY in Supplemental Security Income Case)	☐ Supplemental Security Income
	☐ Continuance of Supplemental Security Income

I disagree with the action taken on the above claim and request review of such action by the Appeals Council, of the Bureau of Hearings and Appeals. My reasons for disagreement are:

_____

_____

_____

Attach to this form, or forward within 10 days to the Appeals Council at the address checked below, any evidence you wish to submit.

Signed by: (Either the claimant or representative should sign - Enter addresses for both)

SIGNATURE OR NAME OF CLAIMANT'S REPRESENTATIVE	CLAIMANT'S SIGNATURE
☐ ATTORNEY ☐ NON-ATTORNEY	
STREET ADDRESS	STREET ADDRESS
CITY, STATE, AND ZIP CODE	CITY, STATE, AND ZIP CODE
TELEPHONE NUMBER	DATE	TELEPHONE NUMBER

Claimant should not fill in below this line

TO BE COMPLETED BY SOCIAL SECURITY ADMINISTRATION

Is this request filed timely?   ☐ Yes   ☐ No

If "No" is checked: (1) attach claimant's explanation for delay; (2) attach any pertinent letter, material or information in Social Security Office.

ACKNOWLEDGMENT OF REQUEST FOR REVIEW OF HEARING DECISION/ORDER

Request for Review of Hearing Decision/Order in this case was filed on _____ at _____.

The APPEALS COUNCIL will notify you of its action on your request.

For the Social Security Administration

☐ Appeals Council
Bureau of Hearings and Appeals, SSA
P.O. Box 2518
Washington, D.C. 20013

☐ Appeals Council
Bureau of Hearings and Appeals, SSA
_____
_____

BY   (Signature)
(Title)
(Street Address)
(City)   (State)   (ZIP Code)

Form HA-520
(9-73)

APPEALS COUNCIL

FORM 12-4

Federal Court Complaint Seeking Review of Determination/Disallowance of Social Security Benefits

UNITED STATES DISTRICT COURT

FOR THE _____ DISTRICT OF _____

_____ DIVISION

_____,

Plaintiff,

v.   Civil Action No.

_____,

Secretary of Department of Health and Human Services,

Defendant.

COMPLAINT SEEKING REVIEW OF DETERMINATION/DISALLOWANCE OF SOCIAL SECURITY BENEFITS

I. NATURE OF THE CASE

1. Plaintiff is seeking judicial review of a final ruling of the Secretary of Health and Human Services concerning an application of social security benefits for _____.

(Insert retirement, supplemental security income or disability.)

II. JURISDICTION

2. Jurisdiction is conferred on this court by 42 U.S.C. § 405(g) (for retirement and disability benefits). 42 U.S.C. § 405(g) and 1383(c) (for supplemental security income).

III. PARTIES

3. Plaintiff, whose social security number is _____, is a resident of the City of _____, State of _____, County of _____. (State whether employed or unemployed, and if employed, state name of employer and location of place of work.)

4. Defendant is the Secretary of the Department of Health and Human Services.

IV. FACTUAL ALLEGATIONS

5. Plaintiff is seeking judicial review of a final decision of the Appeals Council in which plaintiff was the claimant. A copy of the decision of the Appeals Council is attached to this complaint as plaintiff's exhibit number 1.

6. Plaintiff has exhausted all administrative remedies concerning this matter.

V. CAUSE OF ACTION

7. Plaintiff incorporates by reference paragraphs one through six, inclusive.

8. The Appeals Council erred in its decision dated _____ (plaintiff's exhibit number 1) by

_____.

9. The decision of the Appeals Council was arbitrary, capricious, an abuse of discretion, and otherwise contrary to law.

VI. REQUEST FOR RELIEF

WHEREFORE, plaintiff requests:

A. That judgment be entered for plaintiff reversing the decision (or modifying the decision) of the Appeals Council;

B. That plaintiff recover from defendant the costs of this action;

C. That the court grant such other and further relief as it may deem to be just and proper.

(Signature) _____

PLAINTIFF'S NAME
ADDRESS
TELEPHONE NUMBER

PART V: PROTECTING YOUR ENVIRONMENT

13

When Smoke Gets in Your Eyes

You can't file a lawsuit every time someone lights up a cigarette in an elevator. I have represented too many nonsmokers who took the law into their own hands or took on smokers too enthusiastically. Let me reveal my own prejudices: I was an attorney for Action on Smoking and Health, the largest national nonsmokers' rights organization. I am a nonsmoker and strongly feel that nonsmokers have a right to breathe air uncontaminated by tobacco smoke.

The law in the District of Columbia, as in most jurisdictions, prohibts smoking in elevators. One case I handled involved two gentlemen on an elevator who asked a smoker to put out his cigarette. He refused. A government building guard was called, and the smoker argued that he was being wrongly detained. To make a long story short, the smoker sued the nonsmokers for $800,000 for false arrest and other things. I was retained to represent the nonsmokers, who filed a counterclaim for an enormous amount. After several years of legal-paper shuffling, the case was settled, but all sides lost because each party paid attorneys' fees. The lesson: it is not worthwhile getting into a protracted legal battle against an individual smoker.

KNOW THE LAW

In the elevator situation, the most effective method of stopping a smoker is to state, as politely as possible: "Excuse me, sir (madam), but did you know that it is illegal in (name of your city or state) to smoke in elevators?" Most smokers will put out their cigarettes immediately, if you are polite and firm. If they get belligerent, walk away, if possible, from the argument by getting out of the elevator at its next stop.

RESTAURANTS

Many cities and states have passed legislation requiring restaurants to have separate smoking and nonsmoking sections. These laws are being changed frequently, so you must check your local laws. Statewide laws require separate sections in Connecticut, Michigan, Minnesota, Rhode Island, and Utah. Generally, only large restaurants seating fifty or more customers are subject to these laws. Many local areas have similar laws, including Prince George's County, Maryland; Rockland County, New York; Berkeley, California; and Champaign, Illinois.

In areas where there is no law requiring separate sections for smokers and nonsmokers, many restaurants have voluntarily instituted separate sections. For example, CoCo's Famous Hamburgers, Denny's, Furr's, The Magic Pan, Red Lobster, Sambo's, Victoria Station, and Hamburger Hamlet are national chains with a separate section policy. If nonsmokers avoided restaurants which do not restrict smoking, economic realities would convince these restaurants to change their policies.

One example of what you should not do: A nonsmoking client of mine was in a Chinese restaurant. She is very petite in body but not in mind. A large man was smoking a cigar at the table next to her. She politely asked him to stop smoking. He complied at first, but later lit up another cigar. She became incensed, got up and threw water in his face, putting out his cigar. The cigar-smoker convinced a local prosecutor to bring charges against the brave little lady for assault. I represented her and convinced the prosecutor that she was not a danger to society and he dropped the charges. She was a lucky lady. The smoker could have physically beaten her or she could have been jailed because she committed the traditional assault. It is not yet a recognized assault for someone to smoke near you. The best advice would be to ask for the manager of the restaurant, and explain the problem to him or her. He will probably try to find you or the smoker a new table where the two of you will be far apart. Make the restaurant be the intervenor. If the manager won't help you, leave and go to a friendlier watering hole.

PLANES, TRAINS, AND BUSES

Nonsmokers have rights in airplanes, trains, and buses. Airplane rules are the strongest. Unless you are late for a plane or do not have reservations, the airline must provide you with a nonsmoking seat.[1] The airline must expand the smoking section if it is not large enough to accommodate all the nonsmoking passengers. You must be firm with airline personnel. On a Braniff flight, my wife and I were told that we would have to move from the nonsmoking section. We refused to move and cited the Civil Aeronautics Board rule on smoking. The pilot of the plane came out of the cockpit to see what the problem was. He agreed that we were entitled to a nonsmoking seat and would not take off until we were seated in a nonsmoking seat. The nonsmoking section was enlarged to accommodate us, and peace was restored to the skies.

If you feel that an airline has denied you your rights under the CAB rule, you have a right to file a formal complaint. A complaint to the CAB could lead to a fine for the airline. Your normal complaint should include:

1. name of airline
2. flight number
3. date and time
4. cities of origin and destination
5. seat number(s)

Write down all of this information and try to get the names of airline personnel involved in the incident as well as names and addresses of witnesses. A complaint form is enclosed at the end of this chapter for filing with the CAB, Form 13-1. The address of the CAB is:

Civil Aeronautics Board
Office of the Secretary
1825 Connecticut Avenue, N.W.
Washington, DC 20428

Smoking on trains used to be regulated by the Interstate Commerce Commission. Nearly all of the passenger trains in the United States are run by Amtrak, a government-subsidized corporation. Amtrak has smoking on about one half, and no smoking on the other half of its railroad cars. The conductor should be called if someone is smoking in a posted no-smoking car. Unfortunately, dining cars are often smoking cars. Passengers cannot file a formal complaint about smoking on trains since there is no government agency which would hear the complaint. But Amtrak does respond to letter complaints. In fact, the Chief Justice of the United States, Warren Burger, complained that on a New York to Washington, D.C. train, someone was smoking a pipe in a no-smoking car.

If the Chief Justice can write a complaint letter, so can you. The address to write to is:

Amtrak
Consumer Services
400 N. Capitol Street, N.W.
Washington, DC 20001
(202) 383-2121

Smoking on intrastate buses is still regulated by the Interstate Commerce Commission. The ICC regulations provide that there be no more than 30 percent smoking seats on buses, and the smoking section is required to be in the back of the bus.[2] If

---

1. 14 CFR (Code of Federal Regulations) (Part 252) (CAB Rules for smoking aboard aircraft, 1982).

2. 49 CFR (Code of Federal Regulations) Part 1061 (1981).

someone is smoking in the nonsmoking portion of the bus, remind them politely of the rule. If that is not effective, talk to the driver. If that is not effective, you can file a formal complaint with the ICC. The complaint should contain the following:

1. name of the bus company
2. date and time of incident
3. cities of origin and destination

Try to get the name of the driver, the offending smoker, and the witnesses' names and addresses. A formal complaint form is included at the end of this chapter as Form 13-2. The address of the ICC is:

Interstate Commerce Commission
Office of the Secretary
12th and Constitution Avenue, N.W.
Washington, DC 20423

An interesting footnote: Neither the CAB nor the ICC rules require airlines or bus companies to provide smoking sections. Airlines and bus companies have a right to prohibit smoking entirely.

SMOKING IN THE WORKPLACE

Your employer is required by state and federal law to provide you with a safe and healthful work environment. Chapter 11 dealt at length with this right in general. But the right to a safe and healthful work environment includes the right to a relatively smoke-free workplace, especially if you are very sensitive to tobacco smoke. Form 11-1 can be used to file a smoking complaint with the Occupational Safety and Health Administration. You cannot be fired or disciplined for complaining to your employer or to OSHA about work conditions related to safety and health.

One employee took her employer, the Bell Telephone Company of New Jersey, to court to require it to ban smoking at the workplace. The New Jersey court agreed with Donna Shimp and ordered N.J. Bell Telephone to prohibit smoking where Mrs. Shimp worked, except in a smoking lounge.[3] Mrs. Shimp suffered a severe allergic reaction to cigarette smoke, including nose bleeds, severe eye irritation, headaches, nausea, and vomiting. The judge in her case stated that there was no need to fill the

air with toxic tobacco smoke in order to run the phone company. Donna Shimp has established a group to help nonsmokers win their right to a smoke-free workplace. Her address is:

Donna Shimp
Environmental Associates
109 Chestnut Street
Salem, NJ 08079
(609) 935 4200

You do not have to resort to a lawsuit or filing complaints to get nonsmoking areas in which to work. Many employers will voluntarily separate smokers from nonsmokers. Suggest it to your union or employer. A few employers have banned smoking entirely. Studies have shown that nonsmokers have less absenteeism, work harder, and are less expensive to have as employees. Life insurance and health rates are lower for nonsmokers. If your employer pays for your insurance, smokers are costing him money. Convince your employer that nonsmokers deserve to be protected, and that smokers should be encouraged to quit.

Most federal agencies have regulations concerning smoking. If you are a federal employee, ask your union or supervisor for a copy of your agency's regulations on smoking. These regulations are too numerous and they change too often to be listed here. If your agency's regulations are not being enforced, you can file a grievance. The head of your agency is responsible for implementing the Occupational Safety and Health Act. This act requires every agency to have a safe and healthful work environment. Many studies have shown that smoking in a workplace is harmful to the health of nonsmokers.[4]

UNEMPLOYMENT AND DISABILITY PAYMENTS

It is unfortunate that some nonsmokers are forced to leave work because cigarette smoking makes it intolerable for them. But the courts usually rule that quitting work to protect your health does not disqualify the person concerning unem-

---

3. *Shimp* v. *N.J. Bell Tel. Co.,* 145 N.J. Super. 516, 368 A.2d 408 (1976).

4. J. R. White and H. F. Froeb, "Small-Airways Dysfunction in Nonsmokers Chronically Exposed to Tobacco Smoke," New England Journal of Medicine 302, no. 13 (1980) 720–723.

5. *Stevens* v. *Employment Security Commission,* D.C. of Iowa, Polk County, No. CE 6-2934, 11–17–76; Meyer v. C.P. Clare & Co., Iowa Industrial Comm., D.E. 615–78, 11–17–78.

ployment benefits or disability payments.[5] The ninth Circuit Court of Appeals in San Francisco ruled recently that a government worker who developed breathing problems while working with smokers was entitled to $20,000 in disability payments. The court said that unless the Defense Logistics Agency, in San Bruno, California, found Irene Parodi a new job in a smokeless office within 60 days, she would have to be paid disability retirement benefits.[6] The federal appeals court wrote:

> Unlike a person with a physical limitation, a person with an environmental limitation can physically perform assigned work in a proper environment.

_____

6. *Parodi* v. *Merit Systems Protection Board,* 690 F.2d 731 (9th Cir., 1982).

Step-by-step, the courts are inching their way to ruling that a worker has a right to a smoke-free workplace. This process is painstakingly slow, but if every worker complained when the smoke got in his or her eyes, the process would be speedier.

STATE AND LOCAL LAWS

Most states and cities prohibit smoking in elevators, near gasoline stations, and near other dangerous materials. Many ban smoking in grocery stores, theatres, and shopping areas. Because the laws vary and change often, the following list of local nonsmokers' organizations will help you if you want to know the current law in your area. They will also help you concerning other smoking-related problems.

NONSMOKERS' RIGHTS ORGANIZATIONS

NATIONAL

Action on Smoking and Health
2013 H Street, N.W.
Washington, DC 20006
(202) 659-4310

National GASP (Group Against Smokers' Pollution)
P.O. Box 632
College Park, MD 20740
(301) 577-6427

Environmental Associates
109 Chestnut Street
Salem, NJ 08079
(609) 935-4200

STATE AND LOCAL

(If there is no group in your area, call your local Lung Association, as they are usually active in nonsmokers' rights.)

ARIZONA
Smoking and Health Action Coalition
7438 East Juarez Street
Tucson, AZ 85710

CALIFORNIA
California GASP
P.O. Box 1061
Berkeley, CA 94701

COLORADO
GASP of Colorado
P.O. Box 39692
Denver, CO 80239

FLORIDA
Miami GASP
3614 Coral Way
Miami, FL 33145

GEORGIA
GASP
1383 Spring Street
Atlanta, GA 30309

HAWAII
Nonsmokers' Rights Council of Hawaii
P.O. Box 3439
Honolulu, HI 96813

ILLINOIS
Central Illinois GASP
2327 W. Madeira Court
Peoria, IL 61614

MARYLAND
Maryland GASP
P.O. Box 863
Bowie, MD 20715

MASSACHUSETTS
Massachusetts GASP
P.O. Box 242
Brookline, MA 02146

MICHIGAN
GASP of Houghton
1013 Lake Street
Houghton, MI 49931

MINNESOTA
Association for Nonsmokers' Rights
14 Portland Avenue
St. Paul, MN 55102

NEW JERSEY
New Jersey GASP
105 Mountain Avenue
Summit, NJ 07901

NEW YORK
Greater New York Council Against Public Smoking
P.O. Box 348
Lennox Hill Station
New York, NY 10021

Long Island GASP
7 Maxine Avenue
Plainview, NY 11803

NORTH CAROLINA
Charlotte GASP
1229 Marlwood Terrace
Charlotte, NC 28209

Greenville GASP
507 Lancelot Drive
Simpsonville, NC 29681

OHIO
Cincinnati GASP
5525 Stokeswood Court
Cincinnati, OH 45238

PENNSYLVANIA
Pittsburgh GASP
P.O. Box 5983
Pittsburgh, PA 15206

RHODE ISLAND
Rhode Island GASP
149 Plantation Drive
Cranston, RI 02920

TENNESSEE
GASP of Chattanooga
P.O. Box 6074
Chattanooga, TN 37401

VIRGINIA
Northern Virginia GASP
6904 Barneck Drive
Springfield, VA 22152

WYOMING
Wyoming GASP
P.O. Box 213
Cheyenne, WY 82001

FORM 13-1

Complaint Regarding Smoking on Aircraft (for CAB)

BEFORE THE CIVIL AERONAUTICS BOARD
WASHINGTON, DC 20428

In the matter of violations of Part 252 concerning smoking on _____   Docket No.
Airlines.

COMPLAINT

1. _____ complainant, had reservations on _____ airline, on
flight number _____, on _____ (date) to fly from _____ to _____
_____.

2. On _____ (date) complainant checked in for this flight _____ minutes before the
plane was scheduled to depart.

3. I was refused a non-smoking seat, (or) smoking was allowed in non-smoking sections, (or
otherwise state your complaint).

WHEREFORE, I request that _____ airline be fined $1000.00 for violating Part
252 of the Board's regulations.

(Signature) _____
NAME
ADDRESS
TELEPHONE NUMBER

Subscribed and sworn to before me this _____ day of _____.

_____
NOTARY PUBLIC

FORM 13-2

Complaint Regarding Smoking on Buses (for ICC)

BEFORE THE INTERSTATE COMMERCE COMMISSION
WASHINGTON, DC 20423

In the matter of violations of 49 C.F.R. Part
1061 concerning smoking on _____   Docket No.
_____ buslines.

COMPLAINT

1. _____ complainant, bought a ticket from _____ buslines, on bus number _____, on _____ (date) for a bus from _____ to _____.

2. On _____ (date) complainant boarded this bus _____ minutes before it was scheduled to leave.

3. I was refused a non-smoking seat, (or) smoking was allowed in the non-smoking portion of the bus, (or otherwise state your complaint).

WHEREFORE, I request that _____ bus company be fined _____ for violating Part 1061 of Title 49, Code of Federal Regulations.

(Signature)_____

NAME
ADDRESS
TELEPHONE NUMBER

Subscribed and sworn to before me this _____ day of _____.

_____

NOTARY PUBLIC

14

How to Fight Your Local Airport

Modern airport noise litigation began in 1958 when Thomas Griggs brought suit against the Greater Pittsburgh Airport.[1] Mr. Griggs had purchased 20 acres of farmland long before an airport moved next door to him. At first, Mr. Griggs was awarded $12,690 for damage to his property caused by the airport. The award took into consideration noise, vibration, fear of disaster, anxiety, and general interference with the peaceful and quiet enjoyment of his property.

But the airport appealed the decision and the Supreme Court of Pennsylvania ruled that Mr. Griggs, although recognizing that he had been injured, could not sue the airport for damages. Finally, in 1962, the United States Supreme Court ruled in favor of Mr. Griggs. The Supreme Court held that when airplanes fly so low and so often over your property you can sue the airport operator for taking your property rights. The Fifth Amendment to the Constitution formed the basis for the Court's ruling: "No person shall be . . . deprived of . . . property, without due process of law; nor shall private property be taken for public use, without just compensation."

Because the Supreme Court ruled that airport owners are liable to homeowners for aircraft noise, it does not mean that your local airport will settle with you or cave in if you sue them. Your local airport will defend itself with a variety of legal techniques. It will raise at least two major defenses, the statute of limitations, and whether the planes go directly above your property. These two defenses are contradictory, as I will explain, but that won't stop the airport from raising them.

The statute of limitations is different in every state. It may be as little as two or three years. However, most states allow property owners to sue for 15 or 20 years to evict persons who trespass on their land. You may have heard the term *adverse possession*. Generally, if you are a squatter on someone's land for 15 or 20 years, you can gain title to it by possessing it "adverse" to the owner's rights. If someone uses your property as a shortcut for 15 or 20 years, they have created an "easement" through your property. Some courts have, in effect, ruled airplane flights above your property as "overflight easements." In other words, the airport may have created a right-of-way over your land by adverse possession. At least one court has ruled that it would not allow a government-owned airport to gain an easement by adverse possession.[2]

The contradiction in the two defenses is: If the airport denies overflights, they are denying one of the elements of an easement; but if they haven't flown over the property continuously for 15 or 20 years, they don't have an easement, and thus must pay the property owner for this easement.

1. *Griggs* v. *Allegheny County,* 369 U.S. 84 (1962).

2. *Petersen* v. *Port of Seattle,* 618 P.2d 67, 94 Wash. 2d 479 (Supreme Court of Washington, *en banc,* 1980).

Another typical defense is the claim that the airport took the property from a former owner of the property, and only that former owner could have sued. The counterargument is that if the easement was acquired from the former owner, why wasn't this easement recorded in the land records office to put future homeowners on notice?

If you file suit for the diminished value of your property due to aircraft noise, you should not do it alone. If your problem is severe enough, others must also have suffered. Join together with others because you will need to raise a lot of money to be able to prove your case at trial. You will need money for a real estate appraiser to prove that you suffered a damage to your property value. You will need the expert testimony of a surveyor who can demonstrate that aircraft fly directly above your property at a certain altitude. This type of lawsuit is difficult, and an attorney's advice should be sought. You may be able to find a sympathetic attorney who will represent you or your group on a contingency fee arrangement. This means that the attorney will only be paid a legal fee if the case is won or successfully settled.

THE NOISE CONTROL ACT

The Federal Noise Control Act was passed in 1972, but has been virtually ineffective in controlling noise from aircraft. The Federal Aviation Administration has certain duties under that act to reduce aircraft noise. No court has ordered the FAA to use all of its authority to reduce noise, even though the Noise Control Act would seem to require it. I have argued, in several aircraft noise cases, that if noise levels near an airport have increased since the Noise Control Act was passed, then the FAA has breached its responsibilities under that law to take all steps within its authority to reduce aircraft noise. In the sample aircraft noise complaint at the end of this chapter, Form 14-1, I have included a claim under the Noise Control Act. Before filing a Noise Control Act suit, you must give the FAA 60 days notice in advance. Form 14-3 is a notice-of-intent-to-sue letter.

THE NATIONAL ENVIRONMENTAL POLICY ACT (NEPA)

The National Environmental Policy Act (NEPA) requires an Environmental Impact Statement (EIS) for major federal actions which affect the environment. Whenever a runway is extended or a new one built, there must be a new EIS prepared, because airport expansion is considered a major federal action. If an airport authority fails to prepare an EIS, construction can be halted. I have included a NEPA claim in the sample complaint.

NUISANCE

The law concerning airport noise is developing and changing. The California courts have been at the forefront of this change and they have ruled, in the main, in favor of homeowners.

The courts in the eastern states have not been as responsive to the interests of homeowners as the California courts have. This is surprising since the communities near airports in Boston, New York, and Washington are much older than those in California. Let's hope that the California decisions are the beginning of a national trend.

A nuisance activity, which although possibly legal, causes unreasonable intereference with the rights of others. Air travel is not a nuisance if operated properly. If airports were located far from residential areas, there would be little problem. If only warehouses and factories were located under flight paths there would be no problem. However, we cannot relocate airports easily or cheaply. But we can operate our existing airports reasonably to minimize the burden on those who live under the flight paths.

This brings me to a David v. Goliath type of story, about two women who took on the San Francisco International Airport and won. They based their case on the nuisance law.

TAKE YOUR LOCAL AIRPORT TO SMALL CLAIMS COURT

Linda Dyson and Delores Huajardo had been complaining about San Francisco International Airport for years. The airport had been expanding during the 1970s, and by 1976, Dyson and Huajardo, no longer able to hear themselves think, began to write letters and organize. They wrote letters to the editors of newspapers, attended dozens of meetings of the airport commission and city councils, and lobbied at the state and national level to strengthen the noise laws.

In 1977, their small group had expanded to 25 like-minded homeowners. They organized a slow car drive-in at the airport arrival terminal to protest the noise source, and they held a press conference as the traffic built up at the airport. The police had an impossible time separating the demonstrators from the ordinary airport traffic, and San Francisco International Airport was tied in knots for hours. The protest did lead to hearings, but the group grew frustrated as no results came of the hearings, meetings, phone calls, and traditional political activity.

During this time, a landmark case on aircraft noise was winding its way through the California legal machinery.[3] In 1979, the California Supreme Court ruled that homeowners could sue for money damages for the nuisance and mental distress caused by aircraft noise, in addition to property loss claims. These damages included compensation for loss of sleep, interference with radio and television reception, and loss of enjoyment of home and yard. This case was brought in Los Angeles.

The group near San Francisco International Airport approached the attorneys that had handled the successful Los Angeles case, but they could not afford the $50,000 fee quoted. Using a guidebook to small claims courts, Mrs. Dyson and Mrs. Huajardo organized workshops to prepare small claims forms, and were joined by 170 of their neighbors. They received legal advice concerning the documents from a local attorney. A copy of the complaint form that they filed is included at the end of this chapter as Form 14-2. On May 13, 1981, they filed 172 complaints in San Francisco against the airport for the then maximum of $750 in small claims court. The court joined all of the cases together and heard five days of testimony in January, 1982. The complainants asked for damages that had occurred in the preceding 100-day period, because they felt that $7.50 per day, or a total of $750 for that period, was a reasonable amount. In general, the judge agreed and awarded the maximum to 116 of the plaintiffs and lesser amounts to the others for a total of about $100,000.

About 200 residents filed claims in the second round of the small claims battle. Meanwhile, at the beginning of 1982, the small claims limit in California was raised to $1500, so the homeowners again sought the maximum.

More than 200 plaintiffs filed claims in the third round battle in the San Francisco small claims court. The airport is appealing these claims, but it may seriously start to consider noise reduction to avoid unending litigation by furious homeowners who are only seeking peace and quiet. The judge who heard the first round of cases stated that the airport has not made reasonable efforts to minimize the noise problem. He criticized the airport's failure to implement a limited curfew so that the residents could sleep at night, and the failure to prohibit the noisiest aircraft from using the airport.

Small claims court might be the most affordable and effective way to reach the bureaucrats that are running the airports of this nation. Use Form 14-2 as the basis for your small claims complaint. Ask your local small claims court for the maximum allowable in your state, and check local requirements for notarization, special forms, and so forth. Filing fees in small claims courts are usually under $5.00. (*Note*: While the lawsuits mentioned above were pending, the California legislature passed a law forbidding future small claims cases against San Francisco Airport. At this writing, the appellate court has not yet ruled on the appeals. The citizens plan to challenge the new California law.).

---

3. *City of Los Angeles* v. *Greater Westchester Homwaeowners Association,* 26 Cal. 3d 86, 160 Cal. Rptr. 733, 603 P.2d 1329, cert. denied 499 U.S. 820 (1980).

FORM 14-1

Court Complaint Regarding Aircraft Noise

UNITED STATES DISTRICT COURT
FOR THE _____ DISTRICT OF _____
_____ DIVISION

_____,

Plaintiff,

v.   Civil Action No.

_____,

Secretary of Department of Health and
Human Services,

Defendant.

COMPLAINT FOR DECLARATORY, INJUNCTIVE
AND COMPENSATORY RELIEF

I. PRELIMINARY STATEMENT

1. This is an action brought by a homeowner and his/her spouse for damages and other relief against the Federal Aviation Administration, and _____ operator of _____ _____ airport for noise from aircraft operating at _____ Airport.

II. JURISDICTION

2. Jurisdiction is conferred on this court by 28 U.S.C. Sections 1331, 1343, 1346 and 1361 and by 42 U.S.C. Section 4911.

3. The amount in controversy exceeds the sum or value of $10,000, exclusive of interest and costs.

III. PLAINTIFFS

4. Plaintiff _____ is the owner and is a resident of the home at _____ _____. Plaintiff _____ has owned the real property for approximately _____ years.

5. Plaintiff _____ is the wife of _____ and has resided at _____ for _____.

IV. DEFENDANTS

6. Defendant _____ is the Administrator of the Federal Aviation Administration.

7. _____ is the owner and operator of _____ Airport.

V. FACTUAL ALLEGATIONS

8. The _____ is responsible for maintenance and operation at _____ Airport.

9. The Federal Aviation Administration and its Administrator are responsible for implementing rules and regulations concerning the operations of _____ Airport.

10. Approximately _____ planes take off or land at _____ per day, an average of _____ plane(s) per minute between the hours of _____ A.M. and _____ P.M., _____ days a week.

11. Since _____, the defendants have dramatically increased the number of planes operating at _____ and have dramatically increased the number of planes flying directly over their residence.

12. The noise and vibrations from aircraft flying into and out of _____ Airport disturb and interfere with plaintiffs' enjoyment of their property by causing them to awake earlier then desired, by interfering with normal conversations, by interfering with radio and television reception and programming, by interfering with telephone conversations, and by causing permanent damage to plaintiffs' hearing and health.

13. The noise and vibrations from aircraft flying into and out of _____ have caused the value of plaintiffs' residence to be less than it would have been without this noise and vibration.

VI. FIRST CAUSE OF ACTION: Fourteenth and Fifth Amendment Violations By the Federal Defendants.

14. Plaintiffs incorporate by reference paragraphs one (1) through thirteen (13) inclusive.

15. The _____ defendant's operation of _____ permitting noisy aircraft to fly directly over their residence at extremely low altitudes, at an average of _____ per minute from _____ A.M. to _____ P.M., _____ days a week, constitutes a taking of property without just compensation, in violation of the Fourteenth and Fifth Amendments to the Constitution of the United States.

VII. SECOND CAUSE OF ACTION: Nuisance (All Defendants Responsible).

16. Plaintiffs incorporate by reference paragraphs one (1) through fifteen (15) inclusive.

17. Defendant's operation of noisy aircraft over the plaintiffs' and other residences, at low altitudes, from _____ A.M. until _____ P.M. and later on many occasions, constitutes a public nuisance.

18. There is no reasonable need to permit aircraft to take off or land from _____ before _____ A.M. on Saturday and Sunday mornings. Any need for this service is far outweighed by the right of plaintiffs and others to sleep, if they so desire, on Saturday or Sunday mornings.

19. Defendants have operated _____ Airport by failing to use all reasonable means at their disposal to reduce noise, including _____.

VIII. CAUSE OF ACTION: Violations of the Noise Control Act
of 1972 By All Defendants

20. Plaintiffs incorporate by reference paragraphs one (1) through nineteen (19) inclusive.

21. The federal defendants have a duty to the "fullest extent consistent with their authority . . . to further the policy declared in section 4901(b) of this title." 42 U.S.C. Section 4903.

22. 42 U.S.C. Section 4901(b) states in part:

> The Congress declares that it is the
> policy of the United States to promote
> an environment for all Americans free
> from noise that jeopardizes their
> health or welfare.

23. Federal defendants have breached their duty to promote an environment free from noise that jeopardizes health and welfare by permitting noise levels at plaintiffs' residence and in other areas to increase during the past _____ years.

IX. FOURTH CASE OF ACTION: Violations of the National
Environmental Policy Act

24. Plaintiffs incorporate by reference paragraphs one (1) through twenty-three (23) inclusive.

25. Defendants have been designing a new runway known as _____.

26. This runway project is a major federal action which will significantly affect the environment.

27. This new runway will cause harm to plaintiffs by _____.

28. Defendants failed to comply with the National Environmental Policy Act because they have failed to prepare an environmental impact statement concerning this runway.

X. INJURY

29. Plaintiffs have suffered and continue to suffer irreparable injury. There is no adequate remedy at law which would fully compensate plaintiffs for the harm which has been and continues to be suffered by them.

30. The residence at _____ has not appreciated as much as it would have had defendants not increased the airplane noise in that area.

31. Plaintiffs have suffered the following injuries as a direct and proximate result of defendant's actions and inactions:

(a) loss of enjoyment of the use of their property;

(b) interference with conversations;

(c) interference with television, radio and stereo reception and listening enjoyment;

(d) an increase in nervous tension;

(e) deterioration of hearing;

(f) increase in the risk of bodily injury and property damage caused by an aircraft accident near their property;

(g) damage to person and property by vibrations, air pollution, and other emissions from aircraft.

XI. REQUEST FOR RELIEF

Plaintiffs request that this Court order:

A. _____ defendant to pay plaintiffs $_____ for taking property without due process of law.

B. Enjoin defendants from flying or permitting aircraft to land or take off at _____ before 8:00 A.M. Monday through Friday, before 10:00 A.M. Saturday and Sunday, or land or take off after 9:00 P.M.

C. Enjoin defendants from working further on runway _____ without first preparing an environmental impact statement acceptable to this Court.

D. Other relief at this Court deems just and appropriate.

(Signature) _____
PLAINTIFF'S NAME
ADDRESS
TELEPHONE NUMBER

FORM 14-2

Small Claims Complaint Concerning Aircraft Noise

Claim of _____
                                    CLAIMANT

      V.

City and County of San Francisco

CLAIM FOR PERSONAL INJURIES
Section 910 of Government Code

TO THE CLERK OF THE CITY AND COUNTY OF SAN FRANCISCO AND TO THE BOARD OF SUPERVISORS:

    YOU ARE NOTIFIED that _____, whose address is _____, _____, California, claims damages from the CITY AND COUNTY OF SAN FRANCISCO in the amount computed as of the date of presentation of this claim of $1,500.00.

    This claim is based upon personal injuries, annoyance, inconvenience, mental suffering, fear, anxiety and distress, which has occurred within 100 days prior to the date of the filing of this claim by reason of the continuing nuisance of the operation of airplanes from the San Francisco International Airport over, near and about the properties of the claimant. Said airplanes deposit noxious fumes, cause vibrations and excessive noise and cause the claimant to fear the danger of a collision or crash, interfering with their sleep, enjoyment of their home and property during waking hours, preventing the enjoyment of the home in visits, the enjoyment of television, causing damage to the home by reason of vibration, causing smut, dust and causing claimant to inhale toxic materials, all to the damage of each in the sum of $1,500.00.

    The damages claimed to date are computed including general damages and special damages such as broken windows, repairs to television, medical expenses and other items of special damage. Future damages will continue to accrue not only as a natural consequence of the damages inflicted to date, but by reason of the continuing nuisance of the operation of the San Francisco International Airport and the airplanes therefrom, in close proximity to the plaintiff's property.

    All notices of other communications with regard to this claim should be sent to the claimant,

_____, California,

DATED:_____

(Signature) _____
NAME

FORM 14-3

Notice of Intent to Sue Under Noise Control Act

CERTIFIED MAIL

RETURN RECEIPT REQUESTED

NAME_____

ADDRESS_____

DATE_____

Administrator
Federal Aviation Administration
Washington, D.C. 20553

RE: NOTICE OF INTENT TO SUE

Dear Mr. Administrator,

This letter serves as notice of intent to sue under the Noise Control Act of 1972. I am writing on behalf of _____.

You have violated the Noise Control Act by allowing noise levels to increase at _____ _____ since 1972 and by _____.

If these violations are not corrected within 60 days I intend to file suit against you on behalf of the persons listed above.

Sincerely yours,

(Signature)_____
NAME

cc: Administrator EPA
Attorney General

AIRCRAFT NOISE ORGANIZATIONS

NATIONAL

Neighbors Opposed to Irritating Sound Emissions
5225 Wisconsin Avenue, N.W.
Suite 601
Washington, DC 20015

STATES

California
Burbank Anti-Noise Group
P.O. Box 6703
Burbank, CA 91510

Linda Dyson
2580 Summit Drive
Burlingame, CA 94010

Westside Federation Against Jet Noise
P.O. Box 49007
Los Angeles, CA 90049

CAN (Californians Against Noise)
1043 Sonoma Avenue
Menlo Park, CA 94025

Mr. James R. Shelton
Chairman for Sounds
255 Heath Street
Milpitas, CA 95035

Montclair Noise Abatement Group
33 Castle Lane
Oakland, CA 94611

Airport Coalition
4434 Casitas Street
San Diego, CA 92107

Airport Relocation Commission
3120 Goldsmith Street
San Diego, CA 92106

Move Lindbergh Field
P.O. Box 7399
San Diego, CA 92107

UAFT
P.O. Box 7399
San Diego, CA 92107

Studio City Residents Association
P.O. Box 1374
Studio City, CA 91604

Sun Valley Homeowners
P.O. Box 1303
Sun Valley, CA 90027

Colorado
W. 6th Avenue Neighbors Association
6380 W. 6th Street
Lakewood, CO 80214

Citizens Against Noise
3011 Country Club Drive
Colorado Springs, CO 80909

Connecticut
Northwest Greenwich Connecticut Association
Riverside Road
Greenwich, CT 06880

District of Columbia
NOISE
5225 Wisconsin Avenue, N.W.
Suite 601
Washington, DC 20015

Florida
ROAR
4311 Playa Court
Orlando, FL 32809

Residents Against Airport Expansion
P.O. Box 2811
West Palm Beach, FL 33402

Hawaii
Citizens Against Noise
P.O. Box 27705
Honolulu, HI 96827

Illinois
NOISE
1420 Miner Street
Des Plaines, IL 60016

O'Hare Airport Noise Group
194 Sherwood
Wood Dale, IL 60191

Citizens Against Noise
2729 West Lunt Avenue
Chicago, IL 60645

Kentucky
NOISE
P.O. Box 5242
Louisville, KY 40205

Maryland
Maryland Citizens Concerned About Aircraft Noise
11 Russell Road
Cabin John, MD 20818

Piscataway Hills Citizens Association, Inc.
P.O. Box 55062
Fort Washington, MD 20022

Massachusetts
Runway 27 Coalition
18 Greenough Avenue
Jamaica Plains, MA 02130

Squantum Airnoise Commission
127 Bayside Road
Squantum, MA 02171

Winthrop Environmental Committee Against Noise
   (WECAN)
17 Bay View Avenue
Winthrop, MA 02152

New Jersey
Ironbound Community Corporation
95 Fleming Avenue
Newark, NJ 07105

New York
Citizens for a Quieter City
P.O. Box 796, Ansonia Station
New York, NY 10023

Oregon
North Portland Citizens
7508 North Hereford
Portland, OR 97203

Texas
Citizens Against Noise
9720 Wisterwood
Dallas, TX 75238

Virginia
Norfolk Noise Abatement Movement, Inc.
5314 Arthur Circle
Norfolk, VA 23502

Washington.
Citizens Against Noise
P.O. Box 7126
Olympia, WA 98507

Beacon Hill Community
5012 26th Avenue South
Seattle, WA 98108

15

How to Fight Hazardous Waste Dumps and Other Dirty Deeds

In the spring of 1978, Lois Gibbs discovered that her son's elementary school was built over a hazardous waste dump. Twenty-thousand tons of toxic chemicals were buried there years ago by the Hooker Chemical Corporation. Michael Gibbs had developed asthma, epilepsy, and blood and urinary disorders. Mrs. Gibbs felt that her son's medical problems were caused by his exposure to chemical wastes.

Lois Gibbs first went to the local board of education to ask them to transfer her son from the contaminated school. They refused to transfer Michael Gibbs. They believed if Michael was transfered, it would mean that the school would have to be closed. The board's reasoning was that if it was too dangerous for Michael Gibbs, it would be too dangerous for all of the young children at the school.

Other local, state, and federal officials claimed that they would investigate Mrs. Gibbs' concerns, but little happened. Mrs. Gibbs went from door to door to talk to her neighbors about the hazards caused by the chemical dump in their backyards. In August, 1978, the Love Canal Homeowners Association was formed.

The Homeowners Association met with scientists and demanded that they explain the health hazards in plain English, not bureaucratese. When the authorities announced that pregnant women and children under two would be evacuated, the homeowners demanded to know why not others? If chil-

dren under two were unsafe in their homes, how safe would a three-year-old be?

The Love Canal Homeowners Association learned the laws that applied to the toxic wastes that were dumped in their back yards, and gathered scientific evidence to show how they were harmed. They made a political issue out of the dumpsite. The governor of New York at the time, Hugh Carey, who was running for reelection, agreed to evacuate all Love Canal families who lived nearest to the dump. As a result of continuing pressure, press conferences, and lobbying by the citizens, President Carter, during the 1980 Presidential Campaign, ordered the remaining families to be evacuated.

The same political pressure led Congress to pass the Comprehensive Environmental Response, Compensation and Liability Act (CERCLA). This law was passed on December 11, 1980, and is known as the Superfund law. The Superfund law instituted a tax on toxic chemicals to provide for cleanup of hazardous waste sites. Because of Lois Gibbs, the rest of us will have an easier time dealing with the dump in our backyards.

HOW TO STOP A NEW DUMP FROM MOVING TO YOUR NEIGHBORHOOD

In July, 1980, Tracy and John Marsh learned from their local newspaper that Stabatrol, a New York-based company, was planning to dump chemical wastes over a 530-acre area near their Pennsylvania home. They were furious. They immediately began calling neighbors and friends to see if there was a way to stop the dump. Soon they organized OUCH (Opposing Unnecessary Chemical Hazards).

The Marsh's investigation revealed that Stabatrol had illegally begun construction. OUCH stirred up public pressure with phone calls and newspaper articles, and in response their township obtained a court injunction barring further construction on the site.

In September of the same year, the Pennsylvania Department of Environmental Resources held a public hearing. Over 3,000 area residents attended the hearing, and OUCH submitted a petition against the dump, containing 40,000 signatures. Nonetheless, the DER granted Stabatrol an operating permit.

OUCH petitioned the DER to revoke Stabatrol's operating permit in March of 1981. Because of mounting citizen pressure, the Department investigated the Stabatrol company's operations throughout Pennsylvania and turned up strong evidence of water pollution caused by the dumpsites. DER then suspended all Stabatrol operations in the state.

OUCH joined with 16 other activist groups throughout Pennsylvania to fight against all dump locations in the state. Publicity and perseverance were the primary qualities that caused OUCH to succeed.

THE EPA SUPERFUND

The Superfund was established by Congress in the Comprehensive Environmental Response, Compensation, and Liability Act (CERCLA) in December, 1980, in response to disasters from massive unregulated toxic dumpsites around the United States, including in the Love Canal. The Environmental Protection Agency is responsible for managing the Superfund Program.

The fund is financed by a tax on the sale and disposal of chemicals. In 1982, the fund included $1.6 billion for cleanup costs of these toxic waste sites.

The legislation was not without compromise. Some of the proposed laws included compensation for the victims of ground pollution. However, the law currently only provides funds for clean-up costs. The only remedy that victims have is to sue the polluters directly. However, some states, such as New York, have paid victims for moving costs, and bought homes, such as the Love Canal sites, when there was no ability to sell contaminated homes to others for residential uses.

A list of the worst sites identified for clean-up by EPA is included at the end of this chapter. EPA has a toll-free hotline concerning the Superfund. The number is 800-424-9346. In the District of Columbia, the number is 382-3000. There is a list of organizations at the end of this chapter who can help you get rid of hazardous wastes.

Lois Gibbs has formed the Citizen's Clearinghouse for Hazardous Wastes, Inc. They can be contacted at:

Citizen's Clearninghouse for
Hazardous Wastes, Inc.
P.O. Box 7097
Arlington, VA 22207
(703) 532-6816

At the end of this section of the book there is a state by state list of environmental organizations. These organizations will help you or refer you to someone who can.

CERCLA INTERIM PRIORITY LIST

Alabama
Triana (Redstone Arsenal)

American Samoa
Taputimu Farm

Arizona
19th Avenue Landfill

Arkansas
Fritt Industries
Allen Transformer
Mid-South Wood Products
Vertac, Inc.

California
Aerojet General Corporation
Iron Mountain Mines, Inc.
Stringfellow Acid Pits

Colorado
Denver Radium Sites

Connecticut
Laurel Park Landfill

Delaware
Delaware Sand and Gravel–Llangollen
   Army Creek Landfill
Stauffer Chemical
Tybouts Corners

District of Columbia
Fort Lincoln Barrel Site

Florida
Alpha Chemical Corporation
American Creosote Works
Biscayne Aquifer (Northwest 58th
   Street Landfill, Miami Drum, Varsol Spill)
Broward County Solid Waste
   Disposal Facility
Coleman–Evans Wood
   Preserving Company
Gold Coast Oil Corporation
Hollingsworth Solderless
   Terminal Company
Picketville Road Landfill
Pioneer Sand Company
Reeves Southeastern Corporation
Sapp Battery Salvage
Taylor Road Landfill
Timber Lake Battery Disposal
Tower Chemical Company
Whitehouse Waste Oil Pits
Zellwood Ground Water
   Contamination Site

Guam
Ordot Landfill

Georgia
Luminous Processes, Inc.

Illinois
Outboard Marine Corporation

Indiana
Neal's Landfill
Seymour Recycling Corporation

Iowa
Aidex Corporation

Kansas
Arkansas City Dump Site

Kentucky
A L Taylor Site ("Valley of
   the Drums")

Maine
Winthrop Town Landfill

Maryland
Chemical Metals Industries, Inc.

Massachusetts
Charles George Land
   Reclamation Trust
Mark Phillip Trust (Woburn)
Nyanza Chemical Waste Dump
Re-Solve, Inc.

Michigan
Gratiot County Landfill

Minnesota
Andover Sites
Koppers Gas and Coke Plant
National Lead–Taracorp Site
Oakdale Dump Sites
Reilly Tar and Chemical Corp.

Mississippi
Walcotte Chemical Company

Missouri
Ellisville Area Sites
Fulbright Landfill

New Hampshire
Keefe Environmental Services
Ottati & Goss/Kingston
   Steel Drum
Sylvester's

New Jersey
Bridgeport Rental and
   Oil Services
Burnt Fly Bog
Chemical Control
D'Imperio Property
Goose Farm
Kin Buc Landfill
Lipari Landfill
Lone Pine Landfill
Pijack Farm
Price Landfill
Spence Farm
Upper Freehold

New Mexico
AT & SF Railroad (Clovis)
Homestake Mining
United Nuclear Corporation

New York
Batavia Landfill
Facet Enterprises
Love Canal
Marathon Battery Corporation
Niagara County Refuse Site
Old Bethpage Landfill
Olean Well Fields
Pollution Abatement Services

North Carolina
PCB Spills in North Carolina

North Dakota
Arsenic Trioxide Disposal Site

Ohio
Chem-Dyne Corporation
Chemicals and Minerals Reclamation
Fields Brook
Summit National Liquid
  Disposal Services

Oklahoma
Criner Waste Disposal
Tar Creek

Pennsylvania
ABM-Wade
Bruin Lagoon
Butler Tunnel
Hranica Landfill
Lehigh Electric and
  Engineering
Lindane Dump
Lord-Shope Landfill
McAdoo Associates

Rhode Island
Davis Liquid Chemical Waste
  Disposal Site
Picillo Farm Site
Western Sand and Gravel Site

South Carolina
South Carolina Recycling and
  Disposal Co. (Bluff Road)

South Dakota
Whitewood Creek

Tennesee
North Hollywood Dump

Texas
Bioecology Systems, Inc.
French Limited Disposal Site
Motco
Sikes Disposal Pits

Utah
Rose Park

Vermont
Pine Street Canal

Virginia
Chisman Creek Disposal
Mathews Electroplating

Washington
Commencement Bay

West Virginia
West Virginia Ordinance Site

SUPERFUND PRIORITY SITES

Arizona
Globe
Tucson Airport

Colorado
Central City
Marshall L/F
Woodbury Chemical

Delaware
Harvey & Knott L/F

Illinois
A & F Greenup
ACME Solvents
Wauconda Sand & Gravel

Kentucky
Distler Farm
Lee's Lane L/F

Louisiana
Bayou Sorrel
Old Inger

Massachusetts
New Bedford
Silresim

Michigan
Berlin & Farro
Rose Township Dump
G & H Landfill
Liquid Disposal
Northernaire Plating
OTT/Story
Verona Well Field

Minnesota
Burlington Northern
FMC Corporation
LeHillier
New Brighton
Waste Disposal Engineering

Mississippi
Plastifax Inc.

New Jersey
Gloucester Environment
Helen Kramer L/F
Krysowaty Farm
Swope Oil
Syncon Resins

New Mexico
South Valley

New York
Kentucky Avenue Wellfield
Sinclair Refining
York Oil

Ohio
Laskin/Poplar

Pennsylvania
Drake Chemical
Osborne Dump

South Carolina
SCRDI Dixiana

Texas
Crystal Chemical
Harris Site
Highlands Acid

Washington
Western Processing

16

What You Can Do About Air Pollution

The Clean Air Act was passed by Congress in 1970 to start the long process of cleaning this nation's polluted air. Air pollution is divided into categories by its sources. There are three basic types of sources of air pollution, (1) stationary sources, (2) mobile sources, and (3) indirect sources.

An example of a stationary source is a power plant or an incinerator. Automobiles, trucks, and airplanes are examples of mobile sources. Indirect sources of pollution are places like airports, shopping centers, and parking lots, which do not in themselves pollute, but attract mobile sources of pollution.

Mobile sources are regulated on the national level. The pollution control devices on your automobile are required by the Clean Air Act.

Other sources of pollution are regulated at the state level. Each state and the District of Columbia must submit a plan for reducing air pollution to the federal Environmental Protection Agency (EPA) for approval. If the plan is rejected, the EPA has the right to institute a plan of its own. If the plan is approved, the state regulations in the plan become a part of the federal law.

The Clean Air Act has a citizens suit provision which allows citizens to file suit to correct violations of the Act. This provision of the Clean Air Act has become the prototype for allowing citizens to bring environmental suits.

Publicity is often enough to stop air pollution. In 1979, I represented a public interest group who had learned that the Capitol Power Plant was violating the local clean air laws. This plant supplies heat and cooling to Congress and the United States Supreme Court.

Under the federal Clean Air Act, citizens are required to give polluters 60 days notice before filing suit. The purpose of this time period is to give the polluter a chance to correct the violation. Formal notice was served on Thomas P. ("Tip") O'Neill, Jr., the Speaker of the House of Representatives, President Pro Tempore of the Senate, Chairman of various committees, and Administrator of the EPA. Also, informal notice, by press release, was given to the *Washington Post* and television and radio stations. The Washington media loved the story. The *Post* ran it on page one, and every television station covered it.

The lead for most of the stories was that Congress, who passed the Clean Air Act in the first place, was being accused of violating it. All of this publicity came before suit was filed. And the powerbrokers in Congress did not want this publicity to continue, so it was ordained that the suit would be settled. The case was settled quickly and the power plant has cleaned up its act. However, not every case of air pollution is this juicy.

INVESTIGATE

At first you must have a hunch that a power plant, steel mill, or other pollution source is violating the law. Your local pollution control officials may help you. Then again they may not, depending on the political pressures on them.

I met with the District of Columbia officials concerning the Capitol Power Plant. They were furious about the plant because they had tried to serve notice of violation on the engineer for the plant, and he refused to accept it. The D.C. officials went no further, probably not wanting to ruffle Congressional feathers. Your local inspectors, or other officials, may likewise not want to upset the local industry. Washington, like many cities, is a company town: the company is the Federal Government.

You will need to find clear violations of the air pollution laws. The federal Clean Air Act requires the state to submit a plan for reducing air pollution. Every state has submitted a plan, which is basically a list of local statutes designed to reduce air pollution. These local statutes, when approved by the federal EPA, have the force and effect of federal law.

You may have to use your state's Freedom of Information Act to obtain an inspector's report concerning violations at a particular plant. See Chapter 25, which discusses the federal Freedom of Information Act.

If you do not get evidence from your state or local officials of pollution violations, you may have to hire a scientist to measure pollution from the plant and be available to testify that it violates the law. When you get the necessary proof, you are ready for the next step.

NOTICE OF INTENT TO FILE SUIT

Before filing suit, you must give formal notice that you intend to file suit to correct the violations. You must give notice to three parties:

1. the polluter
2. the Administrator of the Environmental Protection Agency, 401 M Street, S.W., Washington DC 20460
3. the Governor of the state in which the pollution occurs.

A sample notice letter is included at the end of this chapter as Form 16-1. This notice, and the copies to the Administrator of the EPA and the governor, should be sent by certified mail, return receipt requested, to provide you with proof that you gave the proper notice.

At the time that you mail this notice, it would be appropriate to hold a press conference or to send out a press release. At the press conference or with the press release, you should include copies of the notice letter and evidence you have concerning the violations, such as pollution measuring machine readouts, photographs, or an expert's report concerning the violations.

BEFORE FILING SUIT

If you file suit against the U.S. Steel Corporation, they will paper you to death. You will need help. A list of environmental organizations is included at the end of this part of the book. Contact environmental groups in your area for assistance and advice.

You will need top-notch expert witnesses to prove your case. A university in your area may be a starting point. A professor of environmental engineering may be interested in your cause and be willing to give you his or her services at a reduced rate. If you prevail in the case, you can be awarded expert witness fees and attorney's fees.

Environmental law is exceedingly and unnecessarily complicated. A sample complaint is included in this chapter as Form 16-2, but after you have modified the complaint to fit your situation, sit down with an attorney familiar with the Clean Air Act, and have him review your draft before filing it in court. An attorney may be willing to represent you on a reduced-fee basis, if you agree to help with research and footwork. The Clean Air Act provides that if you win, the other side has to pay for your attorney's fees.

If your state EPA or the federal EPA has brought suit concerning the same violations as you are complaining about, you cannot file a separate lawsuit; but you may intervene in the pending case. You must base your case on a specific violation of a precise standard. For example, a state plan called for the closing of a certain incinerator. The court held that this was precise enough for a citizens' suit under the Clean Air Act. The basis of your suit must rest on one or more of the following:

1. violation of an emission standard or limitation
2. violation of an order issued by a state or the EPA

Other examples of what constitutes a precise emission standard or limitation are reducing parking in certain areas, imposing tolls on a bridge, and banning taxis from cruising.

FORM 16-1

Notice of Intent to Sue Under Clean Air Act

CERTIFIED MAIL
RETURN RECEIPT REQUESTED
DATE _____

(Address letter to Polluter.)

RE: NOTICE OF INTENT TO SUE
FOR CLEAN AIR ACT VIOLATIONS

Dear _____,

This letter serves as notice, pursuant to 40 C.F.R. Part 54, issued under 42 U.S.C. Section 7604, of the intention of _____ to file suit concerning the violations of the Clean Air Act described below.

Your company has violated the _____ regulations of _____, which were approved as a part of the State Implementation Plan, by the Environmental Protection Agency. These violations have occurred continuously since _____ (date).

Unless these violations are abated within 60 days, suit will be filed to protect the health and welfare of the residents in the area of _____.

Sincerely yours,

(Signature) _____
NAME

cc: Administrator, U.S.
Environmental Protection Agency
401 M Street, S.E.
Washington, DC 20460

Governor
State of _____

FORM 16-2

Federal Court Complaint Concerning Air Pollution

UNITED STATES DISTRICT COURT

FOR THE _____ DISTRICT OF _____

_____ DIVISION

_____,

Plaintiff,

v.   Civil Action No.

_____,

Defendant,

COMPLAINT FOR DECLARATORY, COMPENSATORY AND INJUNCTIVE RELIEF;
JURY TRIAL DEMANDED

I. NATURE OF THE CASE

1. This is a citizens' suit brought under 42 U.S.C. Section 7604 to en____ __at the _____ _____ is brought into compliance with the _____ Air Quality Control Regulations and the Clean Air Act.

II. JURISDICTION

2. Jurisdiction is conferred on this court by 42 U.S.C. Sections 7413 and 7418 (Clean Air Act) and by 28 U.S.C. Sections 1331 (federal question), 1346 (United States as defendant), 1361 (action to compel officer of the United States to perform his duty) and 2201 and 2202 (declaratory judgment).

3. Notice of intent to file suit was served upon the defendant or its agents, _____ ____ Governor, State of _____, and the Administrator of the United States Environmental Protection Agency. A copy of the notice on intent to sue is attached to the complaint as plaintiff's exhibit 1.

4. More than sixty days have passed since receipt of the notices described in paragraph three (3), the violations complained of have not been corrected and an enforcement action has not been brought by either the State of _____ or by the Administrator of the Environmental Protection Agency.

III. PLAINTIFF

5. Plaintiff _____ lives and works in close proximity to the _____ _____ and breathes the air contaminated by the _____.

IV. DEFENDANT

6. Defendant_____

_____

_____

V. FACTUAL ALLEGATIONS

7. Emissions from the _____ have been and continue to be in violation of _____ (Air Quality Regulations).

8. Visible and particulate emissions from the _____ are harmful to the health of plaintiff and others who must breathe the air into which these pollutants are discharged.

VI. FIRST CAUSE OF ACTION: Violations of the Clean Air Act

9. Plaintiffs incorporate by reference paragraphs one (1) through eight (8), inclusive.

10. The Air Quality Control Regulations of the State of _____ were submitted as a part of the State Implementation Plan of the State of _____ to the United States Environmental Protection Agency (EPA), in accordance with Section 110 of the Clean Air Act (42 U.S.C. Section 7410) and were approved by EPA (40 C.F.R. Part _____, _____ Fed. Reg. _____ (date) and the revisions were approved, _____ Fed. Reg. _____ (date) and _____ Fed. Reg. _____ (date).

11. The approval by EPA made the Air Quality Control Regulations enforceable as federal law under Section 304 of the Clean Air Act (42 U.S.C. Section 7604).

VII. SECOND CAUSE OF ACTION: Violations of the _____ of _____ Air Quality Control Regulations.

12. Plaintiff incorporates by reference paragraphs one (1) through eleven (11), inclusive.

13. The Defendant has not sought a variance from the requirements of the regulations cited in paragraph seven (7), nor has the _____ sought an exemption under Section 118 of the Clean Air Act, 42 U.S.C. Section 7418(b).

14. Visible and particulate emissions from the _____ continue to be in excess of the allowable levels established by the State of _____ Air Quality Control Regulations. These emissions are detrimental to the quality of the air in the State of _____ and cause deterioration of the public health, welfare, comfort, convenience, and enjoyment of the plaintiff and other persons in the State of _____.

VIII. THIRD CAUSE OF ACTION: Negligence *Per Se*

15. Plaintiff incorporates by reference paragraphs one (1) through fourteen (14), inclusive.

16. Defendant's violations of the Clean Air Act and the State of _____ Air Quality Control Regulations constitutes negligence *per se.*

IX. FOURTH CAUSE OF ACTION: Nuisance

17. Plaintiff incorporates by reference paragraphs one (1) through sixteen (16), inclusive.

18. Defendant's operation of the _____ is a public nuisance detrimental to public health and welfare which can be abated by currently available technology at reasonable cost.

X. IRREPARABLE INJURY

19. Plaintiff has suffered and continues to suffer injury to his health and welfare as a direct result of the actions and omissions of the defendant. Plaintiff's injury cannot be adequately compensated with monetary relief. Plaintiff's injury continues to irreparably increase every day.

XI. REQUEST FOR RELIEF

WHEREFORE, plaintiff requests that this Court grant the following relief:

A. Declare that the defendant is operating the _____ in violation of the State of _____ Air Quality Control Regulations, in violation of the Clean Air Act and by these violations is maintaining a public nuisance.

B. Enter an order directing the defendants to immediately cease operations at the _____ _____ that result in violations of state and federal law;

C. Enter an order directing the defendant to install the latest available pollution abatement equipment at the _____ according to a timetable established by the court as reasonable;

D. Award plaintiff costs and reasonable attorney's fees; and

E. Award plaintiff damages in the amount of $_____.

F. Order such further relief as the court deems just and appropriate.

(Signature) _____
PLAINTIFF'S NAME
ADDRESS
TELEPHONE NUMBER

JURY DEMAND

Plaintiff demands a trial by jury.

(Signature) _____
PLAINTIFF'S NAME
ADDRESS
TELEPHONE NUMBER

17

How to Make a Federal Case out of Water Pollution

In the 1970s, Congress created a powerful weapon for citizens' groups fighting water pollution. If the State or Federal environmental agencies will not sue a polluter, citizens can legally take the law into their own hands. The Federal Water Pollution Control Act provides citizens with this power.

BASICS OF THE WATER POLLUTION CONTROL ACT

The water pollution control law provides that "the discharge of any pollutant by any person" into waters of the United States is illegal. However, the law provides that the federal Environmental Protection Agency may issue permits for discharging pollutants into waters of the United States. Federal law also permits landfill and dredging operations which are approved by the Army Corps of Engineers.[1]

What are "waters of the United States"? The term has been broadly interpreted to include nearly every body of water in the United States. It includes all streams, man-made canals, wetlands, swamplands above the mean high water line, coastal waters, and intrastate lakes. The only safe exclusion from the law is a pond solely on one person's land. Otherwise, it is fair to assume that the Water Pollution Control Act applies to nearly all surface waters in the United States.

CITIZENS' SUITS

If a polluter is discharging anything but pure water into a river, lake, or ocean, a citizen can sue him or her directly, unless the polluter has a permit allowing the discharge of the pollutant. If there is no permit or if the terms of the permit are being violated, you must give 60 days notice of your intention to file suit. You must send the notice of intention to sue to:

1. the polluter
2. the Administrator of the U.S. Environmental Protection Agency
3. the Governor of the State(s) involved

You should send the notice by certified mail, return receipt requested, so that you will have proof that you gave proper notice.

It is a good idea to send copies of the notice letter to counties involved, and other state and local agencies concerned with natural resources or environmental protection. As I have stated concerning clean air notices, newspapers and radio and television stations are interested in knowing about violations of environmental laws. A press release or a press conference are appropriate at the time of giv-

---

1. Section 404 of the law provides for these permits, which are known as "404" permits.

ing notice. Corporations despise bad publicity, and may be convinced to clean up their operations if they want to avoid further bad publicity. A copy of a notice of intent to sue under the Federal Water Pollution Control Act is included at the end of this chapter as Form 17-1.

Citizens in Friendship Heights and Somerset, Maryland, both suburbs of Washington, D.C., noticed oil and cement being discharged into a local stream. They investigated and discovered that the pollution was from a construction site for the regional subway authority, the Washington Metropolitan Area Transit Authority, known as Metro. Four contractors were working at the site, including Bechtel, one of the largest construction firms in the world. The citizens learned that no one had bothered to obtain a permit for the discharge of pollutants.

The group of citizens found powerful allies in their towns and in several local businesses, including the Prudential Insurance Company. They retained an attorney who gave all the construction companies and Metro notices of intent to sue. The local news media jumped on the story and brought pressure on Metro to stop polluting the Little Falls stream.

Negotiations for a settlement began immediately. Nevertheless, after the 60-day waiting period expired, the group of citizens, companies, and the local town filed suit in federal court. Within a few months there was a settlement, and the pollution source has been eliminated. The combination of legal pressure and media publicity gave the citizen coalition the result they wanted.

Form 17-2 is a complaint for filing in federal court for injunctive relief and for monetary damages. Since the law permits the court to award successful plaintiff's attorney's fees, you may find an attorney who is willing to represent you on a contingency basis. At the end of this chapter there is a list of environmental organizations in every state who can help you with your case. If they cannot help you, they should be able to refer you to another organization or an attorney who can represent you in filing a complaint under the federal Water Pollution Control Act.

FORM 17-1

Notice of Intent to Sue for Water Pollution

CERTIFIED MAIL
RETURN RECEIPT REQUESTED
Date _____

To: Polluter

RE: NOTICE OF INTENT TO SUE UNDER THE
FEDERAL WATER POLLUTION CONTROL ACT

Dear _____,

This letter serves as notice of intent to sue pursuant to the Federal Water Pollution Control Act, 33 U.S.C. Section 1365. If the violations listed in this notice are not permanently terminated and the environmental damage caused by the violations is not remedied within 60 days, the complainants may commence civil action against you. They have the right to seek abatement of the violation, penalties, damages, attorneys fees, and costs pursuant to the Act.

The violations consist of the discharge of pollution into the _____ in the town of _____, State of _____, without a permit issued pursuant to Section 402 of the Act and in violation of _____ of the laws of the State of _____. The pollutants and the location of the violations are as follows:

               Location   *Pollutant*

The complainants believe that the violations occur as follows: _____
_____.

In addition to constituting violations of Section 301(a) of the Act for discharging without a permit, the discharges in question are in violation of the prohibitions and limitation established by the State of _____, under the law of the State, _____. Since the State of _____ operates its own permit program, which has been approved by the U.S. Environmental Protection Agency pursuant to Section 402(b) of the Act, these violations also constitute violations of the effluent limitations as defined by the Act.

Sincerely yours,

(Signatures) _____
COMPLAINANTS

FORM 17-2

Federal Court Complaint for Water Pollution

THE UNITED STATES DISTRICT COURT

FOR THE _____ DISTRICT OF _____

_____ DIVISION

_____,

Plaintiff,

v.   Civil Action No.

_____,

Defendant.

COMPLAINT FOR DAMAGES AND INJUNCTIVE RELIEF
AND FOR IMPOSITION OF CIVIL PENALTIES

I. NATURE OF THE CASE

1. This is a suit brought under Section 505 of the Federal Water Pollution Control Act ("the Act"), 33 U.S.C. § 1365, and for common law negligence, trespass, and nuisance, relating to defendant's negligent discharge of pollutants into _____ without a permit, in violation of Section 301(a) of the Act, 33 U.S.C. § 1311(a). Plaintiffs seek damages, imposition of civil penalties, attorneys' fees and costs, and injunctive relief, including among other things an order compelling defendant to restore _____ to its natural condition in mitigation of the damage caused by the unpermitted discharges.

II. JURISDICTION

2. Jurisdiction is conferred on this Court by Section 505 of the Act, 33 U.S.C. § 1365, and by the Court's pendent jurisdiction over claims derived from a common nucleus of operative fact.

3. Notice of intent to file suit was served, in accordance with 40 C.F.R. § 135.2, by hand of defendant on _____.

4. More than 60 days have passed since the notice was served on defendant. The violations complained of have not ceased; _____ has not been restored to its natural condition; _____ remains; and neither the State of _____ _____, nor the Administrator of the Environmental Protection Agency has commenced and diligently prosecuted a civil or criminal action in court to redress the violations.

III. PLAINTIFFS

5. Plaintiffs _____ are _____ residents whose homes are located near or adjacent to _____. They have been damaged by experiencing unpleasant odors and other detrimental effects, including a lessening of their enjoyment of their property, as a result of defendant's unpermitted discharges.

IV. DEFENDANT

6. The defendant is _____, who is in the business of _____, a resident of _____.

V. FACTUAL ALLEGATIONS

7. (State locations, type, date and duration of pollution.)

8. Defendant does not now have, nor has it ever had, a permit issued by the Environmental Protection Agency or the State of _____ pursuant to Section 402 of the Act, 33 U.S.C. § 1342, allowing the discharges of _____ and other pollutants into the _____.

9. Defendant's discharges of _____ and other pollutants have caused _____ to be polluted, spoiled, and defaced. As a result, the plaintiffs, living in proximity to the _____ have experienced noxious odors, have not been able to use the _____ for recreational purposes, have had the enjoyment of their property decreased, and have been harmed in other ways.

10. _____ and _____ are waters of the United States.

VI. CLAIMS FOR RELIEF

11. Paragraphs 1–10 above are here incorporated as necessary for the purpose of each and every claim for relief set forth below.

First Claim: Violation of the Federal Water Pollution Control Act

12. The discharge of _____ and _____ pollutants by defendant and the others operating under defendant's authority and control, without a permit, into _____ in _____ constitutes a violation of Section 301(a) of the Act, 33 U.S.C. § 1311(a).

Second Claim: Negligence *Per Se*

13. Defendant's discharges of pollutants into _____ and into _____, being in violation of section 301(a) of the Act, constitute negligence *per se.*

Third Claim: Negligence

14. Defendant's operation of the _____ without the exercise of reasonable care in the circumstances, so as to create _____, constitutes negligence.

Fourth Claim: Nuisance

15. Defendant's operation of the _____ constitutes a nuisance detrimental to plaintiffs that can be abated and the resulting damage mitigated by currently available technology at a reasonable cost.

16. Defendant's wrongful pollution of the ground water beneath _____, which has caused and continues to cause damage, inconvenience, discomfort, and injury to the plaintiffs in the legitimate enjoyment and use of its property, constitutes a nuisance.

Fifth Claim: Trespass

17. Defendant's wrongful pollution of the ground water beneath _____ constitutes a subterranean trespass which has caused, and continues to cause great damage and injury to the use by the plaintiffs of its property.

VII. IRREPARABLE INJURY

18. As a direct result of violations alleged above, plaintiffs have suffered and will continue to suffer injury which is irreparable and cannot be adequately compensated with monetary relief alone.

VIII. REQUEST FOR RELIEF

WHEREFORE, Plaintiffs request that this Court grant the following relief:

A. Declare that defendant has been and continues to be in violation of Section 301(a) of the Act by discharging pollutants into _____ without a permit issued under Section 402 of the Act, 33 U.S.C. § 1342.

B. Enter an order directing defendant to cease immediately these unpermitted pollutant discharges.

C. Enter an order directing defendant to:

(1) install pollution control equipment in accordance with Section 301(b) of the Act, 33 U.S.C. § 1311(b), to treat its discharges of pollutants into _____ _____ and the _____;

(2) institute an appropriate program for inspection, operation, and maintenance of such pollution control equipment;

(3) obtain a permit from the Environmental Protection Agency and/or the State of _____, as appropriate, pursuant to Section 402 of the Act, 33 U.S.C. § 1342, for its discharges into _____ and the _____;

(4) take all steps necessary to fixate, contain, or remove the underground _____ _____;

(5) institute an appropriate program of inspection, operation and maintenance of the _____ to prevent the recurrence of _____ and its consequent discharge of pollutants;

(6) assume the expense of removing _____; and

(7) take such steps as are necessary to restore _____ to its natural condition.

D. Award plaintiffs compensatory, consequential, and economic damages.

E. Assess civil penalties pursuant to Sections 309(d) and 505(a) of the Act, 33 U.S.C. § 1319(d) and 1365(a), against defendants of up to $10,000 for each day of violation.

F. Award plaintiffs their costs of litigation, including a reasonable attorney's fee and expenses, pursuant to Section 505(d) of the Act, 33 U.S.C. § 1365(d).

G. Order such additional relief as the Court deems just and necessary.

Signature of Plaintiff _____

PLAINTIFF'S NAME
ADDRESS
TELEPHONE NUMBER

ENVIRONMENTAL ORGANIZATIONS

Alabama
The Alabama Conservancy
1818-A 28th Avenue South
Birmingham, AL 35209
(205) 871-0389

Alaska
Alaska Public Interest Research Group
P.O. Box 1093
Anchorage, AK 99510
(907) 278-3661

Sierra Club
545 East 4th Avenue #5
Anchorage, AK 99501
(907) 274-2318

Arkansas
Arkansas Wildlife Federation
7509 Cantrell Road
Little Rock, AR 72207
(501) 663-7256

Arizona
Arizona Center for Law in the Public Interest
112 N. 5th Avenue
Phoenix, AZ 85004
(602) 252-4904
(other office in Tucson)

California
California Public Interest Research Group
2490 Channing Way #200
Berkeley, CA 94704
(415) 642-9952

Ecology Center
2701 College Avenue
Berkeley, CA 94705
(415) 548-2220

Environmental Defense Fund
2606 Dwight Way
Berkeley, CA 94704
(415) 548-8906

Redwood Community Action Agency
904 G Street
Eureka, CA 95501
(707) 445-0881

Sierra Club
Beverly Boulevard
Los Angeles, CA 90057
(213) 387-6528

Ecology Action Educational Institute
P.O. Box 3895
Modesto, CA 95352
(209) 538-1698

Sierra Club
6014 College Avenue
Oakland, CA 94618
(415) 654-9562

Sierra Club
1228 N Street
Suite 31
Sacramento, CA 95814
(916) 444-2180

Friends of the River
1228 N Street
Sacramento, CA 95814
(916) 442-3155

Environmental Action Clearinghouse
Fort Mason Center
Building C
San Francisco, CA 94123
(415) 776-0265

Friends of the Earth
124 Spear Street
San Francisco, CA 94105
(415) 495-4477

Public Advocates, Inc.
1535 Mission Street
San Francisco, CA 94103
(415) 431-7430

Public Interest Clearinghouse
198 McAlister Street
San Francisco, CA 94102
(415) 557-4014

Sierra Club
530 Bush Street
San Francisco, CA 94108
(415) 981-8634

Community Environmental Council, Inc.
924 Anacapa Street
Suite B-4
Santa Barbara, CA 93101
(805) 962-2210

Ocean Park Community Organization
237 Hill
Santa Monica, CA 90405
(213) 392-8461

Colorado
Colorado Public Interest Research Group
1315 Broadway
Boulder, CO 80302
(303) 492-5086
(other offices in Greeley and Fort Collins)

Environmental Defense Fund
1405 Arapahoe Avenue
Boulder, CO 80302
(303) 440-4901

Colorado Open Space Concil
2239 E. Colfax Avenue
Denver, CO 80206
(303) 393-0466
(other office in Montrose)

Connecticut
Conservation Law Foundation of New England
118 Oak Street
Hartford, CT 06106
(203) 787-9203

Connecticut Public Interest Group
P.O. Box 6000
Trinity College
Hartford, CT 06106
(203) 247-2735
(other office in Storrs)

Connecticut Fund for the Environment
152 Temple Street
New Haven, CT 06510
(203) 787-0646

Oceanic Society
Stamford Marine Center
Stamford, CT (203) 327-9786

Delaware
Community Legal Aid Society
913 Washington Street
Wilmington, DE 19801
(302) 575-0660

District of Columbia
Clean Water Action Project
1341 G Street, N.W.
Washington, DC 20005
(202) 638-1196

Conservation Foundation
1717 Massachusetts Avenue, N.W.
Washington, DC 20036
(202) 797-4300

Defenders of Wildlife
1244 19th Street, N.W.
Washington, DC 20036
(202) 659-9510

Environmental Action
1346 Connecticut Avenue, N.W.
Suite 731
Washington. DC 20036
(202) 833-1845

Environmental Defense Fund
1525 18th Street, N.W.
Washington, DC 20036
(202) 833-1484

National Wildlife Federal
1412 16th Street, N.W.
Washington, DC 20036
(202) 797-6895

Natural Resources Defense Council
1725 1 Street, N.W.
Washington, DC 20006
(202) 223-8210

Sierra Club
330 Pennsylvania Avenue, S.E.
Washington, DC 20036
(202) 547-1141

Florida
Florida Defenders of the Environment
622 N. Main
Gainsville, FL 32601
(904) 372-6965

Florida Public Interest Research Group
326 University Union
Tallahassee, FL 32306
(904) 644-2826

Florida Wildlife Federation
4080 N. Haverhill Road
West Palm Beach, FL 33407
(305) 683-2328

Georgia
Georgia Clean Air Council
1383 Spring Street, N.W.
Atlanta, GA 30367
(404) 876-3601

Georgia Environmental Council
3110 Maple Drive
Suite 407
Atlanta, GA 30305
(404) 993-7124

Hawaii
Conservation Council for Hawaii
P.O. Box 2923
Honolulu, HI 96802
(808) 847-3511

Idaho
Idaho Conservation League
P.O. Box 844
Boise, ID 83701
(208) 354-6933
(other offices in Coeur d'Alene and Salmon)

Snake River Alliance
P.O. Box 1731
Boise, ID 83701
(208) 344-9161

Panhandle Environmental League
P.O. Box 963
Sandpoint, ID 83864

Illinois
Households Involved in Pollution Solutions
P.O. Box 1775
Champaign, IL 61820
(217) 643-3355

Lake Michigan Federation
53 West Jackson Boulevard
Suite 1710
Chicago, IL 60604
(312) 427-5121

Illinois Public Interest Research Group
P.O. Box 168
SIU-E
Edwardsville, IL 62026
(618) 692-2930
(other office in Carbondale)

Illinois South Project
701 North Park
Herrin, IL 62948
(618) 942-6613

Indiana
Indiana Public Interest Research Group
406 N. Fess
Bloomington, IN 47405
(812) 337-7575

Citizens Action Coalition of Indiana
311 W. Washington
Indianapolis, IN 46204
(317) 636-3642
(other offices in Fort Wayne and South Bend)

Iowa
Iowa Wildlife Federation
721 Keeler Street
Boone, IA 50036
(515) 432-4904

Kansas
Kansas Natural Resource Council
5130 Mission Road
Shawnee Mission, KS 66205
(913) 362-5932

Kentucky
Appalachia Science in the Public Interest
180 N. Market Street
Lexington, KY 40507
(606) 254-1425
(other office in Livingston)

Kentucky Rivers Coalition
P.O. Box 1306
Lexington, KY 40590
(606) 233-7227
(other offices in Harlan and Casey County)

Environmental Alternatives
818 E. Chestnut Street
Louisville, KY 40205
(502) 587-3028

Louisiana
American Lung Association
333 St. Charles Avenue
Suite 500
New Orleans, LA 70130
(504) 523-LUNG

Maine
Natural Resources Council of Maine
271 State Street
Augusta, ME 04330
(207) 622-3101

Maryland
Chesapeake Bay Foundation
162 Prince George Street
Annapolis, MD 21401
(301) 268-8816

Audubon Society
8940 Jones Mill Road
Chevy Chase, MD 20815
(301) 652-9188

Maryland Public Interest Research Group
3110 Main Dining Hall
University of Maryland
College Park, MD 20742
(301) 454-5601
(other offices in Baltimore and Towson)

Massachusetts
Hitchcock Center for the Environment
525 S. Pleasant Street
Amherst, MA 01002
(413) 256-6006

Conservation Law Foundation of New England
3 Joy Street
Boston, MA 02108
(617) 742-2540

Massachusetts Public Interest Research Group
120 Boylston Street
Suite 323
Boston, MA 02116
(617) 423-1796
(other offices in Amherst, Framingham, Medford,
  Newton, Salem, Westfield, and Worcester)

Union of Concerned Scientists
1384 Massachusetts Avenue
Cambridge, MA 02230
(617) 547-5552

Michigan
Ecology Center of Ann Arbor
417 Detroit Street
Ann Arbor, MI 48104
(313) 761-3168

Kalamazoo Nature Center Inc.
7000 N. Westnedge
Kalamazoo, MI 49007
(616) 381-1574

Citizens Against Chemical Contamination
11463 Bringold Avenue
Lake, MI 48632
(517) 588-9845

Public Interest Research Group in Michigan
590 Hollister Building
106 W. Allegan
Lansing, MI 48933

Minnesota
Clean Air—Clean Water Unlimited
111 E. Franklin Avenue
Minneapolis, MN 55404
(612) 646-0113

Minnesota Public Interest Research Group
2412 University Avenue S.E.
Minneapolis, MN 55417
(612) 376-7554

Mississippi
Committee for Leaving the Environment Natural
P.O. Box 103
Starkville, MS 39759
(601) 323-0491

Missouri
Coalition for the Environment
6267 Delmar Boulevard
St. Louis, MO 63130
(314) 727-0600

Montana
Montana Environmental Information Center
P.O. Box 1184
Helena, MT 59624
(406) 443-2520

Montana Land Reliance
P.O. Box 355
Helena, MT 59601
(406) 443-7027

Northern Rockies Action Group
9 Placer Street
Helena, MT 59601
(406) 442-6615

Nebraska
Sierra Club
421 S. 9th Street
Suite 210
Lincoln, NE 68508
(402) 476-7192

Nevada
Nevada Wildlife Federation
P.O. Box 8022
University Station
Reno, NV 89507
(702) 825-7823

New Hampshire
The Environmental Coalition
P.O. Box 757
Concord, NH 03301
(603) 895-9058

New Jersey
New Jersey Environmental Lobby
204 W. State Street
Trenton, NJ 08608
(609) 393-7474

New Jersey Public Interest Research Group
204 W. State Street
Trenton, NJ 08608
(609) 393-7474
(other offices in New Brunswick, Newark, Camden, and
  Mahwah)

New Mexico
American Indian Environmental Council
P.O. Box 7082
Albuquerque, NM 87194
(505) 265-1509

New Mexico Public Interest Research Group
P.O. Box 4564
Albuquerque, NM 87106
(505) 277-2757

Sierra Club
1709 Paseo de Peralta
Santa Fe, NM 87501
(505) 983-6331

New York
Environmental Defense Fund
444 Park Avenue South
New York, NY 10016
(212) 686-4191

Natural Resources Defense Council
122 E. 42nd Street
New York, NY 10168
(212) 949-0049

New York Public Interest Group
5 Beekman Street
New York, NY 10038
(212) 349-6460
(other offices in Albany, Buffalo, Binghamton,
    Syracuse, Cortland, New Platz, Westchester, Nassau,
    Suffolk, Brooklyn, Bronx, Queens, and Staten Island)

Sierra Club
228 East 45th Street
14th Floor
New York, NY 10017
(212) 687-2950

North Carolina
Conservation Council of North Carolina
307 Granville Road
Chapel Hill, NC 27514
(919) 942-7935
(other office in Asheville)

North Carolina Public Interest Research Group
P.O. Box 2901
Durham, NC 27705
(919) 286-2275

North Carolina Wildlife Federation
P.O. Box 10626
Raleigh, NC 27605
(919) 782-5418

North Dakota
Dakota Resource Council
113 1st Street W.
P.O. Box 254
Dickinson, ND 58601
(701) 227-1851

North Dakota Wildlife Federation
P.O. Box 66
Erie, ND 58029
(701) 668-2304

Ohio
Southwest Ohio Lung Association
2330 Victory Parkway
Cincinnati, OH 45206
(513) 751-3650

Ohio Public Interest Campaign
1120 Chester Avenue
Cleveland, OH 44114
(216) 861-5200
(other offices in Columbus, Cincinnati, Akron, Dayton,
    Toledo, and Youngston)

Ohio Environmental Council
850 Michigan Avenue
Columbus, OH 43215
(614) 221-0898

Kent Environmental Council
125 West Day Street
Kent, OH 44240
(216) 673-4097

Oklahoma
Oklahoma Wildlife Federation
P.O. Box 1292
Norman, OK 73069
(405) 364-3609

Oregon
Oregon Environmental Council
2637 SW Water Street
Portland, OR 97210
(503) 222-1963

Oregon Student Public Interest Research Group
P.O. Box 751
Portland State University
Portland, OR 97207
(503) 229-4500
(other offices in Salem, Eugene, Ashland, and Corvallis)

Pennsylvania
Clean Air Council
Juniper & Locust Streets
2nd Floor
Philadelphia, PA 19107
(215) 545-1832

Public Interest Law Center of Philadelphia
1315 Walnut Street
16th Floor
Philadelphia, PA 19107
(215) 735-7200

Group Against Smog and Pollution
P.O. Box 5165
Pittsburgh, PA 15206
(412) 444-6650

Rhode Island
Environment Council of Rhode Island
40 Bowen Street
Providence, RI 02903
(401) 521-1670

South Carolina
South Carolina Environmental
    Coalition, Inc.
P.O. Box 5761
Columbia, SC 29250
(803) 799-0321

South Dakota
South Dakota Resources Coalition
Drawer G
Brookings, SD 57007
(605) 627-5543

Black Hills Alliance
P.O. Box 2508
Rapid City, SD 57709
(605) 342-5127
(other office in Vermillion)

Tennessee
Sierra Club
P.O. Box 11248
Knoxville, TN 37919
(615) 588-1892

Tennessee Environmental Council
P.O. Box 1422
Nashville, TN 37203
(615) 251-1110

Texas
Texas Committee on
    Natural Resources
4719 West Lovers Lane
Dallas, TX 75209
(214) 351-2322

Texas Public Interest
    Research Group
University of Houston
P.O. Box 237
Houston, TX 77004
(713) 749-3130

Utah
Sierra Club
615 S. 300 East
Salt Lake City, UT 84111
(801) 364-9431

Vermont
Vermont Natural Resources Council
7 Main Street
Montpelier, VT 05602
(802) 223-2328

Virginia
Izaak Walton League
1800 N Kent Street
Arlington, VA 22209
(703) 528-1818

Institute for Ecological Policies
9208 Christopher Street
Fairfax, VA 22031
(703) 691-1271

Virginia Public Interest
    Research Group
Campus Center
College of William and Mary
Williamsburg, VA 23185
(804) 253-0381

Washington
Sierra Club
1516 Melrose Avenue
Seattle, WA 98122
(206) 621-1696

Washington Environmental Council
107 South Main Street
Seattle, WA 98104
(206) 623-1483
(other office in Olympia)

Washington Public Interest
    Research Group
HUB 304 G, FK-30
University of Washington
Seattle, WA 98195
(206) 543-0434

West Virginia
West Virginia Citizen Action Group
1324 Virginia Street E.
Charleston, WV 25301
(304) 346-5891

West Virginia Public Interest
    Research Group
Student Organizing Wing,
    Mountain Lair
Morgantown, WV 26505
(304) 293-2108

Wisconsin
Sierra Club
142 W. Gorham Street
Madison, WI 53703
(608) 257-4994

Wisconsin's Environmental
    Decade, Inc.
302 E. Washington Avenue
Madison, WI 53703
(608) 251-7020

Citizens for a Better Environment
536 W. Wisconsin Avenue
Suite 502
Milwaukee, WI 53203
(414) 271-7280
(other offices in Appelton and
    Madison)

Wyoming
Wyoming Outdoor Council
P.O. Box 1184
Cheyenne, WY 82001
(307) 635-3416

Sierra Club
P.O. Box 1078
Lander, WY 82520
(307) 332-9824

Powder River Basin Resource
    Council
48 N. Main
Sheridan, WY 82801
(307) 672-5809

18

How to Fight Your Landlord

Tenants' rights are not only for the poor. I have represented millionaire tenants with a leaking ceiling in their posh penthouse apartments and recovered thousands of dollars for their inconvenience and the interference with the use of their apartments. Many of your rights as a tenant are determined by the lease that you have signed. Not all leases are written; you may have an oral lease agreement with your landlord.

LEASES

A lease is a contract for the use of real estate between a landlord and a tenant. Contracts may be oral or written. If you have a written lease, you should examine it carefully. The lease may provide that your tenancy expires at a specific time and that you may not stay after this period ends. If this is the case, the landlord may evict you immediately, if you stay one day after the lease period ends. If the lease agreement does not specifically require you to leave at the end of the lease period, you may continue living there, one month at a time, at your existing rent. However, if your landlord gives you 30 days notice of a rent increase, or 30 days notice that he wants the apartment back, he is within his rights.

Many leases ask you to waive your legal rights. Your lease may provide that you give up your right to a jury trial, written notice, or other rights. Many

courts have ruled that these attempted waivers are invalid because they are contrary to public policy. However, you can try to negotiate these clauses out of your lease with your landlord if you renew your lease.

RENEWING YOUR LEASE

If you have been a good tenant and paid your rent on time, you will be in a good position to negotiate a new lease. By that time you will have found problems with the apartment. If the toilet isn't working properly or the apartment needs painting, you can write these terms into the new lease. You can ask for a longer lease to guarantee your rent if you intend to stay for a long period of time. A new lease gives you an opportunity to strike out positions of the lease that are attempts to waive your legal rights. If you have paid your rent on time for a year, you can argue to your landlord that he or she does not need you to waive notice or the right to a jury trial.

NOTICES

Even if you have only an oral lease, you are entitled to receive notices in writing. These notices are notices of rent increases or notices to quit. A notice to quit is a formal request for you to leave the apartment. Both notices to quit and notices of rent increase ordinarily must be given 30 days in advance. Every state law varies, so check the specific law in your area. The only general exception to a 30 day notice is when your rent is late. However, even if it is late your landlord must give you a written notice before he can begin eviction proceedings; but a notice to pay rent or quit may be given as little as three days in advance.

HOUSING CODES

Housing codes set the minimum standards for rental housing in every state. These codes are also called building codes or health and safety codes in some areas. The codes require heat in winter and utilities year round, and they prohibit roaches, rodents, and peeling paint. The codes vary from city to city, and state to state, so it is a good idea to get a copy of the code for your own use. Your city housing or health department will provide a copy of the code for little or no cost. Your city or state has a building inspection department, or a department under a similar name, which is responsible for enforcing housing codes.

Nearly every apartment has at least a few minor housing code violations. You have a right to ask your housing inspector to inspect your apartment unit. If the inspection reveals housing code violations, your landlord will be ordered to correct them, or else subject himself to fines or possibly a short jail term, if the violations are repeated and serious.

DOES YOUR STATE PROTECT TENANTS' RIGHTS?

Court decisions and statutes have been moving in the direction of increasing tenants' rights in the past twenty years. The most important trend has been to create an implied warranty that your apartment is "habitable." This means that your landlord is giving you a warranty that essential services will not fail you. For example, if your heat is off in January, and it is below freezing, your landlord has breached the warranty of habitability. Similarly, if the ceiling is leaking badly, the warranty is breached. In these cases, the tenant can withhold rent and have a valid defense against eviction. Thirty-nine states and the District of Columbia recognize the warranty of habitability. The table on pages 133–134 lists the states that do and do not. This represents a drastic change in landlord-tenant law. In 1968, no state recognized the warranty of habitability; tenants were required to pay rent even if the heat was turned off and the ceiling had fallen in!

Repair-and-deduct is a concept that half of the states recognize. This means that if you give your landlord a reasonable opportunity to make a repair, and he or she fails to do so you have the right, up to certain limits, to make the needed repairs, and then to deduct the cost of the repairs from your rent check. If your state allows repair-and-deduct, first write your landlord a letter. Send the letter by certified mail, return receipt requested, so that you will have written proof of its delivery. A sample Notice of Defective Conditions letter is included at the end of this chapter as Form 18-1. Give the landlord a deadline in the letter, leaving him a reasonable amount of time to make the repairs. If the repairs have not been made by that date, you should get two repair estimates before commencing work. You are permitted to do the repairs yourself in some jurisdictions, and you can deduct a certain amount for your labor. When your next rent check is due, send a letter explaining the deduction and enclose a copy of the receipts for the repair work. Those states recognizing the right to repair-and-deduct are listed on pages 133–134.

If you are evicted for complaining to your landlord about repairs, or for complaining to the housing authorities about housing code violations, it is called retaliatory eviction. Twenty-eight states and the District of Columbia prohibit retaliatory evictions. In the other states a good argument can be made that such evictions violate the constitutional rights of free speech and of your right to petition the government for redress of grievances. The state would be condoning the landlord's actions by allowing its state courts to evict you. If you are threatened with eviction and your state does not protect you against retaliatory actions, consult with an attorney to protect the exercising of your rights. A list of states who have made retaliatory evictions illegal is included on pages 133–134.

CHART OF TENANTS' RIGHTS

State	Implied Warranty of Habitability	Repair and Deduct	Retaliatory Eviction Illegal
Alabama	No	No	No
Alaska	Yes	Yes	Yes
Arizona	Yes	Yes	Yes
Arkansas	No	No	No
California	Yes	Yes	Yes
Colorado	No	Yes	No
Connecticut	Yes	No	Yes
Delaware	Yes	Yes	Yes
District of Columbia	Yes	No	Yes
Florida	Yes	No	Yes
Georgia	Yes	Yes	No
Hawaii	Yes	Yes	Yes
Idaho	Yes	No	No
Illinois	Yes	Yes	Yes
Indiana	No	No	No
Iowa	Yes	Yes	Yes
Kansas	Yes	No	No
Kentucky	Yes	Yes	Yes
Louisiana	No	Yes	No
Maine	Yes	No	Yes
Maryland	Yes	No	Yes
Massachusetts	Yes	Yes	Yes
Michigan	Yes	Yes	Yes
Minnesota	Yes	No	Yes
Mississippi	No	No	No
Missouri	Yes	No	No
Montana	No	Yes	No
Nebraska	Yes	Yes	Yes
Nevada	Yes*	Yes	Yes
New Hampshire	Yes	No	Yes
New Jersey	Yes	Yes	Yes
New Mexico	Yes	No	No
New York	Yes	No	Yes
North Carolina	Yes	No	No
North Dakota	Yes	Yes	No
Ohio	Yes	Yes	Yes
Oklahoma	Yes	Yes	No
Oregon	Yes	Yes	Yes
Pennsylvania	Yes	Yes	Yes
Rhode Island	Yes	No	Yes

---

* Yes if landlord owns 7 or more units.

CHART OF TENANTS' RIGHTS (Continued)

State	Implied Warranty of Habitability	Repair and Deduct	Retaliatory Eviction Illegal
South Carolina	No	No	No
South Dakota	No	Yes	No
Tennessee	Yes	No	Yes
Texas	Yes	No	No
Utah	No	No	No
Vermont	Yes	No	No
Virginia	Yes	Yes	Yes
Washington	Yes	Yes	Yes
West Virginia	Yes	No	No
Wisconsin	Yes	Yes	Yes
Wyoming	No	No	No
Totals of Yes	40 (78%)	26 (51%)	29 (57%)

EVICTION PROCEDURES

You can be legally evicted for three reasons:

1. Failure to pay rent
2. Breach of lease term
3. End of your tenancy

The failure to pay rent is by far the most common reason for eviction. Even if you have failed to pay rent, you must be given notice that you will be evicted if you don't pay by a certain date.

If you have a dog and the lease prohibits pets, you can be evicted. But, again, you must be given notice and an opportunity to get rid of the pet before an eviction paper can be filed in court.

If your tenancy has ended and you are a "hold-over" tenant, you can be evicted without notice, when your lease specifically states that you must be out by a certain date.

An eviction can proceed very quickly. If you fail to pay rent you could be out on the street in as little as a month. For example, if you fail to pay rent due on the first day of the month, the landlord can hand-deliver a "Notice to Quit" the next day, giving you as little as three days to pay up. If you fail to pay by the fifth of the month, the landlord can file a suit for eviction the next day. You could be served with a summons and a complaint for eviction that same day. The summons will require you to appear in court in a week or two after you receive it. On your court date there will be a speedy trial, usually 15 minutes or less. If you fail to appear, or if you have no valid reason for not paying, the judge or clerk will declare: "judgment for posession (eviction) is entered against you." In as little as two or three days later, the local sheriff, marshal, or constable may pay you a visit to remove the belongings from your apartment and put them out on the street or sidewalk.

SELF-HELP

Nearly every state prohibits landlords from evicting a tenant without court supervision.[1] Evictions by landlords without court supervision are known as "self-help" evictions. When a landlord turns off utilities or locks tenants out, it is also known as self-help. Utility cut-offs and lock-outs are considered by the courts to be evictions and are illegal where self-help evictions are illegal.

Tenants who are wrongfully evicted have a right to sue their landlords for "wrongful eviction." Some attorneys handle wrongful eviction cases on a contingency fee basis, which means they do not get paid for their legal work unless they win the case. If you believe that you have been wrongfully evicted, contact an attorney in your area. If you do not know an attorney, legal aid bureau, or any neighborhood legal services, the Bar Association in your town may be able to recommend one for you.

---

1. Courts in Iowa (1909), Wyoming (1945), and Montana (1960), have permitted self-help evictions.

JURY TRIAL

You can put a wrench into all this judicial machinery by asking for a jury trial. The Supreme Court has ruled that you have a right to a jury trial in a landlord-tenant case.[2] Despite this ruling, some states will not give you a jury trial. Always make a demand for a jury trial; even if the court refuses your demand, you have not lost anything. Requesting a jury trial will delay your case for months, in some cases for years. A jury demand will cost you a jury fee, which varies from state to state. The court clerk will tell you the fees. You must demand a jury trial at the first instance, or you may be considered to have waived your right to it. Your lease may have waived your right to a jury trial, but you can argue that such a waiver is contrary to public policy and your constitutional rights.

DEFENDING AN EVICTION

If you hire an attorney to represent you in landlord-tenant court it will cost no less than $100, at the very minimum. If you are very poor the court may appoint an attorney or a law student to represent you. Ask the court to appoint an attorney for you. Your request for legal counsel may cause the court to delay the case in order to allow you to talk to an attorney. If your income is low you may qualify for free or low-cost legal assistance for a group such as Legal Aid, Legal Services, Neighborhood Legal Services (or Assistance), a local Bar Association, or a law school's Legal Clinic. Look under these headings in the telephone directory, or call a law school in your area for assistance.

In many cases you can represent yourself. If you paid the rent but the landlord's records do not reflect this, bring a cancelled check or receipt to court and explain this to the landlord's attorney or the the judge.

If you made a repair and deducted the amount of the repair from the rent, bring a copy of the notice that you sent to the landlord and a receipt for the repairs, and explain this to the judge.

An improper notice of a rent increase or an improper notice to quit is a good defense to an eviction. Bring copies of the notices with you to court; mark on them the date that you received the notice.

A witness who can confirm the date you received a notice will strengthen your case.

If your ceiling is leaking badly take photographs and bring them to court to prove the failure of your landlord to provide a habitable apartment. You can bring witnesses with you to confirm the condition of your apartment. You have the right to subpoena, or compel to testify, the housing inspector who found housing code violations at your apartment.

If you feel unsure of your rights but cannot afford $100 or more for an attorney, you can consult with an attorney for less. The consultation may put you at ease, or it may convince you that you are wrong. You always have the right to pay back rent to avoid an eviction, even if the sheriff has come to evict you.

SECURITY DEPOSITS

Normally your landlord should return your security deposit within 30 days of your leaving the apartment, as long as you have given proper notice and have not damaged the apartment. A letter giving notice that you are vacating the apartment is included at the end of this chapter as Form 18-2. If your landlord fails to return your security deposit, you can sue for its return in small claims court. Some states allow double or triple damages for failure to return a security deposit. Call a Legal Aid, Legal Clinic, or neighborhood Legal Services office in your area and ask if you are entitled to double or triple damages concerning security deposits. A small claims complaint for return of a security deposit is included at the end of this chapter as Form 18-3.

FORMING A TENANTS' ORGANIZATION

As stated throughout this book, it is best to complain in concert with others who are in a similar position. If the entire roof in your apartment leaks, it should not be difficult to find other tenants who are willing to join with you.

Tenants' unions or organizations can be helpful in luxury apartment buildings as well as inexpensive ones. I was involved with a group of tenants in a luxury building who wanted additional security in the building and a master television antenna installed on the roof. A majority of the tenants organized, and the landlord agreed to meet with them.

---

2. *Pernell* v. *Southall Realty*, 416 U.S. 363 (1974).

The landlord agreed that if a majority of the tenants wanted these features, he would install them, but the costs would be added to the rent.

To organize a tenants' union, there must be a strong issue common to most of the tenants. If there is, you should have little trouble organizing. First you can talk to the tenants that you know. Then you can split up the building and walk door-to-door. It is easy to hand out leaflets by slipping them under apartment doors.

There is a nationwide tenants group called the National Tenants' Organization (NTO). NTO can provide you with information since it serves as a clearinghouse for tenants' rights. The address and telephone number is:

National Tenants Organization
348 W. 121st Street
New York, NY 10027
(212) 749-4500

A tenants' organization can often form the basis for an offer to purchase a building from a landlord. If a landlord wants to sell, the tenants are the logical choice to purchase. They already live in the building. I have often said that if you can afford to rent something, you can afford to buy it. The tenants' organization can purchase the building as a cooperative, or the individual tenants can purchase the apartment units as condominiums. In a cooperative, each tenant owns stock in the cooperative corporation and rents his or her apartment from the co-op. In a condominium each tenant owns the apartment unit in which they reside. One advantage to a cooperative is that the co-op can assume the old mortgage, while a condominium cannot. However, if the cooperative has trouble making mortgage payments, all tenants may lose their building. In a condominium, if you make your mortgage payment, your individual condo unit is safe and secure.

FORM 18-1

Letter to Landlord Concerning Housing Code Violations

CERTIFIED MAIL
RETURN RECEIPT REQUESTED

Date _____

To Landlord (Name and address)

RE: NOTICE OF DEFECTIVE CONDITIONS

Dear Landlord,

I am a tenant in apartment number _____ at _____ _____.
Certain defective conditions and/or housing violations exist at this apartment. They are:
_____
_____
_____

I would appreciate it if you would repair these defective conditions by _____.
Should these conditions remain unrepaired, I intend to exercise my rights under law, including code enforcement, affirmative actions, rent withholding, repair and deduct or quitting the apartment. Thank you for your cooperation.

Sincerely yours,

_____
(Tenant's Signature)
NAME

cc: your attorney

FORM 18-2

Letter to Landlord of Intention to Vacate Apartment

CERTIFIED MAIL
RETURN RECEIPT REQUESTED

Date _____

To Landlord (Name and Address)

RE: THIRTY DAY NOTICE OF
TERMINATION OF TENANCY

Dear Landlord:

I am a tenant in apartment number _____ at _____ _____.
Please regard this letter as notice of my intention to terminate the month-to-month tenancy (or year, as the case may be) under which I have occupied this apartment. I intend to vacate this apartment on _____ (at least 30 days from receipt of this notice).

The apartment will be left clean and in good condition. I will expect my security deposit of $_____ to be sent to me at _____ within _____ days of my departure.

Sincerely yours,

(Tenant's Signature) _____
NAME

19

What You Can Do About Problems with Your Home or Condominium

Problems with water, whether a damp basement, flooding, a leaking roof, or freezing pipes, are the most common household complaints. These problems are not confined to residential quarters; the Kennedy Center for the Performing Arts in Washington, D.C., has had a costly legal and engineering battle to stop a badly leaking roof.

NEW HOMES WITH WARRANTIES

Nearly every new home comes with a warranty, usually for one or more years. Make a list of every defect in your new home, and periodically inform the builder of your complaints. Before the warranty period has ended, make a final list of problems that need to be corrected, and send a letter to your builder by certified mail, return receipt requested, so that you can prove that you complained of the problems within your warranty period.

Depending on the severity of the problem, if the builder fails to correct the defects within a reasonable time you can:

1. Sue the builder with or without an attorney;
2. Complain to a local television, radio, or newspaper consumer service; or
3. Complain to a government consumer protection agency.

Concerning legal action, if your problem is common to other homes in your development, you should meet with the other homeowners and hire an attorney. One group of homeowners in Maryland who had heating system problems, successfully sued a developer and received new furnaces.

If your problem concerns only your home, and the amount of needed repairs is $1000 or less, small claims court may be your answer. A small claims complaint for breach of warranty is included at the end of this chapter as Form 19-1.

Many local radio and television stations and newspapers run consumer complaint services. They can settle many disputes because companies want to avoid the negative publicity that can result if the complaint service believes that you have a bona fide complaint.

Many cities and states have consumer protection offices to handle complaints. A list of these offices is included at the end of this chapter. The Federal Trade Commission's Bureau of Consumer Protection may be able to help you if your problem involves a warranty matter, or a claim of false advertising. Write them at:

Bureau of Consumer Protection
Federal Trade Commission
Washington, DC 20580

The Federal Trade Commission generally does not act on the basis of a single complaint, but you may have the same problem as many other individuals. If you are working with a group of homeowners, a complaint to the FTC signed by 20 homeowners probably will be investigated. The FTC has regional offices throughout the nation. A list of these offices is included in Chapter 21.

PROBLEMS WITH OLDER HOMES

If you have purchased an older home, you may have bought someone else's problems. Before buying any home, you should have a professional engineer inspect it. If you did hire an engineer or inspection service, and it failed to find defects with the home that it should have found, you may be able to sue the inspection service.

The home seller and real estate broker may have lied to you about the condition of the house they sold to you. You may be able to sue them for fraudulent misrepresentation if they lied to you. A case based on fraud is very difficult to prove, so you should retain an attorney to pursue a case of this type. Generally, there are two kinds of defects in a home or condominium. One is called "latent," which means that the defect is not obvious. The other kind of defect is "patent," a defect that should be noticed upon reasonable inspection. An example of a latent defect is a damp basement that did not appear damp when you inspected it. You can only sue for fraudulent misrepresentation where there is a latent defect. The former homeowner and the real estate broker have an obligation to tell you of latent defects.

OTHER HOUSING PROBLEMS DEALT WITH ELSEWHERE IN THIS BOOK

If after moving into a home you notice that airplanes are disturbing your sleep, see Chapter 14—How to Fight Your Local Airport. If you are in default on your mortgage, read Chapter 7—How to Stop a Foreclosure Sale. For advice concerning housing discrimination, see Chapter 20.

WHEN YOUR HOUSE WAS IMPROPERLY DESIGNED

As mentioned earlier, the Kennedy Center had a major roof leaking problem, which cost millions of dollars to repair. It turned out that the architect designed the roof improperly, and was liable for damages caused by the leaks. The well known architect of the Kennedy Center, Edward Durell Stone, who is highly respected in his profession, was insured for "architectural malpractice," which paid for some of the damages. The time period during which you can file a claim against an architect for improper design is usually very long, sometimes up to twenty years after the building was constructed. Suits against architects are complicated and require the use of an attorney who specializes in these cases. Many expert witnesses are needed to prove this type of case. However, often a letter from an attorney, if the liability of the architect is clear, can settle these matters without a lengthy court battle.

WHEN THE GOVERNMENT WAS AT FAULT

Flooding is often caused by poor planning by the city or county authority responsible for storm sewers. The harmless looking creek in your back yard can turn into a raging torrent, if too much rainwater is directed into it. To get results you may have to organize your neighbors and lobby the city council for relief. In these cases the city may be immune from suits for damages. You should consult an attorney in your community if you believe that your wet basement was caused by your city, town, or county. Federal flood control projects may cause your land to be flooded during certain times of the year. The federal government is required to compensate you if its dam or other flood control project causes your land to be under water. This type of case is similar to an aircraft noise case, since the government has taken part of your property for a public use. A lawsuit against the federal government concerning flood damages requires the use of an attorney who specializes in condemnation law or eminent domain law. Consult with an attorney in one of these specialties if your problem involves the federal government causing flooding.

WHEN YOUR INSPECTOR GOOFED

If you hired a building specialist or a professional engineer to inspect your house and he or she failed to notice defects, you may have a claim against the inspection service. Most states require a termite inspection before a house is sold. If the inspector failed to find termites you may have a valid claim against the inspection service. If your damages are not too large you may want to file a complaint in small claims court against the inspection service. Rather than fight your small claims case, the service may be willing to pay for some or all of the damages that you suffered. A small claims complaint against an inspection service is included at the end of this chapter as Form 19-2. Before filing a small claims case, you should write to the inspection service and tell them of your complaint. This will give them an opportunity to settle the claim with you before going to court. While you are not required to give notice in advance of suit, it is a reasonable way to compromise disputes.

CONDOMINIUMS

Your condominium association may be required to make certain repairs to your unit. Generally, the condominium association is responsible for common area maintenance, which usually includes hallways, roofs, common walls, and exterior areas. Every condominium association has condominium documents or bylaws which provide details as to when the condominium association is responsible for repairs.

If the developer of the condominium failed to complete construction in common areas, or failed to correct building defects, the condominium association can sue the developer. If these defects involve warranty work, see the beginning of this chapter, which deals with homeowner's warranties.

An individual condominium unit owner has the right to sue the condominium association if it fails to make common area repairs. These matters should be addressed at condominium association meetings, because all of the owners will share in the costs of repairs and of attorneys, if they are needed.

COOPERATIVES

Owners of cooperatives are actually tenants of the cooperative corporation. You can be evicted from your cooperative unit if you fail to pay the rent on time. Co-op owners are tenants, even though they own shares in the cooperative corporation.

If you live in a co-op, you have all of the rights of a tenant as I discussed in Chapter 18. Before evicting you, the co-op must give you notice, and then it must file a complaint for "possession." You have the same defenses to an eviction as a tenant in a traditional apartment building.

If you fail to pay rent for a co-op you are jeopardizing all of the owners of the cooperative, because if the mortgage for the co-op is not paid, the bank or savings and loan company holding the mortgage can foreclose on it, selling the building at an auction. The buyer can then evict all of the tenants, if it so chooses, or it can raise the rents. See Chapter 7 concerning how a foreclosure sale can be avoided.

FORM 19-1

Small Claims Complaint Concerning House or Condominium Warranty Problems

_____;
                                        Plaintiff,

v.   Case No.

_____,
                                        Defendant.

STATEMENT OF THE CLAIM

1. Plaintiff purchased a home/condominium unit from defendant on _____ (date).

2. The house/condominium unit is covered by a warranty for defects in workmanship and materials for a period of _____ years. A copy of the warranty agreement is attached to this complaint as plaintiff's exhibit no. 1.

3. Before the warranty expired, plaintiff notified defendant that there were defects. A copy of the letter giving defendant notice is attached to this complaint as plaintiff's exhibit no. 2.

4. Defendant received a copy of these defects within the warranty period. A copy of the return receipt from the certified mail notice to defendant is attached to this complaint as plaintiff's exhibit no. 3.

5. Defendant failed to correct the defects which are _____
_____.

WHEREFORE PLAINTIFF seeks judgment against defendant in the amount of _____.

(Signature) _____
PLAINTIFF'S NAME
ADDRESS
TELEPHONE NUMBER

Subscribed and sworn to before me this _____ day of _____.

_____
NOTARY PUBLIC

Small Claims Complaint Against
Home Inspection Company

_____;
                    Plaintiff,
     v.   Case No.

_____,
                    Defendant.

STATEMENT OF THE CLAIM

1. Plaintiff hired the defendant to inspect the home or condominium located at _____
_____. (If you have a written contract attach it and state in this paragraph that a copy of the contract is attached.)

2. Defendant inspected the property on _____ (date) and supplied a written report, a copy of which is attached to this complaint as plaintiff's exhibit no. _____.

3. On _____ (date) plaintiff noticed the following defects in the property: _____.

4. Defendant failed to notice the defects listed in paragraph 3.

5. To repair these defects it will cost plaintiff $_____.

6. Defendant breached the contract with plaintiff by failing to make a proper and complete inspection of the property. A properly qualified engineer/inspection service would have identified the defects listed in paragraph three (3).

7. Defendant was negligent in failing to identify the defects listed in paragraph three (3).

WHEREFORE, plaintiff demands judgment against defendant in the amount of $_____.

(Signature) _____
PLAINTIFF'S NAME
ADDRESS
TELEPHONE NUMBER

Subscribed and sworn to before me this _____ day of _____.

_____
NOTARY PUBLIC

20

How to Combat Housing Discrimination

The federal Fair Housing Act prohibits discrimination in the rental or sale of housing because of race, religion, national origin, or sex. The Act does not apply to rentals if the landlord lives in the house or apartment and owns four or less units, or if the landlord owns three or less single family houses.

The Fair Housing Act is enforced by the Department of Housing and Urban Development (HUD). The Fair Housing division of HUD operates a national, toll-free hotline for housing discrimination information and complaints. Its address and number are:

Fair Housing
Department of Housing and
Urban Development
Washington, DC 20410
(800) 424-8590

HUD investigates complaints filed with its fair housing office. A complaint form is included at the end of this chapter as Form 20-1. Complaints should be filed at the regional offices of the fair housing department.

Below are the regional offices of HUD's fair housing offices, where complaints of discrimination should be filed:

Region I
Boston (Connecticut, Maine, Massachusetts, New Hampshire, Rhode Island, Vermont)

HUD–Fair Housing and Equal Opportunity (FHEO)
John F. Kennedy Federal Building
Boston, MA 02203

Region II
New York (New Jersey, New York, Puerto Rico, Virgin Islands)

HUD–Fair Housing and Equal Opportunity (FHEO)
26 Federal Plaza
New York, NY 10007

Region III
Philadelphia (Delaware, District of Columbia, Maryland, Pennsylvania, Virginia, West Virginia)

HUD–Fair Housing and Equal Opportunity (FHEO)
Curtis Building
6th and Walnut Streets
Philadelphia, PA 19106

Region IV
Atlanta (Alabama, Florida, Georgia, Kentucky, Mississippi, North Carolina, South Carolina, Tennessee)

HUD–Fair Housing and Equal Opportunity (FHEO)
75 Spring Street, S.W.
Atlanta, GA 30303

Region V
Chicago (Illinois, Indiana, Michigan, Minnesota, Ohio, Wisconsin)

HUD–Fair Housing and Equal Opportunity (FHEO)
300 South Wacker Drive
Chicago, IL 60606

Region VI
Fort Worth (Arkansas, Louisiana, New Mexico,
  Oklahoma, Texas)

HUD–Fair Housing and Equal Opportunity (FHEO)
221 West Lancaster Avenue
P.O. Box 2905
Fort Worth, TX 76113

Region VII
Kansas City (Iowa, Kansas, Missouri, Nebraska)

HUD–Fair Housing and Equal Opportunity (FHEO)
Professional Building
Room 1200
1103 Grand Avenue
Kansas City, MO 64106

Region VIII
Denver (Colorado, Montana, North Dakota, South
  Dakota, Utah, Wyoming)

HUD–Fair Housing and Equal Opportunity (FHEO)
Executive Tower Building
1405 Curtis Street
Denver, CO 80202

Region IX
San Francisco (Arizona, California, Hawaii, Nevada,
  Guam, American Samoa)

HUD–Fair Housing and Equal Opportunity (FHEO)
450 Golden Gate Avenue
P.O. Box 36003
San Francisco, CA 94102

Region X
Seattle (Alaska, Idaho, Oregon, Washington)

HUD–Fair Housing and Equal Opportunity (FHEO)
Arcade Plaza Building
1321 Second Avenue
Seattle, WA 98101

You must file your complaint within 180 days of
the discriminatory act. HUD's fair housing office
will investigate the complaint and may attempt to
conciliate the case, or it may inform you that you
can file a complaint in court. In very strong cases,
usually those involving more than one individual,
HUD will refer the case to the Attorney General of
the United States for action.

COURT ACTION

Unlike the Civil Rights Act provisions regarding
equal employment opportunities, the fair housing
law provides that you can file suit in court immediately, rather than first filing with HUD. Another
major difference between housing and employment
laws is that in housing discrimination cases the Supreme Court has ruled that you have the right to a
jury trial.

If you do not file a complaint with HUD you can
file a court suit within 180 days of the discriminatory action. If you filed a complaint with HUD, you
may be given a notice that allows you to go to court
within 30–60 days after the agency declines to proceed with the matter. Your housing discrimination
case can be filed in either state or local court. Form
20-2 is a complaint for filing in federal court.

REAL ESTATE BROKERS

The fair housing law allows you to sue a real
estate broker who refused to show you housing or
who steered you toward or away from certain housing because of your race, sex, or national origin. If
a landlord or homeowner who does not come
within the fair housing law hires a broker, that
broker can be sued.

COURT INJUNCTIONS

The courts have the power to issue an injunction
to prevent a house or apartment from being rented
or sold until your case is decided. I recommend that
you hire an attorney if you need a court injunction.
The housing law provides that if you win, the losing
party must pay for your attorney's fee, as well as
court costs and damages that you have suffered. An
injunction and a temporary restraining order (a
short-term injunction of 10 days or less) is requested in Form 20-2. However, most judges and
courts will require a separate motion and a brief in
support of the motion. If you do not have an attorney, or do not have time to get one you can file the
complaint and the clerk and judge may set the case
for an immediate hearing. Court clerks are usually
very helpful to unrepresented plaintiffs (known as
pro se, or *pro per*).

Your local chapter of the American Civil Liberties Union (ACLU), the National Association for
the Advancement of Colored People (NAACP), or
the National Organization for Women (NOW) may
be able to help you, or to find you an organization
or an attorney to help you. If your complaint involves national origin discrimination, contact an

FORM 20-1: Housing Discrimination Complaint (for HUD)   Form Approved
OMB No. 63-R1226

U.S. DEPARTMENT OF HOUSING AND URBAN DEVELOPMENT

HOUSING DISCRIMINATION COMPLAINT

	FOR HUD USE ONLY

Number _____

Date _____

Filing Date _____

STATE OR LOCAL

FEDERAL COVERAGE

PRIOR ACTION

PRELIMINARY DETERMINATION

INSTRUCTIONS: Read this form and the instructions on reverse carefully before completing. All questions should be answered. However, if you do not know the answer or if a question is not applicable, leave the question unanswered and fill out as much of the form as you can. Your complaint should be signed, dated and, if possible, notarized. Where more than one individual or organization is filing the same complaint, and all information is the same, each additional individual or organization should complete boxes 1 and 7 of a separate complaint form and attach it to the original form. Complaints may be (1) mailed to the Regional Office covering the State where the complaint arose (see list at end of form), to an Area Office, or to Fair Housing, HUD, Washington, D.C. 20410, or (2) filed or presented in person at HUD in Washington, D.C. or at any HUD Regional or Area Office.

PLEASE TYPE OR PRINT

TELEPHONE NUMBER   Home   Business

1. Name of aggrieved person or organization *(Last Name-First Name-Middle Initial) (Mr. Mrs. Miss, Ms.)*

Street Address, City, County, State and ZIP Code

2. Against whom is this complaint being filed?

Name *(Last Name-First Name-Middle Initial)*	Street Address, City, County, State and ZIP Code	Telephone Number

Is the party named above a: *(Check applicable box or boxes)*

☐ Builder   ☐ Owner   ☐ Broker   ☐ Salesperson   ☐ Supt. or Manager   ☐ Bank or Other Lender   ☐ Other

If you have named an individual above who appeared to be acting for a company in this case, check this box ☐ and write the name and address *(Street, City, County, State and ZIP Code)* of the company, in this space.

Name and Identify Others *(if any)* you believe violated the law in this case

3. What did the person you are complaining against do? *(Check applicable box or boxes)*

☐ Refuse to rent, sell, or deal with you

☐ Discriminate in the conditions or terms of sale, rental, occupancy, or in services or facilities

☐ Advertise in a discriminatory way

☐ Falsely deny housing was available

☐ Engage in blockbusting

☐ Discriminate in financing

☐ Discriminate in broker's services

☐ Other *(Explain in box 6 below)*

When did act or acts occur? *(Be sure to include most recent date, if several dates are involved)*

4. Do you believe there was discrimination because of? *(Check applicable box.) See back of this sheet for Racial Categories)*

☐ Race or Color

☐ White   ☐ Hispanic
☐ Black   ☐ Asian or Pacific Islander
☐ American Indian and Alaskan Native

☐ Religion *(Specify)*

☐ Sex
☐ Male   ☐ Female

☐ National Origin *(Specify)*

5. What kind of house or property was involved?

☐ Single family house

☐ A house or building for 2, 3, or 4 families

☐ A building for 5 families or more

☐ Other, including vacant land held for residential use *(Explain in box 6)*

Did the owner live there?

☐ Yes   ☐ No   ☐ Unknown

Is the house or property *(Check applicable box)*

☐ Being sold   ☐ Being rented

What is the address of the house or property?

Street _____

City _____

County _____ State _____

6. Summarize in your own words what happened. Use this space for a brief and concise statement of the facts. Additional details of what happened may be provided on an attachment.

NOTE: HUD will furnish a copy of the complaint to the person or organization against whom the complaint is made.

7. I swear or affirm that I have read this complaint *(including any attachments)* and that it is true to the best of my knowledge, information, and belief.

_____   _____
(Signature)   *(Date)*

8.   NOTARIZATION

Subscribed and sworn to before me this _____ day of _____ 19 ___

_____   _____
(Name)   *(Title)*

IF IT IS DIFFICULT FOR YOU TO GET A NOTARY PUBLIC TO SIGN THIS, SIGN YOUR OWN NAME AND MAIL IT WITHOUT NOTARIZATION. HUD WILL HELP YOU GET YOUR COMPLAINT SWORN TO.

Previous edition is obsolete   HUD-903 (1-80)

FORM 20-2

Federal Court Complaint for Housing Discrimination

UNITED STATES DISTRICT COURT
FOR THE _____ DISTRICT OF _____
_____ DIVISION

_____,
Plaintiff(s),

v.   Civil Action No.

_____,
Defendant(s).

COMPLAINT

I. NATURE OF THE CASE

1. This is an action for declaratory and injunctive relief and for damages for discrimination in housing.

II. JURISDICTION

2. This Court had jurisdiction under 28 USC § 1343(4), and 42 USC § 3612, Declaratory relief is sought 28 USC § 2201.

III. PLAINTIFF

3. Plaintiff is, and at all relevant times was, a _____ (black, female, etc.) citizen of the United States, and resides in the City of _____, County of _____, State of _____.

IV. DEFENDANT

4. Defendant _____ (broker) is an agent for _____ (owner); defendant _____ is the manager of _____ (apartment building); defendant _____ is the owner of an apartment building known as _____, located at _____ (address) in the City of _____, State of _____.

V. FACTUAL ALLEGATIONS

5. On or about _____, 19_____, and continuing to the present time, defendants refused and continue to refuse to rent, or to negotiate the rental (or sale) of, and to otherwise make unavailable to plaintiff a unit in the apartment building described in paragraph four (4) because plaintiff is a_____ (black, female, etc.).

6. The above-described unit desired by plaintiff has been, and at all relevant times was, available for rental, and plaintiff was and is ready, willing, and able to rent such unit at the rental price set by defendants. (Insert purchase terms if a sale was denied.)

VI. CAUSE OF ACTION: ILLEGAL HOUSING DISCRIMINATION

7. Plaintiff incorporates by reference, paragraphs one (1) through seven (7), inclusive.

8. In refusing to rent/sell the unit to plaintiff, defendants have acted and continue to act intentionally and maliciously, and they were and are guilty of wanton and willful disregard of the rights and feelings of plaintiff, in violation of Title VIII of the Civil Rights Act, 42 USC 3601 and the Civil Rights Act of 1866, 42 USC § 1982. (Omit the Civil Rights Act of 1866 if case is not a race case.)

VII. IRREPARABLE INJURY

Plaintiff has no adequate remedy at law, or otherwise, for the harm done by defendants; and plaintiff has suffered and continues to suffer great and irreparable loss, damage, and injury as a proximate result of the described acts and conduct of defendants, and plaintiff will continue to so suffer unless such acts and conduct of defendants are enjoined.

WHEREFORE, plaintiff requests that this Court:

A. Declare that plaintiff cannot be denied the right to rent/purchase the subject apartment unit on the grounds of his/her _____ (race, sex, national origin).

B. Issue a temporary restraining order and a preliminary injunction restraining and enjoining defendants, the officers, agents, and employees of defendant _____, and all those persons in active concert or participation with defendants from refusing to rent the apartment unit to plaintiff and from renting it to anyone other than plaintiff, pending the final hearing and determination of this cause.

C. Following the final hearing and determination herein, issue an injunction permanently enjoining defendants from refusing to rent the apartment unit to plaintiff.

D. Award plaintiff actual damages in the amount of $_____ and punitive damages in the amount of $_____.

E. Award plaintiff a reasonable attorney's fee and costs of this action; and

F. Award such other and further relief as this Court deems just and proper. Dated _____ _____, 19_____.

(Signature) _____

ADDRESS

TELEPHONE NUMBER

Subscribed and sworn to before me this _____ day of _____.

_____

NOTARY PUBLIC

organization in your area that represents people from your country.

HOMOSEXUALS

Discrimination in housing against homosexuals is illegal statewide only in Pennsylvania and Wisconsin. However, various cities and counties outlaw discrimination against gays. They are: Tucson, Arizona; Los Angeles, San Francisco, and San Mateo County, California; Aspen, Colorado; Champaign and Evanston, Illinois; Howard County, Maryland; Amherst, Massachusetts; Ann Arbor, Detroit, and East Lansing, Michigan; Marshall and Minneapolis, Minnesota; Alfred, New York; Columbus and Yellowsprings, Ohio; Austin, Texas; King County, Pullman, and Seattle, Washington; and Washington, D.C.

21

How to Resolve Problems Concerning Consumer Products

Everyone has had problems with consumer products and services. However, most of these problems are minor, such as that the quality of the produce was poor, or the dishwasher repair man kept you waiting all day. If you sued someone in small claims court for every minor consumer transgression, you would spend your life in small claims court.

The first step, then, is to divide the minor problems from the major ones—not always an easy task because the principles involved are usually more important than the dollar value of the problem. Some minor problems can be resolved by talking to the manager of the store where you bought the product. If the manager is not helpful, a good consumer remedy is to tell the manager that you will not shop at his store anymore, and then don't shop there again.

CONSUMER COMPLAINT LETTER

If you are not satisfied with a consumer product, you should complain to the retail store where you purchased an unsatisfactory product and to the manufacturer. The address of the manufacturer should be on the product or the package that it came in. If the address is not on the product, ask the retail store for the manufacturer's address.

Your letter should be typed, and you should enclose a copy of your receipt. Make a copy of the letter for your records and keep the original receipt. Include the serial number of the product if it has one, the date of purchase, and the store where it was bought. Then explain the problem you are experiencing and describe what you want (a refund, a new product, or whatever). A sample complaint letter is included at the end of this chapter as Form 21-1. At the end of your letter make sure to state when you expect a reply.

HELP!

If you get no response within a reasonable time, or you get a negative response, what are your choices? You basically have six choices (not necessarily in this order):

1. Write to an action line or hot line;
2. Write to the Better Business Bureau;
3. Write to a consumer action panel;
4. Write to a state or local consumer protection agency;
5. Write to a federal agency; or
6. File suit against the company.

Your seventh choice is to do nothing. You will have to weigh the alternatives and decide how much time and money you are willing to invest to correct the problem.

ACTION LINES

Most major cities have action lines or hot lines at newspapers, radio, or television stations. A list of the major action services is included at the end of this chapter.

BETTER BUSINESS BUREAUS

Your local Better Business Bureau may help you to resolve your problem. However, not all companies are members of the bureau, and the bureau can do little to help you if the business is not a member. If your product was manufactured in another city, the local bureau will probably not be able to help you, but a consumer action panel may be able to.

CONSUMER ACTION PANELS

Several major industries have established consumer action panels to help resolve consumer complaints. The major consumer action panels are automotive, furniture, major appliances, and funeral services. The Auto Consumer Action Panel will be discussed in Chapter 22.

Decisions by the furniture panel are not binding on either party, while decisions of the major appliance panel are binding on the manufacturer, but not the consumer. Decisions made by the funeral panel are binding on both the consumer and the funeral parlor.

The addresses for the consumer panels are:

Furniture Industry Consumer Action Panel
Director of Consumer Affairs
P.O. Box 951
High Point, NC 27261
(919) 885-5065

Major Appliance Consumer Action Panel
20 N. Wacker Drive
Chicago, IL 60606
(312) 984-5858

ThanaCAP (complaints about funeral charges)
135 West Wells Street
Milwaukee, WI 53202
(414) 276-2500

STATE AND LOCAL CONSUMER PROTECTION AGENCIES

Every state government has an office which handles consumer complaints concerning products and services. A list of these state agencies is included at the end of this chapter. Many cities and counties also have consumer protection offices. States and cities license or regulate many professions, such as doctors, nurses, accountants, pharmacists, funeral directors, plumbers, electricians, auto repair shops, collection agencies, and electronic repair shops. These licensing boards will help you resolve your dispute. The boards or licensing agencies often have the power to revoke licenses and permits, so they have a lot of clout when dealing with license holders.

Concerning disputes about lawyers, doctors, and dentists, you can complain to your state Bar Association, Medical Association, or Dental Association.

FEDERAL AUTHORITY

Three major federal agencies handle consumer problems. They are the Federal Trade Commission, the Food and Drug Administration, and the Consumer Product Safety Commission. The U.S. Postal Services handles consumer complaints concerning mail fraud.

The Federal Trade Commission (FTC) has regional offices which receive complaints concerning warranties, mail order problems, and complaints of unfair or deceptive trade practices. The FTC does not process individual complaints, but if it notices a pattern of complaints against one company, it will take action on behalf of all consumers who have had similar problems. If you believe that an advertisement is false or misleading, the FTC is the appropriate agency to complain to. The address of their Washington, D.C. office is:

Correspondence Office
Federal Trade Commission
Washington, DC 20580
(202) 523-3567

REGIONAL OFFICES

Atlanta
Alabama
Florida
Georgia
Mississippi
North Carolina
South Carolina
Tennessee
Virginia

1718 Peachtree Street, N.W.
Suite 1000
Atlanta, GA 30367
(404) 881-4836

Boston
Connecticut
Maine
Massachusetts
New Hampshire
Rhode Island
Vermont

150 Causeway Street
Room 1301
Boston, MA 02114
(617) 223-6621

Chicago
Illinois
Indiana
Iowa
Kentucky
Minnesota
Missouri
Wisconsin

55 E. Monroe Street
Suite 1437
Chicago, IL 60603
(312) 353-4423

Cleveland
Delaware
Maryland
Michigan
New York (west of Rochester)
Ohio
Pennsylvania
West Virginia

118 St. Clair Avenue
Suite 500
Cleveland, OH 44114
(216) 552-4207

Dallas
Arizona
Louisiana
New Mexico
Oklahoma
Texas

2001 Bryan Street
Suite 2665
Dallas, TX 75201
(214) 767-0032

Denver
Colorado
Kansas
Montana
Nebraska
North Dakota
South Dakota
Utah
Wyoming

1405 Curtis Street
Suite 2900
Denver, CO 80202
(303) 837-2271

Los Angeles
Arizona
Southern California

11000 Wilshire Boulevard
Los Angeles, CA 90024
(213) 824-7575

San Francisco
Hawaii
Nevada
Northern California

450 Golden Gate Avenue
San Francisco, CA 94102
(415) 556-1270

FTC Field Station
P.O. Box 50169
Honolulu, HI 96850
(808) 546-5685

New York
New Jersey
New York (east of Rochester)

26 Federal Plaza
Room 2243-EB
New York, NY 10278
(212) 264-1207

Seattle
Alaska
Idaho
Oregon
Washington

28th Floor
915 2nd Avenue
Seattle, WA 98174
(206) 442-4655

The Food and Drug Administration (FDA) handles complaints concerning food, drug, and cosmetic products. The FDA can order immediate recalls if a product is likely to cause injury or death. For example, the FDA ordered a recall concerning Tylenol products when there was a series of contaminated Extra-Strength Tylenol bottles. Addresses for the FDA are:

National
Consumer Affairs and Small Business Staff (HFO-22)
Food and Drug Administration
Department of Health and Human Services
5600 Fishers Lane
Room 13-82
Rockville, MD 20857
(301) 443-4166

Region I
Food and Drug Administration
585 Commercial Street
Boston, MA 02109
(617) 223-5857

Region II
Food and Drug Administration
20 Evergreen Place
East Orange, NJ 07018
(201) 645-6356

Food and Drug Administration
850 Third Avenue
Brooklyn, NY 11232
(212) 965-5754

Food and Drug Administration
599 Delaware Avenue
Buffalo, NY 14202
(716) 846-4461

Food and Drug Administration
P.O. Box 54427, Old San Juan Station
San Juan, PR 00905
(809) 723-4465

Region III
Food and Drug Administration
900 Madison Avenue
Baltimore, MD 21201
(301) 962-3593

Food and Drug Administration
U.S. Customhouse, Room 900
2nd and Chestnut Streets
Philadelphia, PA 19106
(215) 597-0837

Food and Drug Administration
Pittsburgh Resident Inspection Post
7 Parkway Center
Suite 645
Pittsburgh, PA 15220
(412) 644-2858

Food and Drug Administration
Falls Church Resident Inspection Post
701 W. Broad Street
Room 309
Falls Church, VA 22046
(703) 285-2578

Region IV
Food and Drug Administration
P.O. Box 118
Orlando, FL 32802
(305) 855-0900

Food and Drug Administration
1182 W. Peachtree Street, N.W.
Atlanta, GA 30309
(404) 881-7355

Food and Drug Administration
297 Plus Park Boulevard
Nashville, TN 37217
(615) 251-7127

Region V
Food and Drug Administration
433 West Van Buren Street
1222 Main Post Office Building
Chicago, IL 60607
(312) 353-7840

Food and Drug Administration
Indianapolis Resident Inspection Post
575 North Pennsylvania
Room 693
Indianapolis, IN 46204
(319) 269-6500

Food and Drug Administration
1560 East Jefferson Avenue
Detroit, MI 48207
(313) 226-6260

Food and Drug Administration
240 Hennepin Avenue
Minneapolis, MN 55401
(612) 725-2121

Food and Drug Administration
1141 Central Parkway
Cincinnati, OH 45202
(513) 684-3501

Food and Drug Administration
U.S. Courthouse Building
85 Marconi Boulevard
Room 231
Columbus, OH 43215
(614) 469-7353

Food and Drug Administration
Cleveland Resident Inspection Post
601 Rockwell Avenue
Room 453
Cleveland, OH 44114
(216) 522-4844

Food and Drug Administration
Milwaukee Resident Inspection Post
615 E. Michigan Street
Milwaukee, WI 53202
(414) 291-3904

Region VI

Food and Drug Administration
500 South Ervay
Suite 470-B
Dallas, TX 75201
(214) 767-5433

Food and Drug Administration
4298 Elysian Fields Avenue
New Orleans, LA 70122
(504) 589-6344

Food and Drug Administration
Houston Station
1440 N. Loop
Suite 250
Houston, TX 77009
(713) 226-5581

Food and Drug Administration
San Antonio Resident Inspection Post
419 S. Main
Room 301
San Antonio, TX 78204
(512) 229-6737

Region VII

Food and Drug Administration
1009 Cherry Street
Kansas City, MO 64106
(816) 374-5623

Food and Drug Administration
St. Louis Station
Laclete's Landing
80B North Collins Street
St. Louis, MO 63102
(314) 425-4137

Food and Drug Administration
Omaha Resident Inspection Post
1619 Howard Street
Omaha, NE 68102
(402) 221-4676

Region VIII

Food and Drug Administration
500 U.S. Customhouse
19th and California Streets
Denver, CO 80202
(303) 837-4915

Region IX

Food and Drug Administration
50 United Nations Plaza
Room 518
San Francisco, CA 94102
(415) 556-2682

Food and Drug Administration
1521 W. Pico Boulevard
Los Angeles, CA 90015
(213) 688-3771

Region X

Food and Drug Administration
909 First Avenue
Federal Office Building
Room 5003
Seattle, WA 98174
(206) 442-5310

The Consumer Product Safety Commission (CPSC) handles complaints concerning consumer products that may be dangerous. The CPSC regulates the safety of toys, bicycles, lawnmowers, insulation, electrical products, and dozens of everyday items. One phone call from a concerned mother led to the recall of millions of dangerous toys that McDonald's was giving away. Call the CPSC toll-free hotline: (800) 638-8326 (Maryland residents call: (800) 492-8363 and residents of Alaska, Hawaii, Puerto Rico, and the Virgin Islands can dial (800) 638-8333.) The CPSC can ban, recall, or regulate unsafe products. Addresses and telephone numbers for the CPSC offices are:

U.S. CONSUMER PRODUCT SAFETY COMMISSION REGIONAL AND DISTRICT OFFICES

Atlanta Regional Office
Alabama
Florida
Georgia
Kentucky
Mississippi
North Carolina
South Carolina
Tennessee

Consumer Product Safety Commission
1330 West Peachtree Street, N.W.
Atlanta, GA 30309
(404) 881-2231

Boston Regional Office
Connecticut
Massachusetts
Maine
New Hampshire
Rhode Island
Vermont

Consumer Product Safety Commission
100 Summer Street
Room 1607
Boston, MA 02110
(617) 223-5576

Chicago Regional Office
Illinois
Indiana
Minnesota
Wisconsin

Consumer Product Safety Commission
230 S. Dearborn Street
Room 2945
Chicago, IL 60604
(312) 353-8260

Cleveland Regional Office
Michigan
Ohio

Consumer Product Safety Commission
Plaza Nine Building
Room 520
55 Erieview Plaza
Cleveland, OH 44114
(216) 522-3886

Denver District Office
Consumer Product Safety Commission
Guaranty Bank Building
Suite 938
817 17th Street
Denver, CO 80202
(303) 837-2904

Kansas City Regional Office
Colorado
Iowa
Kansas
Missouri
Montana
Nebraska
North Dakota
South Dakota
Utah
Wyoming

Consumer Product Safety Commission
Midland Building
Suite 1000
1221 Baltimore Avenue
Kansas City, MO 64105
(816) 374-2034

Los Angeles Regional Office
Arizona
Southern California

Consumer Product Safety Commission
3660 Wilshire Boulevard
Suite 1100
Los Angeles, CA 90010
(213) 688-7272

New York Regional Office
New Jersey
New York
Puerto Rico
Virgin Islands

Consumer Product Safety Commission
6 World Trade Center
Vesey Street
6th Floor
New York, NY 10048
(212) 264-1125

Philadelphia Regional Office
Delaware
Washington, D.C.
Maryland
Pennsylvania
Virginia
West Virginia

Consumer Product Safety Commission
400 Market Street
10th Floor
Philadelphia, PA 19106
(215) 597-9105

San Francisco Regional Office
Alaska
Hawaii
Idaho
Nevada
Northern California
Oregon
Washington

Consumer Product Safety Commission
U.S. Customs House
555 Battery Street
Room 416
San Francisco, CA 94111
(415) 556-1816

Seattle District Office
Consumer Product Safety Commission
3240 Federal Building
915 Second Avenue
Seattle, WA 98174
(206) 442-5276

Twin Cities District Office
Consumer Product Safety Commission
Metro Square,
Suite 580
7th and Robert
Saint Paul, MN 55101
(612) 725-7781

The U.S. Postal Service should be contacted when you believe a business is using the mails for fraudulent purposes. In this event write to the postmaster in your area. Your letter should be addressed simply to: Postmaster, your city, state, and zip code. Mail fraud is a felony and the postmaster will refer cases to the United States Attorney for criminal prosecution.

SUING THE BASTARDS

Small claims courts offer relief to consumers and can award a maximum of from $300 to $5000 depending on the state, with most limits around $750 or $1000. A list of the limit that you can sue for in small claims courts is included at the end of this chapter. Filing fees are low, the lowest is about $2 and the highest $15. In as little as two weeks, you can have a trial and get a judgment against a company.

After filing a small claims case, a company who has ignored your letters will soon respond to you. A corporation usually must hire an attorney to represent it in most courts, even most small claims courts. Let me give you an example. I flew on a chartered airline trip to the Caribbean on Trans National Travel, one of the largest charter companies in the country. When checking in for the flight, Trans National required all passengers to pay a surcharge for a supposed increase in fuel and alleged decreases in the value of the dollar. They had all of the passengers in a bind: either pay the "extortion" charge or ruin your vacation.

Well, we had a group of tourists on the plane who included two attorneys. Many of the passengers were able to stop payment on their surcharge checks before they were cashed. I wasn't so lucky. My check cleared in record time. But I filed suit for the $750 maximum even though my surcharge was only about $300. I added the additional money for punitive damages (to punish the travel company) because I had learned that fuel prices had not increased enough to justify the surcharge, and the dollar had not decreased in value as we were told.

Trans National failed to appear to defend in small claims court, so a default judgment was entered against it for $750, plus court costs. I wrote Trans National and it ignored the judgment. If you are not paid after you get a judgment, you must attach or seize property of the losing party. I learned that the Bar Association was organizing a charter with Trans National. I threatened to attach all of the checks coming in to the Bar Association unless Trans National paid within five days. I received the check within three days; the threat worked.

Sample small claims forms are Forms 18-2, 19-2, and 22-4.

MAIL ORDER DISPUTES

The Federal Trade Commission regulates the mail order industry. The FTC has ruled that you must receive the merchandise when the seller says you will, or you are entitled to a refund. If a specific time for delivery is not mentioned, the seller must ship the item within 30 days after receiving the order. If the seller writes you explaining the reason for the delay, you have a right to cancel. If you fail to respond, it means that you agree to the delay. When you prepay for an item and then cancel, the seller must mail a refund within seven business days. If the sale was on a credit card your account must be adjusted within one billing cycle. When a mail order business fails to comply with these rules, write to the Federal Trade Commission, Washington, DC 20580, or your local postmaster. Make a copy of the mail order advertisement or brochure and send it to the postmaster or the FTC with your complaint letter.

FORM 21-1

Sample Complaint Letter

Your Address

Date _____

Consumers Affairs Office

_____ Company

Address _____

RE: (nature of complaint and product)

Dear _____,

I purchased one of your _____ products on _____ (date) and am very unhappy with it because _____ _____. The serial number of the product is _____, and it is a _____ model. I made this purchase at _____ which is located at _____. A copy of my receipt is enclosed.

Unfortunately, your product (or service) has not performed satisfactorily (or the service was inadequate) because _____ _____. In order to resolve this matter I want you to _____.

I am looking forward to your reply and resolution of this problem, and will wait three weeks (or whatever time limit you want to set) before taking other action to resolve this dispute. Contact me at the above address or by telephone at _____.

Sincerely yours,

(Signature) _____

YOUR NAME

STATE CONSUMER PROTECTION OFFICES

Alabama
Consumer Protection Division
Office of Attorney General
560 South McDonough Street
Montgomery, AL 36104
(205) 832-5936
(809) 392-5658

Alaska
Consumer Protection Section
Office of Attorney General
1049 West Fifth Avenue
Suite 101
Anchorage, AK 99501
(907) 279-0428

Arizona
Financial Fraud Division
Office of Attorney General
207 State Capitol Building
Phoenix, AZ 85007
(602) 255-5763
800-354-8431

Arkansas
Consumer Protection Division
Office of Attorney General
Justice Building
Little Rock, AR 72201
(501) 371-2341
800-482-8982

California
California Department of Consumer Affairs
1020 N Street
Sacramento, CA 95814
(916) 445-0660 (Complaint assistance)
(916) 445-1254 (Consumer information)

Colorado
Anti-Trust and Consumer Protection Section
Office of Attorney General
1525 Sherman Street
2nd Floor
Denver, CO 80203
(303) 866-3611

Connecticut
Department of Consumer Protection
State Office Building
165 Capitol Avenue
Hartford, CT 06115
(203) 566-4999
800-842-2649 (Connecticut only)

Delaware
Delaware Division of Consumer Affairs
Department of Community Affairs and Economic
  Development
820 North French Street
4th Floor
Wilmington, DE 19801
(302) 571-3250

District of Columbia
D.C. Office of Consumer Protection
1424 K Street, NW
2nd Floor
Washington, DC 20005
(202) 727-1158

Florida
Division of Consumer Services
110 Mayo Building
Tallahassee, FL 32301
(904) 488-2221
800-342-2176 (Florida only)

Georgia
Governor's Office of Consumer Affairs
205 Butler Street, S.E.
Suite 356
Plaza Level East Tower
Atlanta, GA 30334
(404) 656-3790
800-282-4900

Hawaii
Governor's Office of Consumer Protection
250 South King Street
P.O. Box 3767
Honolulu, HI 96812
(808) 548-2560

Idaho
Business Regulation Division
Office of Attorney General
State Capitol
Boise, ID 83720
(208) 334-2400

Illinois
Consumer Protection Division
Office of Attorney General
228 North LaSalle
Room 1242
Chicago, IL 60601
(312) 793-3580

Assistant Attorney General and Chief
Consumer Protection Division
Office of Attorney General
500 South Second Street
Springfield, IL 62706
(217) 782-9011

Indiana
Consumer Protection Division
Office of Attorney General
219 State House
Indianapolis, IN 46204
(317) 232-6330 or 6331
800-382-5516 (Indiana only)

Iowa
Assistant Attorney General in Charge
Consumer Protection Division
Office of Attorney General
1300 East Walnut
2nd Floor
Des Moines, IA 50319
(515) 281-5926

Kansas
Deputy Attorney General and Chief
Consumer Protection and Antitrust Division
Office of Attorney General
Kansas Judicial Center
2nd Floor
Topeka, KS 66612
(913) 296-3751
800-432-2310

Kentucky
Assistant Deputy Attorney General
Consumer Protection Division
Office of Attorney General
209 St. Clair Street
Frankfort, KY 40601
(502) 564-2200
800-432-9257 (Kentucky only)

Louisiana
State Office of Consumer Protection
2610A Wooddale Boulevard
P.O. Box 44091, Capitol Station
Baton Rouge, LA 70804
(504) 925-4401
800-272-9868

Maine
Bureau of Consumer Protection
Department of Business Regulation
State House Station No. 35
Augusta, ME 04333
(207) 289-3731

Maryland
Consumer Protection Division
Office of Attorney General
26 South Calvert Street
Baltimore, MD 21202
(301) 659-4300

Massachusetts
Self-Help Consumer Information Office
Executive Office of Consumer Affairs
John W. McCormack Building
One Ashburton Place
Room 1411
Boston, MA 02108
(617) 727-7780

Michigan
Michigan Consumers Council
414 Hollister Building
106 West Allegan Street
Lansing, MI 48933
(517) 373-0947
800-292-5680

Minnesota
Special Assistant Attorney General
Consumer Protection Division
Office of Attorney General
Room 200
117 University Avenue
St. Paul, MN 55155
(612) 296-3353

Mississippi
Consumer Protection Division
Department of Agriculture and Commerce
High and President Streets
P.O. Box 1609
Jackson, MS 39205
(601) 354-6258

Missouri
Missouri Department of Consumer Affairs, Regulation
   and Licensing
P.O. Box 1157
Jefferson City, MO 65102
(314) 751-4996

Montana
Consumer Affairs Unit
Department of Commerce
1424 Ninth Avenue
Helena, MT 59620
(406) 449-3163

Nevada
Consumer Affairs Division
Department of Commerce
State Mail Room Complex
Las Vegas, NV 89158
(702) 386-5293

New Hampshire
Consumer Protection and Antitrust Division
Office of Attorney General
State House Annex
Concord, NH 03301
(603) 271-3641

New Jersey
Division of Consumer Affairs
Department of Law and Public Safety
1100 Raymond Boulevard
Room 504
Newark, NJ 07102
(201) 648-4010

New Mexico
Consumer and Economic Crime Division
Office of Attorney General
P.O. Box 1508
Santa Fe, NM 87503
(505) 982-6916

New York
Chairperson and Executive Director
New York State Consumer Protection Board
99 Washington Avenue
Albany, NY 12210
(518) 474-8583

North Carolina
Special Deputy Attorney General and Chief
Consumer Protection Division
Department of Justice Building
P.O. Box 629
Raleigh, NC 27602
(919) 733-7741

North Dakota
Consumer Affairs Office
State Laboratories Department
P.O. Box 937
Bismarck, ND 58505
(701) 224-2485
800-472-2927 (North Dakota only)

Ohio
Consumer Frauds and Crimes Section
Office of Attorney General
30 East Broad Street, 15th Floor
Columbus, OH 43215
(614) 466-8831 or 4986
1-800-282-0515 (Ohio only)

Oklahoma
Department of Complaints, Investigation and
  Mediation
Oklahoma Corporation Commission
Jim Thorpe Building
Room 680
Oklahoma City, OK 73105
(405) 521-4113

Oregon
Consumer Protection and Services Division
Department of Justice
500 Pacific Building
520 SW Yamhill Street
Portland, OR 97204
(503) 229-5522

Pennsylvania
Bureau of Consumer Protection
Office of Attorney General
Strawberry Square
15th Floor
Harrisburg, PA 17120
(717) 787-9707

Rhode Island
Rhode Island Consumers' Council
365 Broadway
Providence, RI 02909
(401) 277-2764

South Carolina
Department of Consumer Affairs
600 Columbia Building
P.O. Box 5757
Columbia, SC 29250
(803) 758-2040
800-922-1594

South Dakota
Division of Consumer Protection
Office of Attorney General
Insurance Building
Pierre, SD 57501
(605) 773-4400
800-592-1865

Tennessee
Division of Consumer Affairs
Box 40627 Melrose Station
Nashville, TN 37204
(615) 741-1461
800-342-8385

Texas
Assistant Attorney General
Consumer Protection and Antitrust Division
Office of Attorney General
P.O. Box 12548, Capitol Station
Austin, TX 78711
(512) 475-3288

Washington
Consumer Protection and Antitrust Division
Office of Attorney General
1366 Dexter Horton Building
Seattle, WA 98104
(206) 464-7744
800-552-0700

West Virginia
Consumer Protection Division
Office of Attorney General
1204 Kanawha Boulevard East
Charleston, WV 25301
(304) 348-8986

Wisconsin
Division of Trade and Consumer Protection
Department of Agriculture, Trade, and Consumer
   Protection
P.O. Box 8911
801 West Badger Road
Madison, WI 53708
(608) 266-9837
800-362-3020

BETTER BUSINESS BUREAUS

Alabama
2026 Second Avenue N.
Suite 2303
Birmingham, AL 35203
(205) 323-6127

Central Bank Building
Suite 410
West Side Square
P.O. Box 383 (35804)
Huntsville, AL 35801
(205) 533-1640

307 Van Antwerp Building
Mobile, AL 36602
(205) 433-5494

60 Commerce Street
Suite 810
Montgomery, AL 36104
(205) 262-2390

Arizona
4428 North 12th Street
Phoenix, AZ 85013
(602) 264-1721

100 East Alameda Street
Suite 403
Tucson, AZ 84701
Inquiries (602) 622-7651
Complaints (602) 622-7654

Arkansas
1216 South University
Little Rock, AR 72204
(501) 664-7274

California
705 Eigtheenth Street
Bakersfield, CA 93301
(805) 322-2074

1265 North La Cadena
Colton, CA 92324
(714) 825-7280

413 T.W. Patterson Building
Fresno, CA 93721
(209) 268-6424

639 South New Hampshire Avenue
3rd Floor
Los Angeles, CA 90005
(213) 383-0992

360 22nd Street, El Dorado Building
Oakland, CA 94612
(415) 839-5900

74-273½ Highway 111
Palm Desert, CA 92260
(714) 346-2014

1401 21st Street
Suite 305
Sacramento, CA 95814
(916) 443-6843

4310 Orange Avenue
San Diego, CA 92105
(714) 283-3927

2740 Van Ness Avenue
Suite 210
San Francisco, CA 94109
(415) 775-3300

P.O. Box 8110
San Jose, CA 95155
(408) 298-5880

20 North San Mateo Drive
P.O. Box 294
San Mateo, CA 94401
(415) 347-1251, 52,53

P.O. Box 746
Santa Barbara, CA 93102
(805) 963-8657

111 North Center Street
Stockton, CA 95202
(209) 948-4880

17662 Irvine Boulevard
Suite 15
Tustin, CA 92680
Inquiries (714) 544-5842
Complaints (714) 544-6942

Colorado
524 South Cascade
Colorado Springs, CO 80903
(303) 636-1155

841 Delaware Street
Denver, CO 80204
(303) 629-1036

Connecticut
Fairfield Woods Plaza
2345 Black Rock Turnpike
Fairfield, CT 06430
(203) 368-6538

250 Constitution Plaza
Hartford, CT 06103
(203) 247-8700

35 Elm Street
P.O. Box 2015
New Haven, CT 06506
(203) 787-5788

Delaware
20 South Walnut Street
P.O. Box 300
Milford, DE 19963
(302) 856-6969

1901-B West Eleventh Street
P.O. Box 4085
Wilmington, DE 19807
(302) 652-3833

District of Columbia
1334 G Street, N.W.
Prudential Building
6th Floor
Washington, DC 20005
(202) 393-8000

Florida
8600 NE-2nd Avenue
Miami, FL 33138
(305) 757-3446

3015 Exchange Court
West Palm Beach, FL 33409
(305) 686-2200

Georgia
212 Healey Building
57 Forsyth Street, N.W.
Atlanta, GA 30335
(404) 688-4910

P.O. Box 2085
Augusta, GA 30903
(404) 722-1574

Martin Theatre Building
1320 Broadway
Suite 250
Columbus, GA 31902
(404) 324-0712, 13

P.O. Box 13956
Savannah, GA 31406
(912) 234-5336

Hawaii
677 Ala Moana Boulevard
Suite 602
Honolulu, HI 96813
(808) 531-8131, 32, 33

P. O. Box 11414
Lahaina, Maui, HI 96761
(808) 877-4000

Idaho
Idaho Building
Suite 324
Boise, ID 83702
(208) 342-4649

Illinois
35 East Wacker Drive
Chicago, IL 60601
Inquiries (312) 346-3868
Complaints (312) 346-3313

109 S.W. Jefferson Street
Suite 305
Peoria, IL 61602
(309) 673-5194

Indiana
118 South Second Street
P.O. Box 405
Elkhart, IN 46515
(219) 293-5731

Old Courthouse Center
Room 310
Evansville, IN 47708
(812) 422-6879

1203 Webster Street
Fort Wayne, IN 46802
(219) 423-4433

2500 West Ridge Road, Calumet
  Township
Gary, IN 46408
(219) 980-1511

15 East Market Street
Indianapolis, IN 46204
(317) 637-0197

204 Iroquois Building
Marion, IN 46952
(317) 668-8954

Ball State Univ. BBB, Whitinger
  Building
Room 160
Muncie, IN 47306
(317) 285-6375

230 West Jefferson Boulevard
South Bend, IN 46601
(219) 234-0183

105 S. Third Street
Terre Haute, IN 47801
(812) 234-7749

Iowa
619 Kahl Building
Davenport, IA 52801
(319) 322-0782

234 Insurance Exchange Building
Des Moines, IA 50309
(515) 243-8137

Benson Building
Suite 645
7th & Douglas SQTREETS
Sioux City, IA 51101
(712) 252-4501

Kansas
501 Jefferson
Suite 24
Topeka, KS 66607
(913) 232-0454

300 Kaufman Building
Wichita, KS 67202
(316) 263-3146

Kentucky
1523 North Limestone
Lexington, KY 40505
(606) 252-4492

844 S. Fourth Street
Louisville, KY 40202
(502) 583-6546

Louisiana
2055 Wooddale Boulevard
Baton Rouge, LS 70806
(504) 926-3010

300 Bond Street
P.O. Box 9129
Houma, LA 70361
(504) 868-3456

804 Jefferson Street
P.O. Box 3651
Lafayette, LA 70502
(318) 234-8341

1413 Ryan Street, Suite C
P.O. Box 1681
Lake Charles, LA 70602
(318) 433-1633

141 De Siard Street, 141 ONB Building
Suite 503
Monroe, LA 71201
(318) 387-4600

301 Camp Street
Suite 403
New Orleans, LA 70130
(504) 581-6222

320 Milam Street
Shreveport, LA 71101
(318) 221-8352
(Texarkana residents call
(214) 792-7691)

Maryland
401 North Howard Street
Baltimore, MD 21201
(301) 685-6986

6917 Arlington Road
Bethesda, MD 20014
(301) 656-7000

Massachusetts
8 Winter Street
Boston, MA 02108
(617) 482-9151

The Federal Building
Suite 1
78 North Street
Hyannis, MA 02601
(617) 771-3022

316 Essex Street
Lawrence, MA 01840
(617) 687-7666

908 Purchase Street
New Bedford, MA 02745
(617) 999-6060

293 Bridge Street
Suite 324
Springfield, MA 01103
(413) 734-3114

32 Franklin Street
P.O. Box 379
Worcester, MA 01601
(617) 755-2548

Michigan
150 Michigan Avenue
Detroit, MI 48226
(313) 962-7566

1 Peoples Building
Grand Rapids, MI 49503
(616) 774-8236
Holland/Zeeland
(616) 772-6063
Muskegon
(616) 722-0707

Minnesota
1745 University Avenue
St. Paul, MN 55104
(612) 646-4637

Mississippi
P.O. Box 2090
Jackson, MS 39205
(601) 948-4732

Missouri
906 Grand Avenue
Kansas City, MO 64106
(816) 421-7800

Mansion House Center
440 N. Fourth Street
St. Louis, MO 63101
(314) 241-3100

P.O. Box 4331, GS 319
Hollard Building, Park Central
Springfield, MO 65806
(417) 862-9231

Nebraska
719 North 48th Street
Lincoln, NE 68504
(402) 467-5261

417 Farnam Building
1613 Farnam Street
Omaha, NE 68102
(402) 346-3033

Nevada
1829 East Charleston Boulevard
Suite 103
Las Vegas, NV 89104
(702) 382-7141

372-A Casazza Drive
P.O. Box 2932
Reno, NV 89505
(702) 322-0657

New Hampshire
One Pillsbury Street
Concord, NH 03301
(603) 224-1991

New Jersey
836 Haddon Avenue
P.O. Box 303
Collingswood, NJ 08108
(609) 854-8467

Mercer County
Cranbury, NJ 08512
(609) 586-1464

Monmouth County
536-6306

Middelsex, Somerset, and
Hunderton Counties
297-5000

34 Park Place
Newark, NJ 07102
(201) 643-3025

2 Forest Avenue
Paramus, NJ 07652
(201) 845-4044

1721 Route 37 East
Toms River, NJ 06753
(201) 270-5577

New Mexico
2921 Carlisle, N.E.
Albuquerque, NM 87110
(505) 844-0500

2120 East 20th Street
Farmington, NM 87401
(505) 325-1136

Santa Fe Division
227 East Palace Avenue
Suite C
Santa Fe, NM 87501
(505) 988-3648

New York
775 Main Street
Buffalo, NY 14203
(716) 856-7180

435 Old Country Road
Long Island (Westbury),
NY 11590
(516) 334-7662

257 Park Avenue, South
New York, NY 10010
Inquiries & Complaints
(212) 533-6200
Other (212) 533-7500

257 Park Avenue, South
(Harlem)
New York, NY 10010
(212) 533-6200

1122 Sibley Tower
Rochester, NY 14604
(716) 546-6776

120 East Washington Street
Syracuse, NY 13202
(315) 479-6635

209 Elizabeth Street
Utica, NY 13501
(315) 724-3129

158 Westchester Avenue
White Plains, NY 10601
(914) 428-1230, 31

120 East Main
Wappinger Falls, NY 12590
(914) 297-6550

North Carolina
29½ Page Avenue
Asheville, NC 28801
(704) 253-2392

Commerce Center
Suite 1300
Charlotte, NC 28202
(704) 332-7152

3608 West Friendly Avenue
P.O. Box 2400
Greensboro, NC 27410
(919) 852-4240, 41, 42

100 Park Drive Building
Suite 203
P.O. Box 12033
Research Triangle Park, NC 27709
(919) 549-8221

The First Union National Bank Building
Winston-Salem, NC 27101
(919) 725-8348

Ohio
P.O. Box F 596
Akron, OH 44308
(216) 253-4590

500 Cleveland Avenue, North
Canton, OH 44702
(216) 454-9401

26 East Sixth Street
Cincinnati, OH 45202
(513) 421-3015

1720 Keith Building
Cleveland, OH 44115
(216) 241-7678

527 South High Street
Columbus, OH 43215
(614) 221-6336

15 East Fourth Street
Suite 209
Dayton, OH 45402
(513) 222-5825

405 N. Huron Street
Toledo, OH 45604
(419) 241-6276

903 Mahoning Bank Building
P.O. Box 1495 44501
Youngstown, OH 44503
(216) 744-3111

Oklahoma
606 N. Dewey
Oklahoma City, OK 73102
(405) 239-6081, 82,83

4833 South Sheridan
Suite 412
Tulsa, OK 74145
(918) 664-1266

Oregon
623 Corbett Building
Portland, OR 97204
(503) 226-3981

Pennsylvania
528 North New Street, Dodson
  Building
Bethlehem, PA 18018
(215) 866-8780

53 N. Duke Street
Lancaster, PA 17602
(717) 291-1151
Toll Free, York Co. Resident
(717) 846-2700

1218 Chestnut Street
Philadelphia PA 19107
(215) 574-3600

610 Smithfield Street
Pittsburgh, PA 15222
(412) 456-2700

Brooks Building
Scranton, PA 18503
(717) 342-9129

Puerto Rico
P.O. Box BBB, Fernandez
  Juncos Station
San Juan, PR 00910
(809) 724-7474
Cable: BEBUSBU

Rhode Island
248 Weybosset Street
Providence, RI 02903
(401) 272-9800

Tennessee
716 James Building
735 Broad Street
Chattanooga, TN 37402
(615) 266-6144

P.O. Box 3608
Knoxville, TN 37917
(615) 522-2139

1835 Union, Suite 202
P.O. Box 41406
Memphis, TN 38104
(901) 272-9641

506 Nashville City Bank Building
Nashville, TN 37201
(615) 254-5872

Texas
465 Cypress Duffy Building
P.O. Box 3275
Abilene, TX 79604
(915) 677-8071

518 Amarillo Building
Amarillo, TX 79101
(806) 374-3735

American Bank Tower
Suite 720
Austin, TX 78701
(512) 476-6943

P.O. Box 2988
Beaumont, TX 77704
(713) 835-5348

202 Varisco Building
Bryan, TX 77801
(713) 823-8148

109 Chaparral
Suite 101
Corpus Christi, TX 78401
(512) 888-5555

1511 Bryan Street
Dallas, TX 75201
(214) 747-8891

2501 North Mesa Street
Suite 301
El Paso, TX 79902
(915) 533-2431

709 Sinclair Building
106 West 5th Street
Fort Worth, TX 76102
(817) 332-7585

P.O. Box 7499
Houston, TX 77008
(713) 868-9500

1015 15th Street
P.O. Box 1178
Lubbock, TX 79401
(806) 763-0459

Air Terminal Building
P.O. Box 6006
Midland, TX 79701
(915) 563-1880
Complaints (915) 563-1882

337 West Twohig
San Angelo, TX 76903
(915) 653-2318

400 West Market Street
Suite 301
San Antonio, TX 78205
(512) 225-5833

608 New Road
P.O. Box 7203
Waco, TX 76718
(817) 772-7530

First National Bank Building
Suite 600
Wichita Falls, TX 76301
(817) 723-5526

Utah
40 North 100 East
Provo, UT 84601
(801) 377-2611

1588 South Main
Salt Lake City, UT 84115
(801) 487-4656

Virginia
105 East Annandale Road
Suite 210
Falls Church, VA 22046
(703) 533-1900

First & Merchants Bank Building
Suite 620
300 Main Street, E.
P.O. Box 3548
Norfolk, VA 23514
(804) 627-5651
Peninsula area
(804) 851-9101

4020 West Broad Street
Richmond, VA 23230
(804) 355-7902

646 A Crystal Tower
145 West Campbell Avenue, SW
Roanoke, VA 24011
(703) 342-3455

Washington
2332 Sixth Avenue
Seattle, WA 98121
(206) 622-8067, 68

N. 214 Wall
Spokane, WA 99201
(509) 747-1155

950 Pacific Avenue
Tacoma, WA 98402
(206) 383-5561

P.O. Box 1584
424 Washington Mutual Building
Yakima, WA 98907
(509) 248-1326

Wisconsin
740 North Plankinton Avenue
Milwaukee, WI 53203
(414) 273-1600

CALL FOR ACTION AFFILIATES

California
KCBS CFA
One Embarcadero Center
San Francisco, CA 94111
(415) 478-3300
11 a.m.–1 p.m.

Colorado
KLZ CFA
2149 S. Holly Street
Denver, CO 80222
(303) 759-2285
10 a.m.–12 noon

Connecticut
WELI CFA
P.O. Box 85
New Haven, CT 06501
(203) 481-1011
9:30 a.m.–11:30 a.m.

District of Columbia
WTOP CFA
4646 40th Street, N.W.
Washington, DC 20016
(202) 686-8225
11 a.m.–1 p.m.

Florida
WCIX–TV CFA
1111 Brickell Avenue
Miami, FL 33131
(305) 371-6566
11 a.m.–1 p.m.

Illinois
WIND CFA
625 N. Michigan Avenue
Chicago, IL 60611
(312) 644-0560
11 a.m.–1 p.m.

Indiana
WOWO CFA
203 W. Wayne Street
Ft. Wayne, IN 46802
(219) 424-2400
10 a.m.–12 noon

Kansas
KCMO–TV CFA
4500 Johnson Drive
Fairway, KS 66205
(913) 677-7381
11 a.m.–1 p.m.

Maryland
WBAL CFA
3800 Hooper Street
Baltimore, MD 21211
(301) 366-5900
11 a.m.–1 p.m.

Massachusetts
WBZ CFA
1170 Soldiers Field Road
Boston, MA 02134
(617) 787-2300
11 a.m.–1 p.m.

WBSM CFA
P.O. Box J4105
New Bedford, MA 02741
(617) 997-3349
11 a.m.–1 p.m.

Michigan
WJR CFA
Fisher Building
Detroit, MI 48202
(313) 873-8700
11 a.m.–1 p.m.

Missouri
KMOX CFA
One Memorial Drive
St. Louis, MO 63102
(314) 421-1975
11 a.m.–1 p.m.

New York
WIVB-TV CFA
2077 Elmwood Avenue
Buffalo, NY 14207
(716) 874-1700
10 a.m. –12 noon

WGSM CFA
900 Walt Whitman Road
Huntington, NY 11747
(516) 423-1400
11 a.m.–1 p.m.

WMCA CFA
888 Seventh Avenue
New York, NY 10019
(212) 586-6666
11 a.m.–1 p.m.

WGY CFA
1400 Balltown Road
Schenectady, NY 12309
(518) 385-1488
11 a.m.–1 p.m.

WHEN CFA
P.O. Box 6509
Syracuse, NY 13217
(315) 467-6116
11 a.m.–1 p.m.

North Carolina
WRAL-TV CFA
115 E. Chapel Hill Street
Durham, NC 27701
(919) 688-9306
11 a.m.–1 p.m.

WRAL-TV CFA
209 S. McDowell Street
Raleigh, NC 27601
(919) 832-7578
11 a.m.–1 p.m.

Ohio
WJKW-TV CFA
5800 Marginal Road
Cleveland, OH 44103
(216) 578-0700
10 a.m.–12 noon

WFMJ CFA
101 W. Boardman
Youngstown, OH 44503
(216) 744-5155
11 a.m.–1 p.m.

Pennsylvania
WFBG CFA
Logan Valley Boulevard
Altoona, PA 16603
(814) 944-9336
1 p.m.–3 p.m.
7 p.m.–9 p.m. Th

KYW CFA
5th S. Market Street
Philadelphia, PA 19106
(215) 925-1060
11 a.m.–1 p.m.

KDKA CFA
One Gateway Center
Pittsburgh, PA 15222
(412) 333-9370
11 a.m.–1 p.m.

Tennessee
WDIA CFA
P.O. Box 12045
Memphis, TN 38112
(901) 278-6316
11 a.m.–1 p.m.

22

How to Avoid Getting Squeezed by Your Lemon

Next to your home, a car is usually your largest investment. With economy cars selling for $10,000, it is indeed frustrating when the damn vehicle doesn't work properly. There are eleven different steps that you can take when your new, or fairly new, automobile seems to be in the repair shop more often than it is in your garage. These steps can be pursued, not necessarily in this order:

1. Complain to the dealer
2. Complain to manufacturer's zone or regional representatives
3. Complain to the main headquarters of the manufacturer
4. Return your lemon
5. File a complaint with the Automotive Consumer Action Program (AUTOCAP)
6. Write to the Federal Trade Commission
7. Refuse to pay your car loan (in certain cases)
8. Write to the National Highway Traffic Safety Administration
9. Write to the Environmental Protection Agency
10. File a complaint with a State Consumer Protection Office
11. File Suit

THE DEALER

First, unless your car is a total disaster, you should give your dealer an opportunity to repair the car. If the needed repair work is covered by the manufacturer's warranty, the dealer should make the repair. Even if the warranty period has expired, the dealer may be able to make the repair under a so-called "secret" warranty. A secret warranty is made when a manufacturer has had repeated problems with a particular component of the car. It is secret because dealers are told to charge for the repairs unless the customer complains. So by all means, make a vocal complaint. If you suspect that other people are experiencing the same problem you can call or write the Automobile Owners Action Council, or the Center for Auto Safety. Their addresses are:

Automobile Owners Action Council
1010 Vermont Avenue, N.W.
Washington, DC 20005
(202) 638-5550

Center for Auto Safety
1223 DuPont Circle Building
Washington, DC 20036
(202) 659-1126

You can also write to the Better Business Bureau, or to an action line. Addresses of Better Business and action lines are at the end of Chapter 21. Send copies of your complaint letter to as many of these organizations as you want; it might strike a nerve somewhere and provoke assistance.

While the dealer who sold you the car should be responsive to your complaints you can go to any dealer who sells the car that you own. A large dealer may have had more experience with your type of problem. Some dealers have better service departments than others; if you are unhappy with one dealer, try another.

MANUFACTURER'S REPRESENTATIVES

Every auto manufacturer has an internal system for handling consumer complaints. Auto dealers are supervised by regional or zone representatives of the manufacturers. A list of contacts in the automobile industry is included at the end of this chapter. Your dealer will give you the name of the zone rep who services it. The zone rep may be able to handle your complaint by phone, or he may want to meet you at a dealership to inspect your car. A zone or regional representative has the power to authorize warranty repairs, even when your car is not in the warranty period.

CORPORATE HEADQUARTERS

Occasionally, writing to the president of an auto manufacturer gets results. But the standard route is to write to the customer relations office at the corporation's headquarters. A list of these offices is included at the end of this chapter. A sample complaint letter is included at the end of this chapter as Form 22-1.

RETURNING YOUR LEMON

If your problems are substantial, and you have been deprived of the use of your car for a long time, you may be able to take back your lemon for a refund or exchange. Before returning your car, you should consult with an attorney. Returning a car is risky because you may still be liable for car payments while the dispute is being worked out. Taking your car back is a last resort which should only be attempted when it seems that your problems are insoluble. If your car is turned in, make sure that you offer the dealer the keys and title, remove your license plates, and notify your lender and insurance company.

AUTOCAPS

There are 32 regional automobile consumer ac-tion programs, or Autocaps, across the United States. At the end of this chapter there is a list of these Autocaps. The Autocaps have a standard form for filing complaints. This form is included at the end of this chapter as Form 22-2. Each Autocap has a panel composed of half industry representatives and half consumer representatives, which will review your complaint. The panels make a decision within three or four weeks which is usually followed by the manufacturer or dealer, but its decision is not binding on you. If you disagree with the decision of the Autocap panel, you can pursue other remedies, through agencies or in court.

THE FEDERAL TRADE COMMISSION

The Federal Trade Commission (FTC) will investigate cases where warranties are not lived up to or where there have been false or misleading advertisements. The FTC will not usually resolve an individual complaint, but it will step in where a pattern of fraud or warranty violations develops. The FTC has regional offices in major cities and a national office in Washington. The national office has a warranty project. If you have a warranty problem write to:

Warranty Project
Bureau of Consumer Protection
Federal Trade Commission
Washington, DC 20580

Concerning false advertising or other fraudulent practices, write to a regional FTC office. A list of these offices is included at the end of Chapter 21.

WHEN YOU HAVE A RIGHT TO REFUSE TO PAY YOUR CAR LOAN

When the car dealer arranges your loan, you legally are entitled to stop making car payments when there are serious problems with the car. You have a right to stop making payments on your GM car when GMAC provided financing, your Ford product when Ford Motor Credit made your loan, or when Chrysler Credit lent money for your Chrysler product. However, if your credit union or bank made the car loan directly to you, you must continue to make car payments, even when your car is a lemon through and through.

THE NATIONAL HIGHWAY TRAFFIC SAFETY ADMINISTRATION

The National Highway Traffic Safety Administration (NHTSA) is the federal agency which is responsible for most automobile recalls. NHTSA provides a toll-free consumer hotline to receive safety-related automotive complaints. NHTSA's toll-free number and address is:

U.S. Department of Transportation
National Highway Safety Traffic Administration
Auto Safety Hotline, NEF-ll HL
400 7th Street, S.W.
Washington, DC 20590

NHTSA keeps track of all auto recalls, so you can call them to determine whether your car was ever the subject of a recall. If you are buying a used car, you should call the hotline to find out if the car has been recalled, and what it has been recalled for. NHTSA will need the car's vehicle identification number, make, model, and year.

Safety-related defects cover a wide range of automotive problems. For example, excessive rusting can lead to safety problems and has been the subject of recalls. Stalling, brakes, seatbelts, defrosters, turn signals, headlights, and many other problems have been investigated by NHTSA. If your car is recalled because of an order of the traffic safety administration, the repairs will be paid for by the manufacturer even if your warranty expired long ago. Form 22-3 is an NHTSA questionnaire which informs the agency of safety-related problems.

THE ENVIRONMENTAL PROTECTION AGENCY

The Environmental Protection Agency can help you resolve auto complaints that at first glance, do not appear to concern the environment. For example, if your car, with 40,000 miles on it, needs a valve job because it is burning oil, the EPA may be able to get the work done at no cost to you, even though your warranty has expired. The Clean Air laws require all cars to meet emission requirements for 5 years or 50,000 miles. A car that burns oil in excess probably cannot meet the emission limits. Even if you bought the car used, the EPA can still help. If your car is smoking excessively or burning too much oil, or your catalytic converter does not

work anymore, write the EPA a letter. To confirm that you car fails to comply with the air quality laws, you should get it inspected at your state's inspection service (if your state has an inspection program) or at a private inspection service. The address to send your complaint to is:

Director
Mobile Source Enforcement
Environmental Protection Agency
Washington, DC 20460

CONSUMER PROTECTION AGENCIES

Every state has an office to handle consumer complaints. If you have failed elsewhere, your state office may be able to help you. A list of consumer protection agencies in each state is at the end of Chapter 21. A massive case against General Motors began in Illinois when a consumer complained that his Oldsmobile had a Chevy engine in it. The Attorney General of Illinois filed a class action suit against GM, which was settled quickly. Each Oldsmobile owner who received a Chevy engine also received a check from General Motors to compensate for the switch. GM now informs consumers that the engine in its cars may have been manufactured by other GM divisions, and that your Cadillac may have a Buick engine. It only takes one irate consumer to make a difference.

TAKING LEGAL ACTION

If all else has failed, you should bring all your repair records and other documents to a lawyer. A half hour consultation should be worthwhile. The lawyer may convince you that you do not have a case, or may think the case is so good that he or she will represent you on a contingency fee basis. A contingency fee means the lawyer only gets paid if there is a victory. If there is a warranty related problem, the Magnuson-Moss Warranty Act provides that if you win the case the auto company must pay for the lawyer's fees, court costs, and damages. The Automobile Owners Action Council (see page 166), the Center for Auto Safety (page 166), or your local Bar Association may be able to supply you with the names of a few lawyers who will be able to represent you. If there is a small amount at stake, less than $1000, you may want to file a small claim against the dealer and the manufacturer. Form 22-4 on page 173 is a small claims form to be used for this purpose.

ROADSIDE HAZARDS

Occasionally your car is damaged by an obstruction on the highway, or by the highway itself. Potholes, trolley tracks, and other dangerous road conditions may cause auto accidents or otherwise damage your car. I have brought successful lawsuits against cities for the unsafe conditions of their roads. However, in some states, cities are immune from suit. If your car has been damaged because of unsafe roadways, discuss your rights and remedies with a lawyer in your area.

FORM 22-1

Letter to Auto Manufacturer

Name _____
Address _____
Date: _____

Consumer Affair Office
Automobile Manufacturer

RE: Vehicle Identification number _____
Model, year _____
Dealer Purchased from _____

Dear _____,

I purchased the above-described automobile on _____ and have brought it back to the dealer _____ times to correct _____ _____.
I have lost _____ days from work in order to have the car repaired. My salary is _____ per day; I have therefore lost $_____ in time lost from work. In addition I have had to rent a car for $_____ per days for _____ days, or a total of $_____.
Enclosed are copies of repair bills, work orders and _____ which confirm these problems.
I want you to either replace the car with a new one, refund my purchase price of $_____, or pay me $_____ for the damages that I have suffered. I expect your reply by _____. If I do not have a satisfactory response from you by then, I will proceed to seek relief from a court or agency with jurisdiction over the matter.

Sincerely yours,

(Signature) _____
NAME

cc: Automobile Owners Action Council
    Center for Auto Safety
    Action Line

FORM 22-2

AUTOCAP Complaint Form

Automotive Consumer Action Program
(AUTOCAP)

**AUTOMOTIVE TRADE ASSOCIATION
NATIONAL CAPITAL AREA**

4330 East-West Highway, Suite 218
Bethesda, Maryland 20814
(301) 657-3200

Summary of Consumer Complaint

(Note: Before filling out this form, have you given the dealer an opportunity to respond to your problem? If not, we suggest that you contact the appropriate departmental manager [i.e., service manager, sales manager, whatever]. You may find the matter can be resolved without a third party.)

Please print clearly or type. As we are particularly interested in the current status of your problem, please be brief and to the point, leaving out any irrelevant history. Do not make any reference to anyone's honesty or integrity as a copy of this statement will be sent to the company(s) involved.

Name: _____ Date:_____

Address:_____

Daytime Telephone: _____

Dealership Involved: _____ Location: _____

_____

Name(s) of Dealer Representative Dealt with (if Known): _____

_____

Make of Car: _____ Model: _____ Year: _____

Engine Size: _____ Gas: _____ Diesel: _____

Purchased: New_____ Used_____ Demo_____ From: _____

On (Date): _____ Current Mileage: _____

Is the Manufacturer Involved? _____ Which One? _____

Manufacturer's Representative(s) Involved: _____

Are Any Other Agencies Involved? _____ Which One(s)? _____

_____

Where Did You Hear About Autocap? _____

This problem concerns (circle appropriate numbers and letters).

1) Repairs	A) New Car Warranty	D) Financing
2) New Car Sales	B) Used Car Warranty	E) Shop Service
3) Used Car Sales **AND**	C) The Purchase	Guarantee
4) Demo Sale	Agreement	F) Shop Charges

COMPLAINT DESCRIPTION

1. Name parties and include dates (with vehicle mileage everywhere applicable).
2. Note any action or offers by the dealer or manufacturer.
3. Note what it is you are seeking.

_____
_____
_____
_____
_____
_____
_____
_____
_____
_____
_____
_____
_____
_____
_____
_____

Attach copies of all supporting documents such as repair orders, purchase agreements, etc. Original documents are not required and this office assumes no responsibility for returning originals. Limit additional description to _one_ other sheet.

Signature _____

- -

OFFICE USE

Case # _____ Staff Member Handling Case _____

FORM 22-3: National Highway Traffic Safety Administration Auto Safety Form

Form Approved: O.M.B. No. 04-R5640

DEPARTMENT OF TRANSPORTATION
NATIONAL HIGHWAY TRAFFIC SAFETY ADMINISTRATION
VEHICLE OWNER'S QUESTIONNAIRE

The Privacy Act of 1974
Public Law 93-579
This information is requested pursuant to authority vested in the National Highway Traffic Safety Act and subsequent amendments. You are under no obligation to respond to this questionnaire. Your response may be used to assist the NHTSA in determining whether a manufacturer should take appropriate action to correct a defect. If the NHTSA proceeds with administrative enforcement or litigation against a manufacturer, your response, or a statistical summary thereof, may be used in support of the agency's action.

FOR HQ USE ONLY

ODI NO.

HL NO.

OWNER

LAST NAME

FIRST NAME & MIDDLE INITIAL

TELEPHONE NO. *(Area Code)*
Work—
Home—

STREET ADDRESS

CITY

STATE

ZIP CODE

VEHICLE INFORMATION

VEHICLE MAKE & MODEL

MODEL YEAR

BODY STYLE

VEHICLE IDENTIFICATION NO.

ENGINE SIZE (CID/CC)

MILEAGE

DATE PURCHASED _____
☐ New ☐ Used

DEALER'S NAME

AIR CONDITIONED
☐ Yes ☐ No

VEHICLE SPEED AT FAILURE _____
☐ Parked

NO. CYLINDERS _____
POWER STEERING ☐ Yes ☐ No
POWER BRAKES ☐ Yes ☐ No

TRANSMISSION
MANUAL *(Speed)* ☐ 3 ☐ 4 ☐ 5
AUTOMATIC ☐ Yes ☐ No
TYPE _____

FAILED COMPONENT/PART INFORMATION

COMPONENT/PART NAME

LOCATION
☐ Left ☐ Right
☐ Front ☐ Rear

FAILED PART
☐ Original
☐ Replacement

MILEAGE AT FAILURE

NO. OF FAILURES

DESCRIPTION OF FAILURE

FAILED TIRE INFORMATION

MANUFACTURER

TIRE NAME

SIZE

TYPE FAILURE

CONSTRUCTION
☐ Belted ☐ Bias
☐ Radial

FAILED TIRE
☐ Original
☐ Replacement

BELT MATERIAL
☐ Steel ☐ Fiberglass
☐ Aramid

LOCATION
☐ Right Front ☐ Right Rear
☐ Left Front ☐ Left Rear

DOT IDENTIFICATION NO.

APPLICABLE ACCIDENT INFORMATION

ACCIDENT
☐ Yes ☐ No

NO. INJURIES

NO. FATALITIES

DESCRIPTION OF ACCIDENT

SIGNATURE OF OWNER

DATE

HS Form 350B (Rev. 11/78)

DESCRIPTION OF PROBLEM

FORM 22-4

Court Complaint Against Auto Dealer and Manufacturer

_____,
                                    Plaintiff,

         v.   Case No.

_____,
                              (auto dealer)

         and

_____

                         (auto manufacturer),

                              Defendants.

STATEMENT OF THE CLAIM

1. On _____ (date) plaintiff purchased a _____ vehicle identification no. _____ from _____ for $_____.

2. The warranty on this car is for _____. Despite the warranty defendants have (refused) (failed) to repair the car satisfactorily and the car continues to have the following defects: _____

_____

3. Because of this breach of warranty I have suffered the following loss: _____

_____

WHEREFORE, I request damages against defendants in the amount of $_____, plus attorneys fees and court costs.

                         (Signature) _____
                         PLAINTIFF'S NAME
                         ADDRESS
                         TELEPHONE NUMBER

Subscribed and sworn to before me this _____ day of _____.

                         _____
                         NOTARY PUBLIC

AUTOMOBILE CORPORATE CONSUMER CONTACTS

AMERICAN HONDA MOTOR COMPANY, INC.

Corporate Office
Customer Relations Supervisor
American Honda Motor Company, Inc.
100 West Alondra Blvd.
Gardena, CA 90247
(213) 327-8280

AMERICAN MOTOR SALES CORPORATION

Atlanta Zone Office
Owner Relations Department
American Motors Sales Corporation
1640 Stone Ridge Drive
P.O. Box 718
Stone Mountain, GA 30083
(404) 491-3230

Boston Zone Office
Owner Relations Department
American Motors Sales
420 Providence Highway
Westwood, MA 02090
(617) 392-5633

Cincinnati Zone Office
Owner Relations Department
American Motors Sales Corporation
1125 Glendale-Milford Road
Cincinnati, OH 45215
(513) 771-1900

Chicago Zone Office
Owner Relations Department
American Motors Sales Corporation
1600 Busse Road
Elk Grove Village, IL 60007
(312) 346-8600

Dallas Zone Office
Owner Relations Department
American Motors Sales Corporation
7900 Ambassador Row
P.O. Box 47326
Dallas, TX 75247
(214) 689-9634

Denver Zone Office
Owner Relations Department
American Motors Sales Corporation
5005 Lima Street
Denver, CO 80239
(303) 373-5800

Detroit
Owner Relations Department
American Motors Sales Corporation
600 American Center
Southfield, MI 48034
(313) 827-7870

Kansas City Zone Office
Owner Relations Department
American Motors Sales Corporation
P.O. Box 283
Shawnee Mission, KS 66201
(913) 677-7850

Los Angeles Zone Office
Hawaii and Alaska

Owner Relations Department
American Motors Sales Corporation
P.O. Box 92787
Airport Station
Los Angeles, CA 90009
(213) 973-0100
(213) 644-1164

Minneapolis Zone Office
Owner Relations Department
American Motors Sales Corporation
P.O. Box 1273
Minneapolis, MN 55440
(612) 340-8850

New York Zone Office
Owners Relations Department
American Motors Sales Corporation
P.O. Box 500
Elmsford, NY 10523
(914) 997-2823

Philadelphia Zone Office
Owner Relations Department
American Motors Sales Corporation
Mid-Atlantic Industrial Park
P.O. Box 1000
Woodbury, NJ 08096
(609) 853-4400

Pittsburgh Zone Office
Owner Relations Department
American Motors Sales Corporation
150 Commonwealth Drive
Warrendale, PA 15086
(412) 776-4175

Portland Zone Office
Owner Relations Department
American Motors Sales Corporation
8111 N.E. Columbia Boulevard
Portland, OR 97218
(503) 255-4220

Washington, D.C. Zone Office
Owner Relations Department
American Motors Sales Corporation
Post Office Drawer AA
Westgate Research Park
McLean, VA 22101
(703) 893-4600

Corporate Office
Consumer Relations Manager
American Motors Corporation
14250 Plymouth Road
Detroit, MI 48232
(313) 493-2341

BMW OF NORTH AMERICA, INC.

Central Region
Customer Relations Manager
BMW of North America, Inc.
999 Plaza Drive
Suite 500
Schaumburg, IL 60195
(312) 843-4550

Eastern Region
Customer Relations Manager
BMW of North America, Inc.
Campus 3
Montvale, NJ 07645
(201) 573-2000

Southern Region
Customer Relations Manager
BMW of North America, Inc.
Twin Towers
Suite 728
8585 North Stemmons Highway
Dallas, TX 75247
(214) 631-6600

Western Region
Customer Relations Manager
BMW of North America, Inc.
12541 Beatrice Street
Los Angeles, CA 90066
(213) 306-4500

Corporate Office
National Customer Relations Manager
BMW of North America, Inc.
Campus 3
Montvale, NJ 07645
(201) 573-2141

CHRYSLER CORPORATION

Atlanta Zone Office
South Carolina, North Carolina, Tennessee, Alabama, Georgia

Manager, Customer Relations
Chrysler Corporation
P.O. Box 18896
Lenox Square Station
Atlanta, GA 30326
(404) 261-7522

Boston Zone Office
Massachusetts, Connecticut, Rhode Island, Maine, Vermont, New Hampshire

Manager, Customer Relations
Chrysler Corporation
P.O. Box 50
Natick, MA 01760
(617) 655-2810

Chicago Zone Office
Iowa, Illinois, Wisconsin, Indiana

Manager, Customer Relations
Chrysler Corporation
P.O. Box E 367
Elk Grove, IL 60007
(312) 593-3780

Cincinnati Zone Office
Kentucky, Indiana, Ohio

Manager, Customer Relations
Chrysler Corporation
P.O. Box 41902
Cincinnati, OH 45241
(513) 733-8450

Dallas Zone Office
Texas

Manager, Customer Relations
Chrysler Corporation
P.O. Box 34064
Dallas, TX 75234
(214) 242-8462

Denver Zone Office
Wyoming, New Mexico, Colorado, Nebraska, Utah

Manager, Customer Relations
Chrysler Corporation
P.O. Box 39006
Denver, CO 80239
(303) 371-1330

Detroit Zone Office
Michigan, Ohio, Indiana

Manager, Customer Relations
Chrysler Corporation
P.O. Box 300
Troy, MI 48099
(313) 879-0600

Kansas City Zone Office
Oklahoma, Missouri, Nebraska, Kansas, Iowa

Manager, Customer Relations
Chrysler Corporation
Cloverleaf 11 Building
Suite 205
6901 W. 63rd Street
Overland Park, KS 66202
(913) 831-2244

Los Angeles Zone Office
California, Arizona, Hawaii, Nevada

Manager, Customer Relations
Chrysler Corporation
P.O. Box 4120
Fullerton, CA 92631
(714) 870-4000

Memphis Zone Office
Louisiana, Arkansas, Mississippi, Tennessee

Manager, Customer Relations
Chrysler Corporation
P.O. Box 18008
Memphis, TN 38118
(901) 365-4701

Minneapolis Zone Office
South Dakota, Minnesota, Iowa, Wisconsin, North
    Dakota, Nebraska

Manager, Customer Relations
Chrysler Corporation
P.O. Box 1231
Minneapolis, MN 55440
(613) 553-2546

New York Zone Office
New Jersey, New York, Connecticut

Manager, Customer Relations
Chrysler Corporation
500 Route 303
Tappan, NY 10983
(914) 627-2200

Orlando Zone Office
Georgia, Florida, Alabama

Manager, Customer Relations
Chrysler Corporation
P.O. Box 13428
Orlando, FL 32809
(305) 851-6510

Philadelphia Zone Office
Pennsylvania, New Jersey, Delaware

Manager, Customer Relations
Chrysler Corporation
P.O. Box 489
Wayne, PA 19087
(215) 687-6110

Pittsburgh Zone Office
Ohio, Pennsylvania, West Virginia, Maryland

Manager, Customer Relations
Chrysler Corporation
P.O. Box N
Oakdale, PA 15071
(412) 777-3600

Portland Zone Office
Oregon, Alaska, Washington, Montana, Idaho

Manager, Customer Relations
Chrysler Corporation
P.O. Box 744
Beaverton, OR 97005
(503) 641-4170

St. Louis Zone Office
Illinois, Missouri, Kentucky, Indiana

Manager, Customer Relations
Chrysler Corporation
P.O. Box 278
Hazelwood, MO 63042
(314) 731-6742

San Francisco Zone Office
California, Nevada

Manager, Customer Relations
Chrysler Corporation
P.O. Box 5507
San Mateo, CA 94403
(415) 572-0377

Syracuse Zone Office
New York, Pennsylvania

Manager, Customer Relations
Chrysler Corporation
P.O. Box 158
Eastwood Station
Syracuse, NY 13206
(315) 432-4041

Washington, D.C. Zone Office
Maryland, Virginia, North Carolina, Delaware, District
of Columbia

Manager, Customer Relations
P.O. Box 770
Chrysler Corporation
Seabrook, MD 20801
(301) 794-6315

Corporate Office
Manager, Owner Relations
Chrysler Corporation
P.O. Box 1718
Detroit, MI 48288
(313) 956-5970

FIAT MOTORS OF NORTH AMERICA, INC.

Eastern Area
Manager, Customer Relations
Fiat Motors of North America, Inc.
155 Chestnut Ridge Road
Montvale, NJ 97645
(201) 573-3811

Western Area
Manager, Customer Relations
Fiat Motors of North America, Inc.
6600 Katella Avenue
Cypress, CA 90630
(714) 891-4651

Corporate Office
National Customer Relations Department
Fiat Motors of North America, Inc.
155 Chestnut Ridge Road
Montvale, NJ 07645
(201) 573-3840

FORD MOTOR COMPANY

Corporate Office
Owner Relations—Operations Department
The Ford Parts and Service Division
Ford Motor Company
P.O. Box 1805
Dearborn, MI 48126
(313) 337-6950

GENERAL MOTORS CORPORATION

Buick Motor Division
Customer Service Department
General Motors Corporation
902 East Hamilton Avenue
Flint, MI 48550
(313) 766-1240

Cadillac Motor Car Division
Customer Relations
General Motors Corporation
2860 Clark Street
Detroit, MI 48232
(313) 544-5536

Chevrolet Motor Division
Customer Relations Department
General Motors Corporation
Warren, MI 48090
(313) 492-5500

Oldsmobile Division
Customer Service Department
General Motors Corporation
920 Townsend Street
Lansing, MI 48921
(517) 377-5546

Pontiac Motor Division
Customer Service Department
General Motors Corporation
One Pontiac Plaza
Pontiac, MI 48053
(313) 857-1316

Corporate Office
Manager, Customer Relations
General Motors Corporation
8-257 General Motors Building
Detroit, MI 48202
(313) 556-2942

MAZDA MOTORS OF AMERICA (EAST), INC.

East
Alabama, Connecticut, Delaware, Florida, Georgia,
Maine, Maryland, Massachusetts, New Hampshire,
New Jersey, North Carolina, Pennsylvania, Rhode
Island, South Carolina, Vermont, Virginia, District of
Columbia, West Virginia

Customer Relations Manager
Mazda Motors of America (East), Inc.
8313 Baycenter Road
Jacksonville, FL 32216

Great Lakes
Illinois, Indiana, Michigan, Ohio, Wisconsin

Customer Relations Manager
Mazda Distributors Great Lakes
2660 28th Street, S.E.
Grand Rapids, MI 49508
(616) 949-7570

Gulf
Arkansas, Iowa, Kansas, Kentucky, Louisiana,
    Mississippi, Missouri, Nebraska, Oklahoma,
    Tennessee, Texas

Customer Relations Manager
Mazda Distributors Gulf
10445 Corporate Drive
Sugar Land, TX 77478
(713) 491-5800

Northwest
Alaska, Idaho, Minnesota, Montana, North Dakota,
    Oregon, South Dakota, Washington

Customer Relations Manager
Mazda Distributors Northwest
8621 South 180th
Kent, WA 98031

Pacific
Arizona, California, Colorado, Nevada, New Mexico,
    Utah, Wyoming

Customer Relations Manager
Mazda Distributors Pacific
18601 South Susana Road
Compton, CA 90221
(213) 603-8978

Corporate Office
Customer Relations Manager
Mazda Motors of America (East), Inc.
8313 Baycenter Road
Jacksonville, FL 32216
(914) 731-4010

Corporate Office
Manager Consumer Communications
Mazda Motors of America (Central), Inc.
3040 East Ana Street
Compton, CA 90221
(213) 537-2322

MERCEDES-BENZ OF NORTH AMERICA, INC.

Chicago Zone
Service Manager
Mercedes-Benz of North America, Inc.
3333 Charles Street
Franklin Park, IL 60131
(312) 455-9131

Houston Zone
Service Manager
Mercedes-Benz of North America, Inc.
9550 North Loop East
P.O. Box 24396
Houston, TX 77029
(713) 675-6126

Jacksonville Zone
Service Manager
Mercedes-Benz of North America, Inc.
8813 Western Way
P.O. Box 17604F
Jacksonville, FL 32216
(904) 731-4040

Los Angeles Zone
Service Manager
Mercedes-Benz of North America, Inc.
851 East Watsoncenter
P.O. Box 4625
Carson, CA 90749
(213) 835-8315

New York Zone
Service Manager
Mercedes-Benz of North America, Inc.
One Glenview Road
P.O. Box 277
Montvale, NJ 07645
(201) 573-2518

San Francisco Zone
Service Manager
Mercedes-Benz of North America, Inc.
513 Eccles Avenue
San Francisco, CA 94080
(415) 871-5125

Washington, D.C. Zone
Service Manager
Mercedes-Benz of North America, Inc.
5530 Wisconsin Avenue
Chevy Chase, MD 2001
(301) 654-1676

Corporate Office
Owner Services
Mercedes-Benz of North America, Inc.
One Mercedes Drive
Montvale, NJ 07645
(201) 573-0600

NISSAN MOTOR CORPORATION IN U.S.A. (DATSUN)

Boston Regional Office
Maine, Vermont, New Hampshire, Massachusetts,
    Rhode Island, Connecticut, parts of New York

Customer Relations Manager
Nissan Motor Corporation in USA (Datsun)
777 West Street
Mansfield, MA 02048
(617) 339-3721

Chicago Regional Office
Minnesota, Wisconsin, Iowa, Illinois, Missouri

Customer Relations Manager
Nissan Motor Corporation in U.S.A. (Datsun)
51 Shore Drive
Hinsdale, IL 60521
(312) 325-9050

Columbus Regional Office
Michigan, Indiana, Ohio

Customer Relations Manager
Nissan Motor Corporation in U.S.A. (Datsun)
150 E. Wilson Bridge Road
Suite 100
Worthington, OH 43085
(614) 846-6900

Dallas Regional Office
Texas, Oklahoma, Louisiana

Customer Relations Manager
Nissan Motor Corporation in U.S.A. (Datsun)
13405 N. Stemmons Freeway
Farmers Branch, TX 75234
(214) 243-4311

Denver Regional Office
North Dakota, South Dakota, Wyoming, Nebraska,
    Utah, Colorado, Kansas, New Mexico

Customer Relations Manager
Nissan Motor Corporation in U.S.A. (Datsun)
11000 E. 45th Avenue
Denver, CO 80239
(303) 371-4230

Jacksonville Regional
South Carolina, Georgia, Florida

Customer Relations Manager
Nissan Motor Corporation in U.S.A. (Datsun)
8743 Western Way
Jacksonville, FL 32217
(904) 737-7100

Memphis Regional Office
Arkansas, Kentucky, Tennessee, Mississippi, Alabama

Customer Relations Manager
Nissan Motor Corporation in U.S.A. (Datsun)
5775 Summer Trees Drive
Memphis, TN 38134
(901) 372-5700

New York Regional Office
New Jersey, Pennsylvania, New York area

Customer Relations Manager
Nissan Motor Corporation in U.S.A. (Datsun)
No. 4 Corporate Place
Piscataway, NJ 08854
(210) 981-0220

Norfolk Regional Office
Maryland, Delaware, West Virginia, Virginia, North
    Carolina, District of Columbia

Customer Relations Manager
Nissan Motor Corporation in U.S.A. (Datsun)
151 Harbor Drive
Portsmouth, VA 23705
(804) 399-4011

Portland Regional Office
Washington, Montana, Oregon, Idaho, Alaska

Customer Relations Manager
Nissan Motor Corporation in U.S.A. (Datsun)
9575 S.W. Scholls Ferry Road
Portland, OR 97223
(503) 646-0543

San Francisco Regional Office
Northern California, Nevada

Customer Relations Manager
Nissan Motor Corporation in U.S.A. (Datsun)
355 Wigetlane
P.O. Box 8028
Walnut Creek, CA 94596
(415) 871-6684

PEUGEOT MOTORS OF AMERICA, INC.

Central Zone
Customer Relations
Peugeot Motors of America, Inc.
9444 Old Katy Road
Houston, TX 77055
(714) 461-9013

Eastern Zone
Customer Relations
Peugeot Motors of America, Inc.
40 Van Nostrand Avenue
Englewood, NJ 07631
(210) 894-0210

Western Zone
Customer Relations
Peugeot Motors of America, Inc.
1020 East 230th Street
Carson, CA 90745

Customer Relations
Eastern Auto Distributors, Inc.
933 East Little Creek Road
Norfolk, VA 23518
(804) 588-1334

Corporate Office
Customer Relations
Peugeot Motors of America, Inc.
One Peugeot Plaza
Lyndhurst, NJ 07071
(201) 935-8400

PORSCHE AUDI

Atlantic Region
Delaware, Maine, Maryland, Massachusetts, New
   Hampshire, North Carolina, Pennsylvania, Rhode
   Island, Vermont, Virginia, District of Columbia, West
   Virginia

Customer Service Manager
Volkswagen of America, Inc.
Porsche Audi Division
9300 George Palmer Highway
Lanham, MD 20801
(301) 459-7000

Central Region
Illinois, Indiana, Iowa, Kentucky, Michigan, Minnesota,
   North Dakota, Ohio, South Dakota, Wisconsin
   (excluding Rapid City)

Customer Service Manager
Volkswagen of America, Inc.
Porsche Audi Division
106 Wilmot Road
Suite 201
Deerfield, IL 60015
(312) 948-5660

Pacific Region
Arizona, California, Colorado, Hawaii, Nevada, New
   Mexico, South Dakota (Rapid City), Texas (El Paso),
   Utah, Wyoming

Customer Service Manager
Volkswagen of America, Inc.
Porsche Audi Division
11300 Playa Street
Culver City, CA 90230
(213) 390-8011

Southern Region
Alabama, Florida, Georgia, Louisiana, Mississippi,
   Oklahoma, South Carolina, wtennessee, Texas
   (excluding El Paso)

Customer Service Manager
Volkswagen of America, Inc.
Porsche Audi Division
Suite 170
1770 The Exchange
Atlanta, GA 30339
(404) 955-9000

Porsche Audi Northwest, Inc.
Alaska, Idaho, Montana, Oregon, Washington

Customer Service Manager
5 Oaks Industrial Park
Route #1
P.O. Box 220 VW
Hillsboro, OR 97123
(503) 645-5511

Volkswagen Mid-America, Inc
Arkansas, Kansas, Missouri, Nebraska

Customer Service Manager
Porsche Audi Division
8825 Page Boulevard
St. Louis, MO 63114

(314) 429-2141

Porsche Audi Eastern
(A Division of World-Wide Volkswagen Corp.)

Connecticut, New Jersey, New York

Customer Service Manager
Greenbush Road
Orangeburg, NY 10962
(914) 578-5000

Corporate Office
Customer Service Manager
Porsche Audi Division of Volkswagen of America, Inc.
818 Sylvan Avenue
Englewood Cliffs, NJ 07632
(201) 894-5000

SAAB-SCANIA OF AMERICA

Central Regional Customer Relations Manager
Saab-Scania of America
10415 United Parkway
Schiller Park, IL 60176
(312) 671-4920

Eastern Regional Customer Relations Manager
Saab-Scania of America
Saab Drive
P.O. Box 697
Orange, CT 06477
(203) 795-5671

Western Regional Customer Relations Manager
Saab-Scania of America
1225 East Artesia Boulevard
Carson, CA 90746
(213) 537-3901

Corporate Office
Customer Relations Manager
Saab-Scania of America
P.O. Box 697
Orange, CT 06477
(203) 795-5671

SUBARU OF AMERICA, INC.

Subaru of New England
Maine, Vermont, New Hampshire, Massachusetts,
    Rhode Island, Connecticut

Customer Relations Manager
95 Morse Street
Norwood, MA 02062
(617) 769-5100

Subaru Distributor Corp.
New York, North New Nersey

Customer Relations Manager
4 North Street
Walwick, NJ 07463
(201) 445-7350

Penn Jersey Subaru, Inc.
Southern New Jersey, Pennsylvania, Delaware

Customer Relations Manager
Glen Avenue and Forest Road
P.O. Box P
Morristown, NJ 08057
(609) 234-7600

Subaru Atlantic, Inc.
West Virginia, Virginia, North Carolina, Maryland

Customer Relations Manager
9050 Red Branch Road
P.O. Box 308
Columbia, MD 21045
(614) 864-6650

Distributors, Inc.
Georgia, South Carolina, Florida

P.O. Box 3007
West Palm Beach, FL 33402
(305) 683-3066

George Byers Sons, Inc
Kentucky, Ohio, Indiana, Michigan

Customer Relations Manager
401 North Hamilton Road
P.O. Box 16513
Columbus, OH 43215
(614) 864-6650

Subaru of Southern California
Southern California

Customer Relations Manager
1881 Kaiser Avenue
Irvine, CA 92714
(714) 540-8720

Subaru Mid-America, Inc.
Missouri, South Dakota, Minnesota, Wisconsin, Iowa,
    Illinois

Customer Relations Manager
2374 Espes Avenue
Elk Grove, IL 60007
(312) 439-2555

Subaru South, Inc.
Arkansas, Louisiana, Tennessee, Missouri, Alabama

Customer Relations Manager
7700 Frazier Pike
Little Rock, AR 72206
(501) 490-2770

Southwest Subaru Star Corp.
Alaska, Texas

Customer Relations Manager
300 Breesport
P.O. Box 32906
San Antonio, TX 78216
(512) 349-3903

Subaru Inter-Mountain
Nebraska, Kansas, Colorado, New Mexico, Arizona

15000 East 39th Street
P.O. Drawer D
Auroria, CO 80041
(303) 371-3820

Subaru Northwest Corporation
Washington, Oregon, Idaho, Montana, Wyoming

Customer Relations Manager
8040 East 33rd Drive
P.O. Box 11293
Portland, OR 97211
(503)287-4171

Subaru of Northern California
Northern California, Nevada, Utah

Customer Relations Manager
2505 Port Street
P.O. Box 985
West Sacramento, CA 95691
(916) 371-7901

Corporate Office
Customer Relations Department
Subaru of America, Inc.
7040 Central Highway
Pennsauken, NJ 08109
(609) 665-3344

TOYOTA MOTOR SALES, U.S.A.

Boston Regional Office
Main, Vermont, New Hampshire, Massachusetts, Rhode
   Island

Customer Relations Department
Toyota Motor Distributors, Inc.
440 Forbes Boulevard
Mansfield, MA 02048
(617) 339-5701

Chicago Regional Office
Indiana, Illinois, Wisconsin, Minnesota

Customer Relations Department
Toyota Motor Distributors, Inc.
500 Kehoe Boulevard
Carol Stream, IL 60187
(312) 260-6240

Cincinnati Regional Office
Tennessee, Kentucky, Ohio, Michigan

Customer Relations Department
Toyota Motor Distributors, Inc.
4550 Creek Road
Cincinnati, OH 45242
(513) 745-7500

Denver Regional Office
Arizona, New Mexico, Utah, Colorado, Wyoming

Customer Relations Department
Toyota Motor Distributors, Inc.
9033 East Easter Place
Suite 200
Englewood, CO 80112
(303) 773-1404

Gulf States Regional Office
Texas, Oklahoma, Arkansas, Louisiana, Mississippi

Customer Relations Department
Gulf States Toyota, Inc.
10310 Harwin
Houston, TX 77036
(713) 776-6700

Kansas City Regional Office
Kansas, Missouri, Nebraska, Iowa, South Dakota,
   North Dakota

Customer Relations Department
Toyota Motor Distributors, Inc.
11111 NW Airworld Drive
Kansas City, MO 64195
(816) 891-1000

Los Angeles Regional Office
Southern California

Customer Relations Department
Toyota Motor Distributors, Inc.
2800 Jamboree Road
Newport Beach, CA 92660
(714) 833-8123

Mid-Atlantic Regional Office
Virginia, West Virginia, Maryland, Delaware,
   Pennsylvania

Customer Relations Department
Mid-Atlantic Toyota Distributors, Inc.
Toyota Building
6710 Baymeadow
P.O. Box 1030
Glen Burnie, MD 21061
(301) 760-1500

National Customer Relations Manager
Toyota Motor Sales, Inc.
2055 West 190th Street
Torrance, CA 90509
(213) 532-5010

New York Regional Office
New York, New Jersey, Connecticut

Customer Relations Department
Toyota Motor Distributors, Inc.
16 Henderson Drive
West Caldwell, NJ 07006
(201) 575-7600

Portland Regional Office
Washington, Oregon, Indiana, Montana, Hawaii

Customer Relations Department
Toyota Motor Distributors, Inc.
6111 N.E. 87th Avenue
Portland, OR 97220
(503) 255-6440

San Francisco Regional Office
Northern California, Nevada

Customer Relations Department
Toyota Motor Distributors, Inc.
500 Forbes Boulevard
San Francisco, CA 94080
(415) 871-9040

Southeast Regional Office
Alabama, Florida, Georgia, North Carolina, South
 Carolina

Customer Relations Department
Southeast Toyota Distributors, Inc.
1751 Talleyrand Drive
P.O. Box 5287
Jacksonville, FL 32266
(904) 358-3634

VOLKSWAGEN OF AMERICA, INC.

Atlanta Region
Northern Alabama, Northern Georgia, South Carolina,
 Tennessee

Customer Service Manager
Volkswagen of America, Inc.
2625 Cumberland Parkway
Suite 450
Atlanta, GA 30339
(404) 433-0521

Boston Region
Maine, Massachusetts, New Hampshire, Rhode Island,
 Vermont

Customer Service Manager
Volkswagen of America, Inc.
100 Fordham Road
Wilmington, MA 01887
(617) 658-6700

Chicago Region
Illinois, Iowa, Minnesota, North Dakota, South
 Dakota, Wisconsin (excluding Rapid City)

Customer Service Manager
Volkswagen of America, Inc.
3737 Lake Cook Road
Deerfield, IL 60015
(312) 272-5000

Columbus Region
Indiana, Kentucky, Michigan, Ohio

Customer Service Manager
Volkswagen of America, Inc.
1840 MacKenzie Drive
Columbus, OH 43221
(614) 457-2411

Denver Region
Arizona (excluding Yuma), Colorado, Nevada
 (excluding Reno), New Mexico, South Dakota (Rapid
 City), Texas (El Paso), Utah, Wyoming

Customer Service Manager
Volkswagen of America, Inc.
Greenwood Plaza
7503 Marin Drive (3-C)
Englewood, CO 80111
(303) 773-6374

Hawaii Operation
Customer Service Manager
Volkswagen of America, Inc.
2865 Pukoloa Street
P.O. Box 3799
Honolulu, HI 96812
(808) 537-4338 Business Office
(808) 833-1866 Parts Warehouse (Service)
(808) 839-1907 Distribution

Jacksonville Region
Florida, Southern Alabama, Southern Georgia

Customer Service Manager
Volkswagen of America, Inc.
P.O. Box 2274
155 East 21st Street
Jacksonville, FL 32203
(904) 354-8188

Los Angeles Region
Arizona (Yuma), Southern California

Customer Service Manager
Volkswagen of America, Inc.
11300 Playa Street
Culver City, CA 90230
(213) 390-8011

New York Region
Connecticut, New Jersey, New York

Customer Service Manager
World-Wide Volkswagen
Greenbush Road
Orangeburg, NY 10962
(914) 578-5000

Northwestern Region
Alaska, Indiana, Montana, Oregon, Washington

Customer Service Manager
Riviera Motors, Inc.
5 Oaks Industrial Park
Route #1, Box 220 VW
Hillsboro, OR 97123
(503) 645-5511

Mid-Western Region
Arkansas, Kansas, Missouri, Nebraska

Customer Service Manager
Volkswagen Mid-America, Inc.
8825 Page Boulevard
St. Louis MO 63114
(314) 429-2141

San Antonio Region
Louisiana, Mississippi, Oklahoma, Texas (excluding El
   Paso)

Customer Service Manager
Volkswagen of America, Inc.
10515 Gulfdale Drive
Suite 100
San Antonio, TX 78216
(512) 341-8881

San Francisco Region
Nevada (Reno), Northern California

Customer Service Manager
Volkswagen of America, Inc.
7106 Johnson Industrial Drive
Pleasanton, CA 94566
(415) 462-8000

Valley Forge Region
Customer Service Manager
Volkswagen of America, Inc.
P.O. Box 830
1001 South Trooper
Valley Forge, PA 19482
(215) 666-7500

Washington D.C. Region
Maryland, North Carolina, Virginia, District of
   Columbia, West Virginia

Customer Service Manager
Volkswagen of America, Inc.
9300 George Palmer Highway
Lanham, MD 20801
(310) 459-7000

VOLVO NORTH AMERICA

Corporate Office
Consumer Affairs Manager
Volvo North America
One Volvo Drive
Rockleigh, NJ 07647
(201) 768-7300

STATE AND METROPOLITAN AUTOCAP LOCATIONS

Arizona
Arizona Automobile Dealers Association
AUTOCAP
P.O. Box 5438
Phoenix, AZ 85010
(602) 252-2386

California
Northern California Motor Car Dealers Association
AUTOCAP
1244 Larkin Street
San Francisco, CA 94109
(415) 673-2151, 52, or 53

Motor Car Dealers Association of Southern California
AUTOCAP
5757 West Century Boulevard
Los Angeles, CA 90045
(800) 262-1482 (In state)
(213) 776-0054 (Out of state)

San Diego Motor Car Dealers Association
AUTOCAP
2333 Camino Del Rio South
Suite 265
San Diego, CA 92108
(714) 296-2265

Colorado
Colorado Automobile Dealers Association
AUTOCAP
517 E. 16th Avenue
Denver, CO 80203
(303) 831-1722

Connecticut
Connecticut Automotive Trades Association, Inc.
AUTOCAP
18 North Main Street
Hartford, CT 06107
(203) 521-8970

Florida
Jacksonville Automobile Dealers Association
AUTOCAP
9926 Beach Boulevard
Suite 209
Jacksonville, FL 32216
(904) 725-7366 (Duval County only)

South Florida Automobile Dealers Association

AUTOCAP
8600 N.E. Second Avenue
Miami, FL 33138
(305) 522-2886 (Dade & Monroe Counties)
(305) 758-2886 (Broward County)

AUTOCAP
3015 Exchange Court
West Palm Beach, FL 33409
(305) 686-6168 (West Palm Beach)
(305) 272-4445 (Boca Raton & Delray)

Georgia
Georgia Automobile Dealers Association

AUTOCAP
1380 West Paces Ferry Road
Suite 230
Atlanta, GA 30327
(404) 237-1483

Hawaii
Hawaii Automobile Dealers Association

AUTOCAP
P.O. Box 560
Kailua, HI 96734
(808) 833-9011

Illinois
Illinois New Car and Truck Dealers Association

AUTOCAP
828 South Second Street
P.O. Box 3045
Springfield, IL 62708
(217) 753-4513

Kentucky
Kentucky Automobile Dealers Association

AUTOCAP
123 Walnut Street
P.O. Box 498
Frankfort, KY 40601
(502) 695-3310

Maine
Maine Automobile Dealers Association, Inc.

AUTOCAP
P.O. Box 2667
Augusta, ME 04330
(207) 623-3882

Maryland
*Automotive Trade Association of the National Capital
Area*

(Montgomery & Prince Georges Counties only);
See Washington, D.C.

Massachusetts
Massachusetts State Automobile Dealers Assocition

AUTOCAP
59 Temple Place
Room 505
Boston, MA 02111
(617) 451-1048

Michigan
Michigan Automobile Dealers Association

AUTOCAP
1500 Kendale Boulevard
P.O. Box 2525
East Lansing, MI 48823
(800) 292-1923 (In state)
(517) 351-7800 (Out of state)
(Does not cover Macomb, Oakland, or Wayne Counties)

New Mexico
*New Mexico Automobile and Truck Dealers
Association*

AUTOCAP
510 Second Street, N.W.
Suite 202
Albuquerque, NM 87102
(505) 243-1002

New York
Broome County Chamber of Commerce

AUTOCAP
P.O. Box 995
Binghamton, NY 13902
(607) 723-7127
(Broome County only)

Capital District Automobile Dealers Association

AUTOCAP
815 Central Avenue
Albany, NY 12206
(518) 438-0645
(Albany, Saratoga, Schenectady, and Troy Counties
only)

Jefferson County Autocap

P.O. Box 596
Watertown, NY 13601
(315) 782-1600
(Jefferson County only)

Niagara Frontier Automobile Dealers Association

AUTOCAP
1144 Wehrle Drive
Williamsville, NY 14221
(716) 631-8510
(Niagara County only)

Rochester Automobile Dealers Association
AUTOCAP
179 Lake Avenue
Rochester, NY 14221
(716) 458-7150

Greater New York Automobile Dealers Association
AUTOCAP
One Hanson Place
Room 1212
Brooklyn, NY 11243
(1-800) 522-3881
(NYC, LI, & Westchester County)

New York State Automobile Dealers Association
AUTOCAP
37 Elk Street
P.O. Box 7287
Albany, NY 12224
(800) 342-9208 (In state)
(518) 463-1148 (Out of state)
(Serves balance of state)

North Dakota
Automobile Dealers Association of North America
AUTOCAP
1325 23rd Street, South
P.O. Box 2524
Fargo, ND 58108
(701) 293-6822

Ohio
Cleveland Automobile Dealers Association
AUTOCAP
1367 E. 6th Street
Suite 300
Cleveland, OH 44114
(216) 241-2880
(Metropolitan Cleveland only)

Oregon
Oregon Automobile Dealers Association
AUTOCAP
P.O. Box 14460
Portland, OR 97214
(503) 233-5044

South Carolina
South Carolina Automobile and Truck Dealers Association
AUTOCAP
1517 Laurel Street
Columbia, SC 29201
(803) 254-4040

Tennessee
Chattanooga Automotive Trade Association
AUTOCAP
1701 N. Concord Road
Chattanooga, TN 37421
(615) 899-0714
(Chattanooga area only)

Nashville Franchised Automobile Dealers Association
AUTOCAP
P.O. Box 40093
Nashville, TN 37204
(615) 269-4948

Texas
Texas Automobile Dealers Association
AUTOCAP
1108 Lavaca
P.O. Box 1028
Austin, TX 78767
(512) 476-2686

Utah
Utah Automobile Dealers Association
AUTOCAP
1588 South Main
Salt Lake City, UT 84115
(801) 484-8845

Vermont
Vermont Automotive Trade Association
AUTOCAP
148 State Street
P.O. Box 561
Montpelier, VT 05602
(800) 642-5149 (In state)

Virginia
Automotive Trade Association of the National Capital Area
(Northern Virginia only)
See Washington, D.C.

Virginia Automobile Dealers Association
AUTOCAP
1800 West Grace Street
P.O. Box 5407
Richmond, VA 23220
(804) 359-3578
(Serves balance of state)

Washington State
Puget Sound Automobile Dealers Association
AUTOCAP
805 Lenora Street
Seattle, WA 98121
(800) 552-0746 (In state)
(206) 263-2423 (Out of state)

Washington, D.C.
Automotive Trade Association of the National Capital Area
AUTOCAP
4330 East-West Highway
Suite 218
Bethesda, MD 20814
(301) 657-3200
(Washington, D.C.; Northern Virginia; Montgomery and Prince Georges Counties, MD only)

West Virginia
West Virginia Automobile and Truck Dealers Association
AUTOCAP
2101 Washington Street, East
P.O. Box 2028
Charleston, WV 25327
(304) 343-4160

Wyoming
Wyoming Automobile Dealers
AUTOCAP
P.O. Box 2067
Casper, WY 82602
(307) 265-4610

23

Your Constitutional Rights

Many volumes have been written on constitutional rights, so this chapter can only touch on a few of the highpoints. The most valued constitutional rights flow from the First Amendment which guarantees the rights of free speech, free press, freedom of association, and freedom of religion.

The only general exception to free speech rights has been for pornographic materials. The Supreme Court has ruled that you do not have the right to publish pornography, but the court has ruled that you have a right to read pornographic materials. The rulings are somewhat inconsistent, but stand for the general proposition that everyone has the right to read whatever they please in the privacy of their own homes.

The First Amendment is the reason that the Supreme Court forbids prayer in public schools. The court has ruled that everyone has the right to freedom *from* religion as well as freedom *of* religion under the First Amendment. The high court has ruled that Christmas lights paid for by the government are illegal. Despite this the court has refused to decide whether the words "in god we trust" on our currency, violates this principle, and the corollary that church and state must be separate.

Schoolchildren have First Amendment rights also. During the Vietnam war, schoolchildren in Des Moines, Iowa, wore black armbands to protest the war. The students were disciplined for the protest and filed suit against the school board. The

U.S. Supreme Court ruled that the students had a constitutional right to protest.[1]

DOOR-TO-DOOR CAMPAIGNS

Many states and cities have attempted to regulate door-to-door campaigns for public or private causes. Nearly all of these regulations have been ruled unconstitutional. You have a right to knock on doors to talk to neighbors which cannot be regulated; your free speech and free association rights demand it. However, recently the Supreme Court ruled that you do not have a right to put a flyer in your neighbor's mailbox, unless you put a postage stamp on it.[2] This is an unfortunate ruling, based on the mail service monopoly granted to the government. You are allowed to leave notices under someone's door, or in the box designed for newspapers.

SHOPPING CENTERS

You have the right to hand out leaflets on public sidewalks or in other public areas, in front of the White House, city halls, or the halls of Congress.

---

1. *Tinker* v. *Des Moines Independent Community School District,* 393 U.S. 503 (1969).
2. *United States Postal Service* v. *Greenburgh Civic Association,* 453 U.S. 114 (1981).

The Supreme Court recently ruled that citizens have a right to hand out information on the sidewalk in front of the Supreme Court building itself. But the right to hand out leaflets in privately owned shopping centers and malls has met mixed reviews at the court. During the Earl Warren era, the court created a right to distribute flyers even in private shopping centers because they were like public streets, open to everyone. However, the Supreme Court, under the leadership of Warren Burger, changed the shopping center rule. The owner of a shopping mall now has the right to restrict leafletting at the mall.

THE ACLU

The American Civil Liberties Union (ACLU) is the oldest and largest protector of First Amendment rights. The ACLU has offices in nearly every major and not-so-major city, and should be contacted if you believe that your constitutional rights have been violated.

EQUAL PROTECTION OF THE LAWS

The Fifth Amendment and the Fourteenth Amendments require all citizens to have equal protection under the law, regardless of sex, race, or national origin. The sign engraved in the marble arch above the doors to the Supreme Court states: "Equal Justice Under Law." Unfortunately, we have not attained equal justice for all. A proper slogan might be "all the justice money can buy." As a practical matter, large corporations are better able to protect their rights than individual citizens.

RIGHT TO COUNSEL

You are entitled to the representation of an attorney in all criminal cases. If you cannot afford an attorney, the court must appoint one to represent you. You have the right to refuse representation and to represent yourself.

In civil cases, except in certain small claims courts, you have the right to hire an attorney. If you cannot afford an attorney, some courts may appoint a law student to represent you, or refer you to a legal aid office, neighborhood legal services office, or to a law school's legal clinic. If you meet certain income guidelines, you may get an attorney to represent you free of charge.

RIGHT TO SILENCE

The Fifth Amendment guarantees you the right to remain silent. However, if you are granted immunity from criminal prosecution, you give up the right to silence. When questioned by the police you must be informed that you have a right to remain silent and the right to an attorney.

RIGHT TO A JURY TRIAL

You have a right to a jury trial in serious criminal cases and in civil cases involving a claim for more than $20. The Supreme Court has ruled that you have the right to a jury trial in an eviction case. You do not have the right to a jury trial in an employment discrimination case concerning race, sex, or national origin, but you do in a housing discrimination case and in age discrimination cases. The distinctions don't make much sense, but the constitution is what the Supreme Court says it is.

CRUEL AND UNUSUAL PUNISHMENT

The Constitution prohibits "cruel and unusual punishment" as penalties for the commission of crimes. However, the Supreme Court stated recently that it was not cruel and unusual punishment to imprison a man for life for stealing $22.36[3], or to sentence a man for 40 years in prison for possession and distribution of 9 ounces of marijuana.[4] Obviously the prohibition on "cruel and unusual punishment" does not offer us much protection.

INVOLUNTARY SERVITUDE

The Thirteenth Amendment outlaws involuntary servitude. This post-Civil War amendment to prohibit slavery does not make the draft unconstitutional, although if you are drafted it is anything but voluntary. The amendment against involuntary servitude protects workers against court orders to work, except concerning strikes. However, you always have a right to quit your job, even when under contract. You may, however, be sued for breach of contract if you refuse to work when you are obligated to do so.

3. *Rummel* v. *Estelle*, 445 U.S. 263 (1980).
4. *Hutto* v. *Davis*, 70 L. Ed2d 556 (1982).

SEARCH AND SEIZURE

You have the right to be free from unreasonable searches and wiretaps of your house and body, unless a warrant has been issued, or the search is incident to a lawful arrest. However, concerning visual searches through car windows, the Supreme Court has ruled that you have waived your rights by exposing the interior of the car to "public view." The court stated that you do not have a reasonable expectation of privacy in such a case. If you are wrongfully searched or your possessions wrongfully seized, you may have a valid lawsuit against the police who conducted the unconstitutional activity. Consult with an attorney or call the American Civil Liberties Union if you suspect illegal police activity. Police must obtain a warrant in order to tap your phone legally, but they are allowed to record the phone numbers that you have dialed without first obtaining a warrant.

PRIVACY

The Supreme Court ruled that Americans have certain constitutionally protected rights of privacy. The Fourth Amendment prohibition on unreasonable searches and seizures offers some protection. But the right to privacy is broader. The court ruled that you have the right of marital privacy and that contraceptives cannot be outlawed without invading this right. Many cities, which have been conducting strip searches, are under attack for this invasion of privacy. A police officer is allowed to "pat you down" outside your clothing if he has some minimal reason to suspect that you may be carrying a weapon.

DUE PROCESS

Under the "due process" clause in the Constitution you have the right to be notified before your property is taken or you are imprisoned, and you must be given a fair opportunity to defend yourself. If your property is taken from you by the government you must be given just compensation. For example, if a freeway takes part of your land, or airplanes destroy the use of your land, the government responsible must compensate you for interfering with your property rights.

CONTRACT RIGHTS

The constitution guarantees the freedom to enter into contracts. Certain topics of contracts, such as gambling or prostitution, can be restricted without interfering with this right. The freedom of contract has been diminished by legislation which has prohibited certain types of contracts, such as usury laws, minimum wage laws, and child labor laws.

CONCLUSION

The Constitution takes precedence over statutes, so you can always argue that your constitutional rights have been violated. Even though something may clearly appear to violate your rights, it is up to a court of law to interpret the Constitution. It has been argued that the Constitution protects the right to a clean environment, but no court has agreed. The Supreme Court may yet rule that the constitution demands a clean environment, so someone has to make arguments under the Constitution for the interpretations to evolve.

24

How to Sue City Hall for False Arrest

It is very frustrating to be arrested when you are innocent. The first thing you should know is that it is illegal to resist arrest even if the arrest itself is illegal. I was illegally arrested once, and I will never forget the indignity of it. Nor will the policeman, because he has been sued for it and has had his deposition taken. His employer, the city, settled the case and has paid damages, and my "criminal" record has been sealed.

WHAT IS FALSE ARREST?

Not every person found to be innocent has been falsely arrested. As long as the police have "probable cause" for the arrest, or an arrest warrant has been issued, they cannot be sued successfully for false arrest. A false arrest is an arrest when there is no probable cause and no arrest warrant. If you are falsely arrested do not resist. You should be advised of your right to an attorney and your right to remain silent. Do not get belligerent. Be polite, but do not divulge any information, unless you are absolutely certain that the information you are revealing is true and will not incriminate you. If you have any doubts in your mind, do not say anything, except to ask for the telephone to call a lawyer.

DO NOT LIE

A client of mine, who was innocent, lied to the police to cover up his negligence. He was the man-ager of a fast food restaurant. Money was missing from the store when he opened it in the morning. He told the police that he had locked the store the night before, though he had allowed another employee to lock the back door. Since he was supposed to lock the back door himself, he lied, so that his boss would not fire him for allowing another employee to lock the back door. Well, it backfired on him. He had to change his story, and when he did, the police became suspicious. Because he changed his story the police had "probable cause" to believe that he actually took the money and had the right to arrest him and bring him to trial.

PROBABLE CAUSE

Probable cause is not a precise term. It means more than a hunch and less than a sure thing. If your fingerprints were left at the scene of a crime, that constitutes "probable cause" that you committed the crime. It is enough evidence to bring your case to trial, even though it may not be enough to convict you. You can only be convicted if the jury believes "beyond a reasonable doubt" that you committed the crime that you are charged with.

DON'T BE A WISE GUY OR GAL

I was arrested for being a wise guy. I tried to tell the police officer what the law was, and he got angry. He threw me in the back of a police paddy-wagon without telling me what crime he was charging me with. By the time we got to the police station I learned that I was being charged with "depositing trash," an offense the officer concocted during the ride to the stationhouse. I was lucky, because the officer failed to appear at the arraignment. The arraignment is the date set when you plead guilty or not guilty. Since the officer failed to appear, the charged had to be dropped. I later filed suit for false arrest and recovered damages.

FALSE ARREST

To sue a city for false arrest, you must first have been arrested. An arrest occurs when you are deprived of your freedom of movement. If you are being questioned by the police but are free to leave at any time, you have not been arrested. Private citizens can arrest you. For example, there was a bizzare case when a person double parked and blocked a car's movement. The driver blocked in the parking space sued the double parker for false arrest and false imprisonment (nearly identical torts) and won. You must also prove that the person making the arrest did not have probable cause to arrest you. If you committed a crime in the presence of a policeman, he has more than enough probable cause that you committed the crime and does not need a warrant to arrest you.

In some states a citizen may arrest another citizen when a felony is committed in his or her presence. If a citizen arrests you when the crime is not a felony, or when the citizen did not see the crime being committed, you may have a good claim for false arrest. Department stores often have security guards detain suspicious persons if they believe the person has shoplifted. Store personnel must have seen you commit a crime in order to detain you. If you are detained by a security guard or a policeman, ask if you are free to leave. If they will not let you go, you have been arrested.

Many retail stores have been sued successfully for false arrest, as well as invasion of privacy. Store personnel usually do not have the right to "peep" into a dressing room to see if you are stealing their clothing.

STRIP SEARCHES

Many police departments have been strip searching suspects after they have been arrested. Even if you have been arrested legally, strip searches may be illegal, depending on the nature of the crime you have been charged with. Strip searches will add to your damages immensely if you were arrested illegally. A woman in Arlington, Virginia, arrested for playing her stereo too loudly, was taken into the police station and strip searched. She sued the county for damages and recovered a substantial amount.

TALK TO A LAWYER

The law concerning false arrest is changing rapidly and varies from state to state. If you have been arrested, even if the charges have been dropped, you may want to talk to an attorney to see if you were falsely arrested or imprisoned. Some lawyers will handle false arrest cases on a contingency fee basis, which means that it will not cost you any money for their representation, except court costs. If a lawyer is willing to take your case on a contingency fee basis, it means that the lawyer feels the case is worth pursuing.

25

How to Get Your FBI or CIA File and Other Governmental Documents

About half of us have our names on file at the Federal Bureau of Investigation (FBI) or the Central Intelligence Agency (CIA). To test this out I requested my FBI records. The FBI responded in a few weeks, stating that my file could not be disclosed to me because of national security reasons. I was astonished. I assumed that I did not have an FBI file and it turned out that somehow I was involved with a matter of national security.

Well curiosity got the better of me. I appealed within the Bureau. I researched the national security exemption in the law, and reminded the FBI that they could black out those parts of my file that were crucial to our national security. The agency responded by revealing the documents that they had in my file, but put black markings over most of the documents. I learned that someone in Great Britain was keeping records on me and disclosing them to the FBI (I studied at a University in Britain for a year). It could have been Scotland Yard, but the informant was blanked out. I had a right to appeal the decision not to disclose certain information, but I decided that I had learned enough.

WHO HAS THE RECORDS?

The first question that you should ask when seeking government information is: "who maintains the records that I want?" You should make a series of phone calls to make sure that you know where the records that you want are kept. It usually takes five or six phone calls to get an answer. At the end of this chapter is a list of Federal Information Centers who can get you started. If you request records from the FBI's central office but your file is kept in Cleveland, the central office does not have to check with all branches before answering you. It may be necessary to send out multiple requests.

HOW A REQUEST SHOULD BE MADE

The Freedom of Information Act (FOIA) requires federal agencies to supply requesters with information unless that information involves national security, is secret for some other reason, or is deemed to be private information concerning an individual or individuals. The FOIA requires the agency to respond to your request within 10 business days. Their response can state that they are unable to find any information, they can send you the information they have, or explain why they won't give it to you. A large number of the requests are from newspapers and other media who are seeking information for a news story.

If you are requesting your personal files you should have your letter notarized to confirm your identity. In this case you should include your social security number. Requests should be sent by certified mail, return receipt requested, so that you will have proof of the date of receipt.

Your request should give as many details as possible so that the records can be found. Provide dates, social security numbers, locations, and other information that may help them to find the file you are requesting.

You should address your request letter to the FOIA Office, and the outside of your envelope should state "FREEDOM OF INFORMATION REQUEST."

Agencies are permitted to charge for making photocopies; usually five or ten cents per page. The agency may charge for search time if they cannot find your material within half an hour. Tell the agency that you are willing to pay copying and search charges, but give them a maximum charge which you are willing to pay. Every agency is allowed to waive these charges if the request is for information which is of benefit to the public. Always ask that the fees be waived for this reason. A sample freedom of information request is included at the end of this chapter as Form 25-1

WHERE FBI AND CIA REQUESTS SHOULD BE SENT

If you are interested in learning whether the FBI or CIA have kept track of you, write them at:

Information and Privacy Coordinator
Central Intelligence Agency
Washington, DC 20505
(703) 351-1100

and:

Director
Federal Bureau of Investigation
Attention: FOIA and Privacy Act Branch
Washington, DC 20505
(202) 324-5520

OTHER AGENCIES

There are literally hundreds of government agencies. The *U.S. Government Organization Manual;* which is available at all public libraries, contains the addresses and functions of all federal agencies. Every federal agency is required to respond to your Freedom of Information Request within ten business days.

APPEALS

When the agency responds to your request, it will notify you that you have a right to appeal within the agency. You are given 20 days in which to appeal to a higher office in the agency. The appeal is taken by writing a letter, stating the reasons that the first decision was erroneous, to the official named by the agency to receive appeals. If you are unhappy with the agency's decision on your appeal, you have the right to file a complaint in federal district court. A federal complaint form is included at the end of this chapter as Form 25-2

ASSISTANCE

If you need assistance, the following organizations may be able to help you:

Freedom of Information Clearinghouse
P.O. Box 19367
Washington, DC 20036
(202) 785-3704

ACLU National Security Project
122 Maryland Ave., N.E.
Washington, DC 20002
(202) 544-5380

Freedom of Information Service Center
Reporters' Committee for Freedom of
  the Press
1125 15th Street, N.W.
Washington, DC 20005
(202) 466-6312

Your local American Civil Liberties Union office may be able to refer you to an attorney who has handled FOIA cases. Under the law, if you prevail in court the agency may be ordered to pay you attorney's fees and court costs. Freedom of Information Act cases are not complicated and you may be able to handle it by yourself. It may be useful to consult with an attorney after the agency has denied your request, to review the grounds for any exemption that the agency has claimed. The attorney should be able to advise you if the agency had a right to withhold the information from you, and to advise you concerning your chances for winning an appeal.

FORM 25-1

Freedom of Information Act Letter

CERTIFIED MAIL
RETURN RECEIPT REQUESTED
Name _____
Address _____
Daytime phone _____
Date _____

Freedom of Information Office
Agency Address

RE: FREEDOM OF INFORMATION ACT REQUEST

Dear Sir or Madam,

This is a Freedom of Information Act request. I request that you provide the following information:

_____

_____

In order to assist your search for these files I am providing you with the following information:

_____

_____

I also ask that you check for additional records in your offices in the following cities:

_____

_____

If all or part of my request is denied, please list the specific exemption which is being claimed for this denial. If you determine portions of the requested material to be exempt, provide me with the remaining non-exempt portions.

I request that you waive search and copying fees since this request is in the public interest because _____.

If you will not waive fees and charges, I authorize up to $_____ for these charges. Please contact me if the charges may exceed this amount, so that I can select those documents that I want copied.

If you have any question concerning this request please call me at the telephone number that I have listed above.

As provided in the Freedom of Information Act, I will expect your response within ten working days.

Sincerely yours,

_____
(Signature)
NAME
Social Security Number

_____ appeared before me this _____ date of _____.

_____
NOTARY PUBLIC

FORM 25-2

Freedom of Information Act Federal Court Complaint

UNITED STATES DISTRICT COURT

FOR THE _____ DISTRICT OF _____

_____ DIVISION

_____,

Plaintiff,

v.   Civil Action No.

_____,

Defendant.

COMPLAINT FOR INJUNCTIVE RELIEF

I. NATURE OF THE CASE

1. This is an action under the Freedom of Information Act, 5 U.S.C. Section 552, (FOIA), to order the production of agency records, concerning _____, which were improperly withheld from plaintiff.

II. JURISDICTION

2. This court had jurisdiction over this action pursuant to 5 U.S.C. Section 552(a)(4).

III. PARTIES

3. _____, plaintiff, is the requestor of the agency records which have been withheld improperly.

4. Defendant _____ is an agency of the United States, and has possession of the records that plaintiff seeks.

IV. FACTUAL ALLEGATIONS

5. By letter dated _____, plaintiff wrote to defendant seeking access to documents pertaining to _____.

6. Defendant responded by letter dated _____, claiming that the requested information was exempt from disclosure because _____.

7. By letter dated _____ plaintiff appealed the denial of his request.

8. Plaintiff's appeal was denied on _____. A copy of this denial is attached to this complaint as plaintiff's exhibit no. 1. Plaintiff has exhausted his administrative remedies.

V. CAUSE OF ACTION

9. Plaintiff incorporates by reference paragraphs one through eight, inclusive.

10. Plaintiff has a right of access to the requested information under 5 U.S.C. Section 552(a)(3), and there is no legal basis for defendant's denial of this access.

VI. REQUEST FOR RELIEF

WHEREFORE, plaintiff requests that this Court:

A. Order defendant to make the requested information available;

B. Expedite this proceeding as required by 5 U.S.C. Section 552(a)(4)(B);

C. Award plaintiff his costs and reasonable attorney's fees pursuant to 5 U.S.C. Section 552(a)(4)(E);

D. Issue a written finding, pursuant to 5 U.S.C. Section 552(a)(4)(F) that the agency acted arbitrarily and capriciously in withholding the information; and

E. Grant such other relief as the court may deem in the interests of justice.

Respectfully submitted,

(Signature) _____

NAME

ADDRESS

TELEPHONE NUMBER

FEDERAL INFORMATION CENTERS

If you have questions about any program or agency in the Federal government you may want to call the Federal Information Center (FIC) nearest you. FIC staffs are prepared to help consumers find needed information or locate the right agency—usually Federal but sometimes state or local—for help with problems. Each city listed below has an FIC or a tieline—a toll-free local number connecting to an FIC elsewhere:

Alabama
Birmingham
   (205) 322-8591
Mobile
   (205) 438-1421

Alaska
Anchorage
   (907) 271-3650

Arizona
Phoenix
   (602) 261-3313
Tucson
   (602) 622-1511

Arkansas
Little Rock
   (501) 378-6177

California
Los Angeles
   (213) 688-3800
Sacramento
   (916) 440-3344
San Diego
   (714) 293-6030
San Francisco
   (415) 556-6600
San Jose
   (408) 275-7422
Santa Ana
   (714) 836-2386

Colorado
Colorado Springs
   (303) 471-9491
Denver
   (303) 234-7181
Pueblo
   (303) 544-9523

Connecticut
Hartford
   (203) 527-2617

New Haven
   (203) 624-4720

Florida
St. Petersburg
   (813) 893-3495
Tampa
   (813) 229-7911
Other locations
   (800) 282-8556

Georga
Atlanta
   (404) 221-6891

Hawaii
Honolulu
   (808) 546-8620

Illinois
Chicago
   (312) 353-4242

Indiana
Gary/Hammond
   (219) 833-4110
Indianapolis
   (317) 269-7373

Iowa
Des Moines
   (515) 284-4448
Other locations
   (800) 532-1556

Kansas
Topeka
   (913) 295-2866
Other locations
   (800) 432-2934

Kentucky
Louisville
   (502) 582-6261

Louisiana
New Orleans
   (504) 589-6696

Maryland
Baltimore
   (301) 962-4980

Massachusetts
Boston
   (617) 223-7121

Michigan
Detroit
   (313) 226-7016
Grand Rapids
   (616) 451-2628

Minnesota
Minneapolis
   (612) 349-5333

Missouri
Kansas City
   (816) 374- 2466
St. Louis
   (314) 425-4106
Other locations
   within area
   code 314
   (800) 392-7711
Other locations
   within area
   codes 816 and 417
   (800) 892-5808

Nebraska
Omaha
   (402) 221-3353
Other locations
   (800) 642-8383

New Jersey
Newark
   (201) 645-3600
Patterson/Passaic
   (201) 523-0717
Trenton
   (609) 396-4400

New Mexico
Albuquerque
   (505) 766-3091
Santa Fe
   (505) 983-7743

New York
Albany
   (518) 463-4421

Buffalo
   (716) 846-4010
New York
   (212) 264-4464
Rochester
   (716) 546-5075
Syracuse
   (315) 476-8545

North Carolina
Charlotte
   (704) 376-3600

Ohio
Akron
   (216) 375-5638
Cincinnati
   (513) 684-2801
Cleveland
   (216) 522-4040
Columbus
   (614) 221-1014
Dayton
   (513) 223-7377
Toledo
   (419) 241-3223

Oklahoma
Oklahoma
   (405) 231-4868
Tulsa
   (918) 584-4193

Oregon
Portland
   (503) 221-2222

Pennsylvania
Allentown/Bethlehem
   (215) 821-7785
Philadelphia
   (215) 597-7042
Pittsburgh
   (412) 644-3456
Scranton
   (717) 346-7081

Rhode Island
Providence
   (401) 331-5565

Tennessee
Chattanooga
   (615) 265-8231
Memphis
   (901) 521-3285
Nashville
   (615) 242-5056

Texas
Austin
  (512) 472-5494
Dallas
  (214) 767-8585
Fort Worth
  (817) 334-3624
Houston
  (713) 229-2552

San Antonia
  (512) 224-4471

Utah
Ogden
  (801) 399-1347
Salt Lake City
  (801) 524-5353

Virginia
Newport News
  (804) 244-0480
Norfolk
  (804) 441-3101
Richmond
  (804) 643-4928
Roanoke
  (703) 982-8591

Washington
Seattle
  (206) 442-0570
Tacoma
  (206) 383-5230

Wisconsin
Milwaukee
  (414) 271-2273